POSTCARD HISTORY SERIES

The Wildwoods
1920–1970

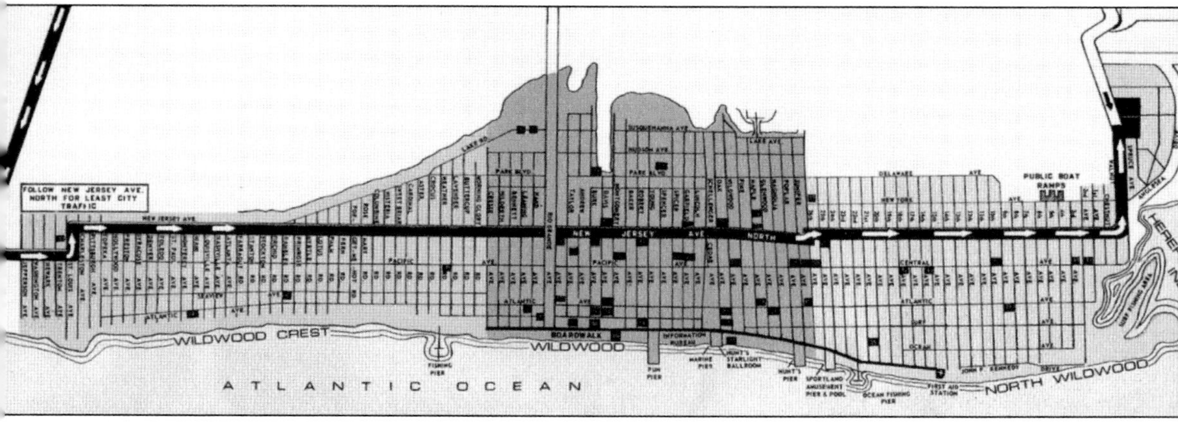

This map shows the Wildwoods, stretching from Jefferson Avenue in Wildwood Crest, through Anglesea Drive in North Wildwood. Typically the oldest structures to be found in the Wildwoods are located in Wildwood proper. From humble beginnings, development spread to the adjacent areas, thus creating Wildwood Crest and North Wildwood.

On the cover: This postcard from 1942 shows a group of beachgoers enjoying a warm summer day at one of Wildwood's beautiful beaches. Along with several prominent boardwalk structures in the background, an amusement pier can be seen jutting into the ocean. More than 60 years later, people still flock to Wildwood every summer to bask in the sun and frolic in the surf. (Author's collection.)

On the back cover: Designed to emulate a passenger ship, the Sun Deck Apartments was located on Ocean Avenue at Andrews Avenue. This postcard from 1944 shows the faux smokestack emerging from the roof, as well as decks featuring strategically placed life preservers. Although the structure would survive and evolve for many decades, nothing remains today of the Sun Deck Apartments. (Author's collection.)

POSTCARD HISTORY SERIES

The Wildwoods
1920–1970

Vincent Martino Jr.

ARCADIA PUBLISHING

ISBN 978-0-7385-5003-9

Published by Arcadia Publishing
Charleston, South Carolina

Printed in the United States of America

Library of Congress Catalog Card Number: 2006940202

For all general information contact Arcadia Publishing at:
Telephone 843-853-2070
Fax 843-853-0044
E-mail sales@arcadiapublishing.com
For customer service and orders:
Toll-Free 1-888-313-2665

Visit us on the Internet at www.arcadiapublishing.com

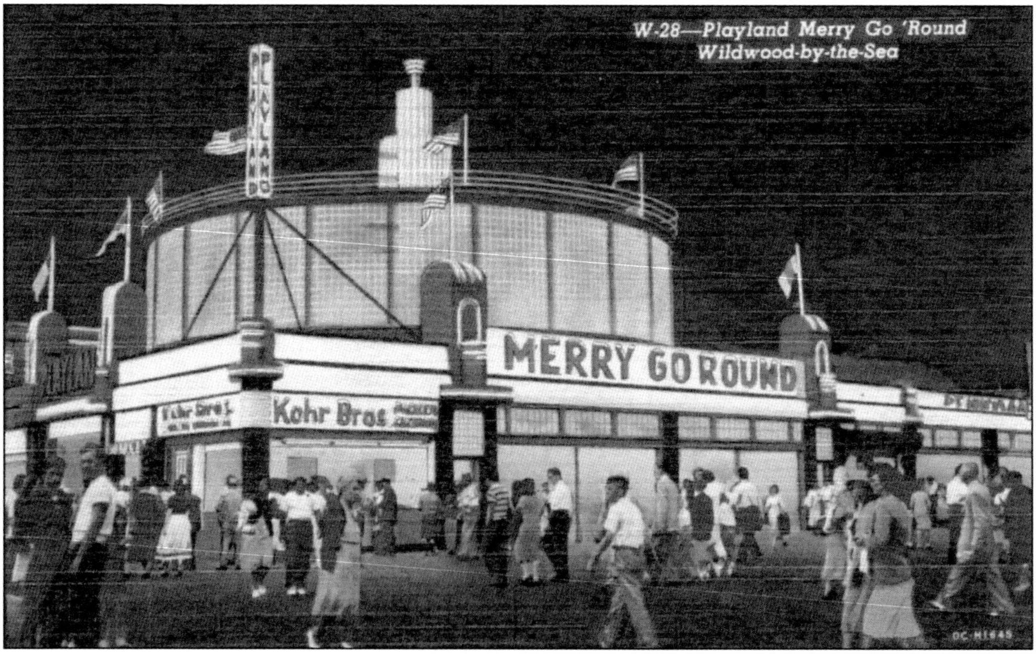

This view from the early 1950s shows the Playland merry-go-round located on the boardwalk at Cedar Avenue. The merry-go-round sat at a very familiar point on the boardwalk, where the straightaway view shifted slightly and changed course. Also visible in this view is the Kohr Brothers Frozen Custard stand, still a boardwalk fixture decades later. Sadly this iconic amusement is no more.

Contents

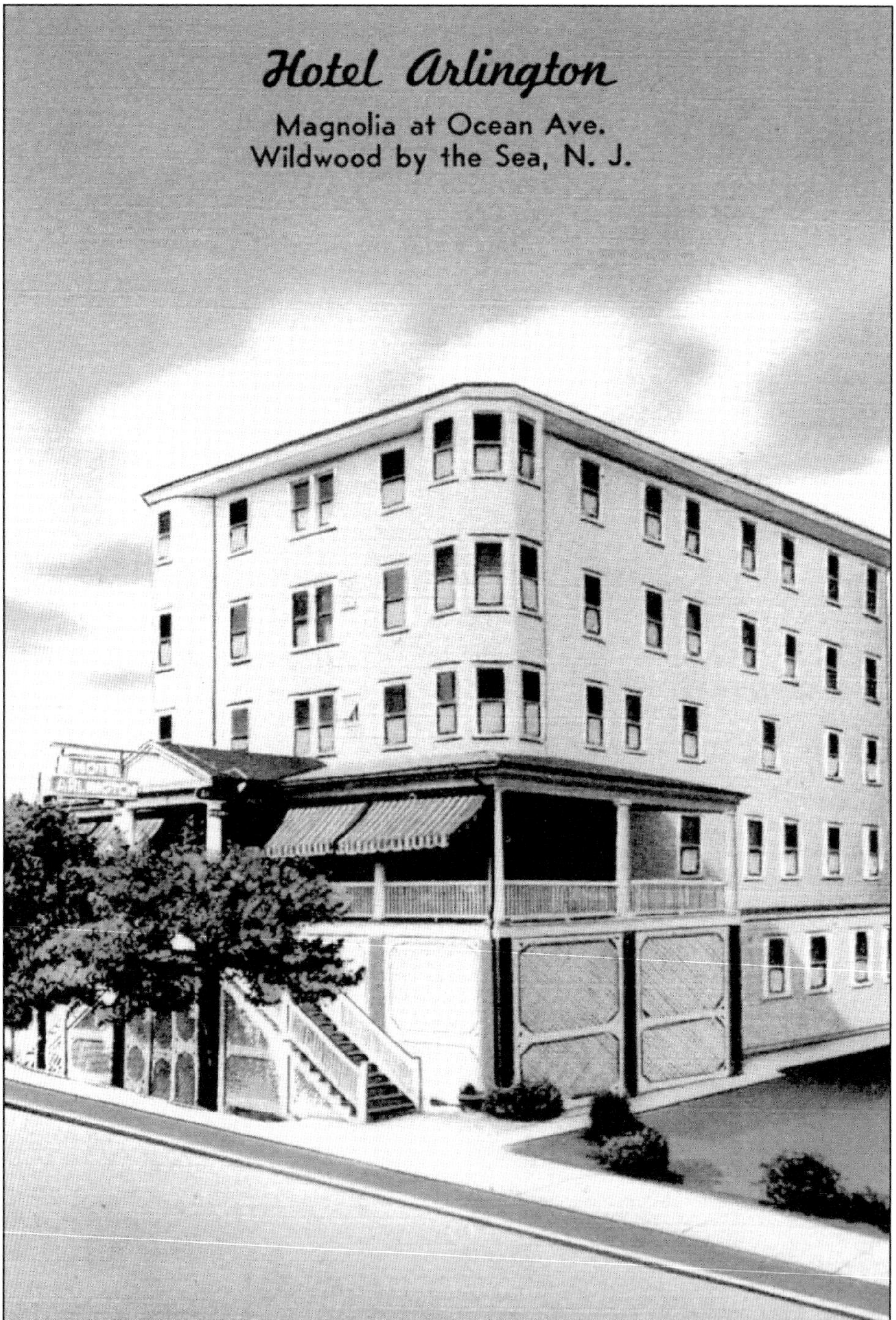

The Hotel Arlington is seen in this postcard from the 1940s.The building is located on Magnolia Avenue, near Ocean Avenue. Although the structure remains to this day, the glory days of old hotels such as the Hotel Arlington have faded long ago. As of 2007, the Hotel Arlington still offers rooms to those visitors that wish to stay in Wildwood and gain experience of a time that has long since passed.

Introduction

The beachside resort area known collectively as the Wildwoods actually encompasses four distinct communities. These are Wildwood proper, West Wildwood, North Wildwood, and Wildwood Crest. Although there is a modest year-round population that has yet to attain five figures in number, the summer vacation season brings throngs of people to this strip of coastal land, swelling its numbers to more than 250,000 at any given point in time. The Wildwoods are more than just a vacation destination for tourists, as a true sense of community developed early on and carries through to this day. There are schools, churches, civic groups, and businesses that were founded with the local populace in mind. But there is no denying that the growth and prosperity of the Wildwoods hinges solidly on its reputation as a family vacation hot spot. Located on the peninsula that is southern New Jersey, the Wildwoods has cultivated a customer base from all over the tri-state area. Vacationers from New York, Pennsylvania, and New Jersey have flocked to the Wildwoods for decades to enjoy its beautiful beaches, amusements, and ample recreation offerings. And as times and tastes have changed, the Wildwoods have been forced to adapt. On the whole, the Wildwoods have evolved quite significantly over the past century. Once it was the domain of grand Victorian homes and quaint seaside cottages; the Wildwoods of today, however, are more densely populated and modern. Many links to the past have been preserved via careful maintenance of irreplaceable structures and a keen intent upon showcasing the area's architectural gems. However, all the progress and strides made by this locale over the years have led to the loss of many grand homes and businesses. For the worthwhile development taking place in the Wildwoods comes at a cost. Fortunately those who have come before us had the forethought to visually document the area's rich history through the production of postcards, some dating back over 100 years. Many were produced at a time when cameras were a luxury for the rich or an instrument of employment for an early photographer. As a result, sometimes the best pictorial evidence of a given subject exists in the form of a postcard. *The Wildwoods: 1920–1970* provides residents and visitors alike with a selection of diverse history that allows for a glimpse into the past.

Our journey through the Wildwoods' past begins with an exploration of the hospitality industry and the many eclectic offerings. As a vacation resort, lodging is very important to attracting visitors and generating revenue. With that in mind, many motels in the Wildwoods were built to be functional but more so to be aesthetically appealing and unique. Beginning in the post–World War II era, hundreds of these motels were built in a style that has lately come to be known as doo-wop, after the popular 1950s-era genre of music. This was a time when the Wildwoods enjoyed their most earnest growth and some of their greatest prosperity. Fortunately many of these motels that came out of this period have survived well into the 21st century, though many, however, have been regrettably lost to time and progress. The Wildwoods are quickly becoming a haven of "second home" ownership. Not withstanding this notion, the advent of affordable air travel has created other options for vacationers beyond those places that could be driven to within a couple hours time. Unfortunately this has meant the demolition of many old motels to make way for dense housing and condominiums. Despite passionate protest and vociferous opposition, many of the Wildwoods' most exceptional and unusual motels have been replaced by residential offerings that fail to capture the community's spirit and character. Many of these motels were a feast for the eyes and often included artistic signage, faux tropical settings, and a genuine nod toward the post-modern era of the 1950s. Even the names are evocative of more exotic locales, including the Ala Moana, Casa Bahama, Palm Beach, Rio, Sans Souci, and Tahiti just to name a few. However, the accommodations are not the only part of the landscape to have changed. The boardwalk and its associated amusements, games, and stores have been reinvented time and again over the years. This has been done sometimes as a result of the owners' innovation, but also as a result of several devastating fires that have plagued various sections of the boardwalk over its many storied years. As fanciful amusement parks rise in the suburbs of the region's major cities, the amusement pier operators must remain vigilant toward emerging industry trends and respond appropriately. Inevitably this results in the replacement of much beloved rides and amusements, in lieu of the more alluring mega-roller coasters and theme park–style rides. And although the Wildwoods can boast several restaurants that have withstood the test of time, many others have come and gone over the years. Perhaps nothing epitomizes the fickle and changing tastes of the consumer more so than the propensity for restaurants to change theme and management on such a frequent basis.

Despite the many observations that center on the inescapable effects of change, the old adage that says "the more things change, the more they stay the same" somehow manages to hold true. Families still take sojourns to the shore, in search of the same things weary travelers have always savored. Fun, relaxation, and merriment await those who have made the Wildwoods a perennial vacation favorite. Now, take a trip back in time to a youth spent in beautiful Wildwood. Revisit the bygone era that was the Wildwoods of the mid-20th century, and nurture the evocative memories that will most assuredly begin to pass through your mind. As you embark on this journey through time, be transfixed with awe in regard to the many great strides brought to us via time and progress. Lament not the passing of yesterday, but embrace the present, and look to the future with hope. Be among the many to celebrate the Wildwoods' regional significance, undeniable charm, and architectural splendor.

One

Accommodations in Wildwood

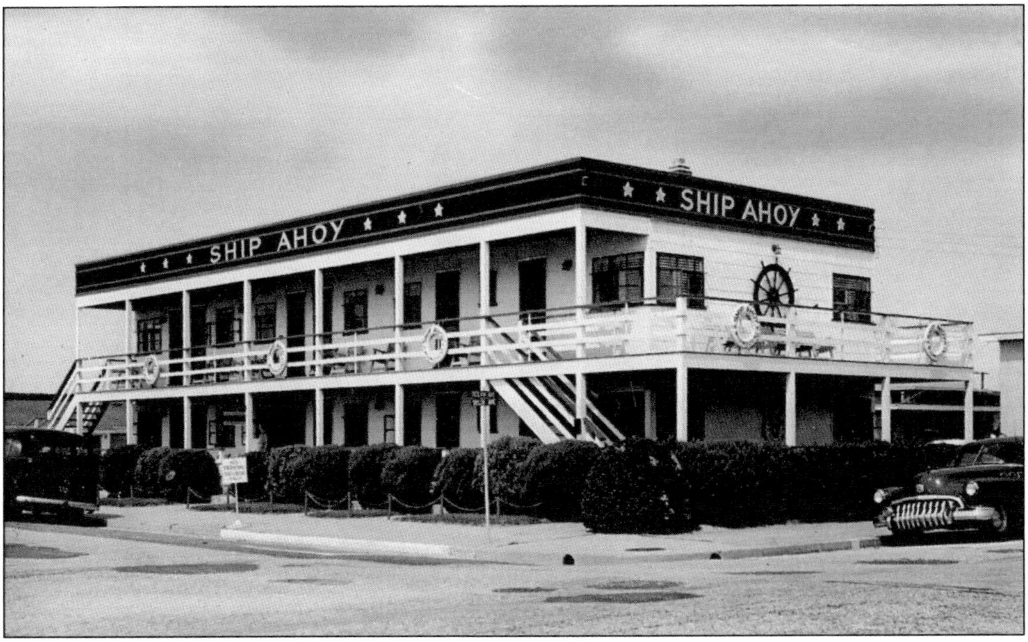

The Ship Ahoy Apartments was located on Ocean Avenue at Taylor Avenue in this postcard from the 1950s. All apartments offered ocean views, and "modern conveniences" such as showers, refrigerators, and continuous hot water. Although the building no longer exists at this location, many residents and visitors will recognize an almost identical facility on Washington Avenue at Baker Avenue in Wildwood.

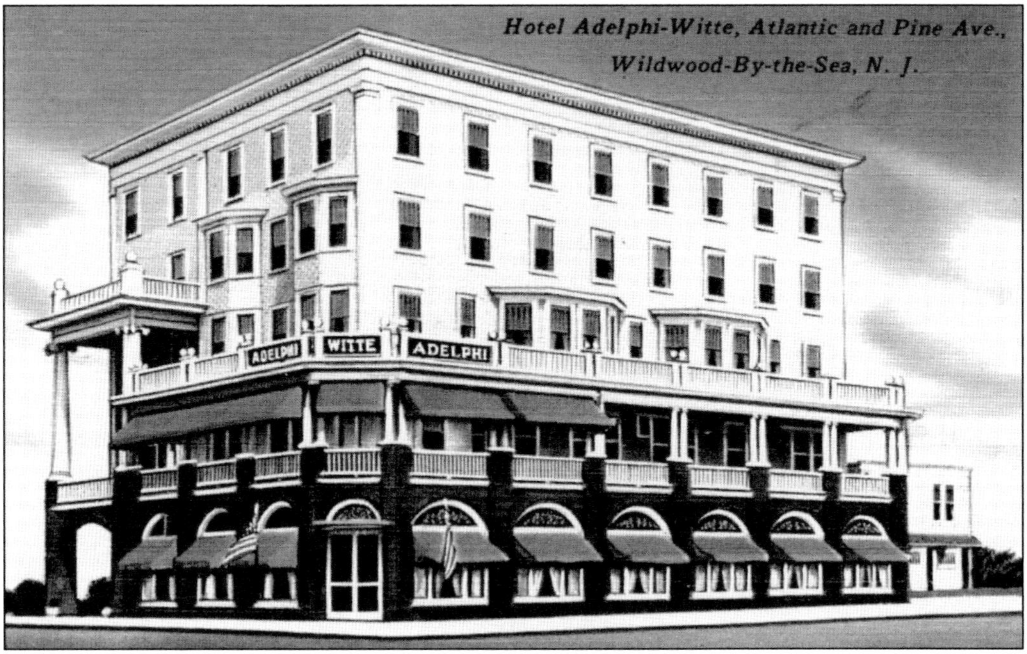

The Hotel Adelphi-Witte is seen in this postcard from the 1940s. The building was located at the prominent intersection of Atlantic Avenue and Pine Avenue. Today the five-story structure is but a memory of the distant past. This area is now home to several businesses and newer hotels.

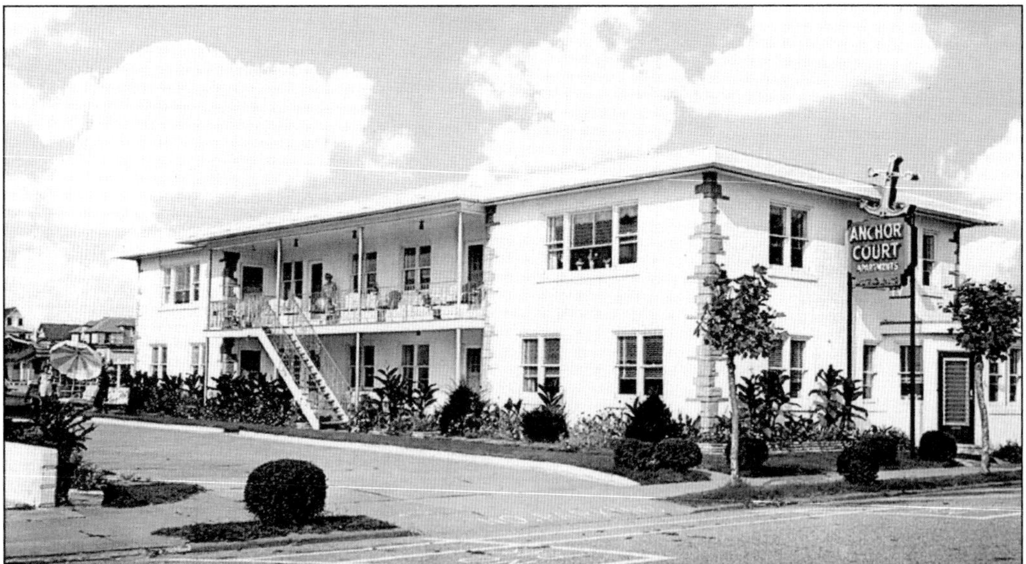

This postcard from the 1950s shows the Anchor Court Apartments located at 240 East Baker Avenue. The facility once offered "modern" one- and two-bedroom apartments, complete with kitchen and bath. The card also proudly boasts "fireproof construction" as one of its amenities. Today the Anchor Court building still stands, although it no longer functions as rental units. The building has been converted to condominium ownership.

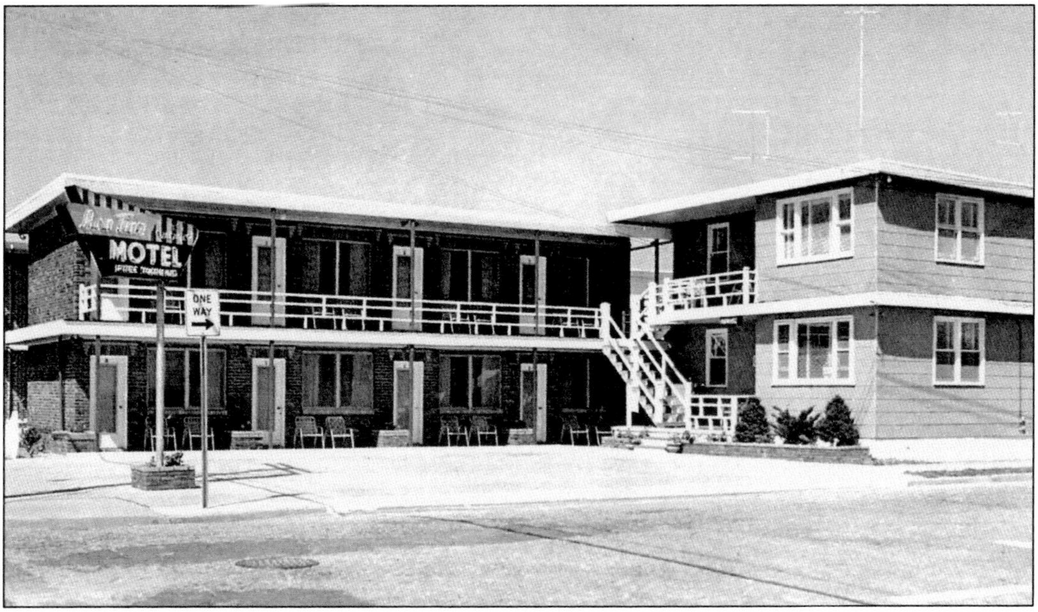

The Ann Tina Motel was located at 4600 Atlantic Avenue, at the corner of Burk Avenue. This quaint motel overlooked Fox Park on busy Atlantic Avenue and was in existence for many years. However, as the brisk pace of development continued in Wildwood, this small motel could not stand the test of time. Today the Ann Tina Motel is just a memory.

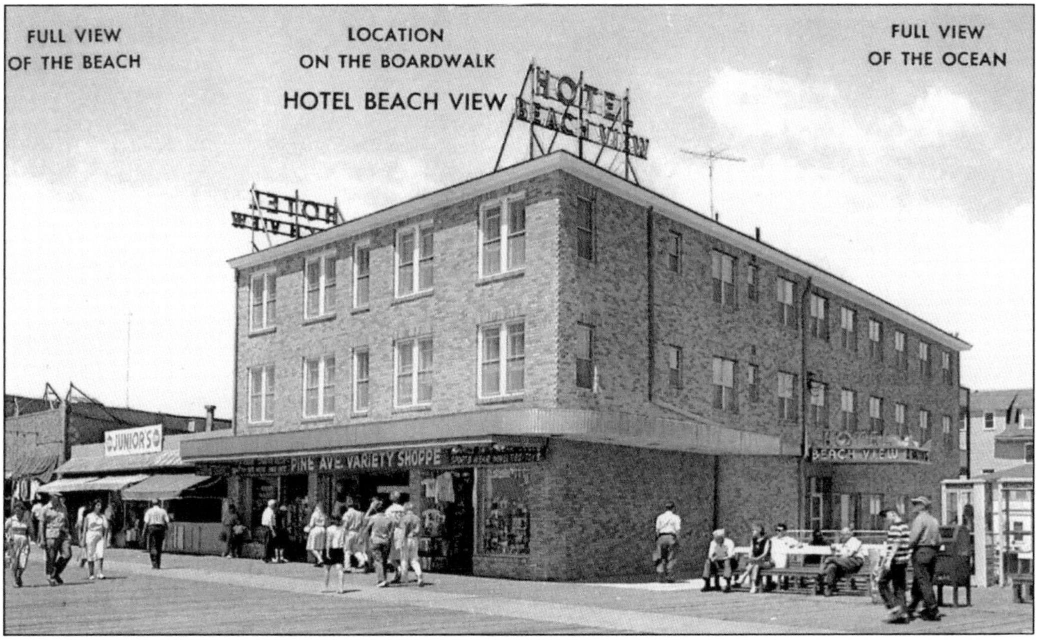

The Hotel Beach View was located on the boardwalk at Pine Avenue when this postcard was created in the 1950s. The three-story building had a side entrance, as the ground floor facing the boardwalk was occupied by shops. Today the hotel is long gone, as the upper floors have been removed. The building's first floor remains at 3200 Boardwalk and is occupied by some shops.

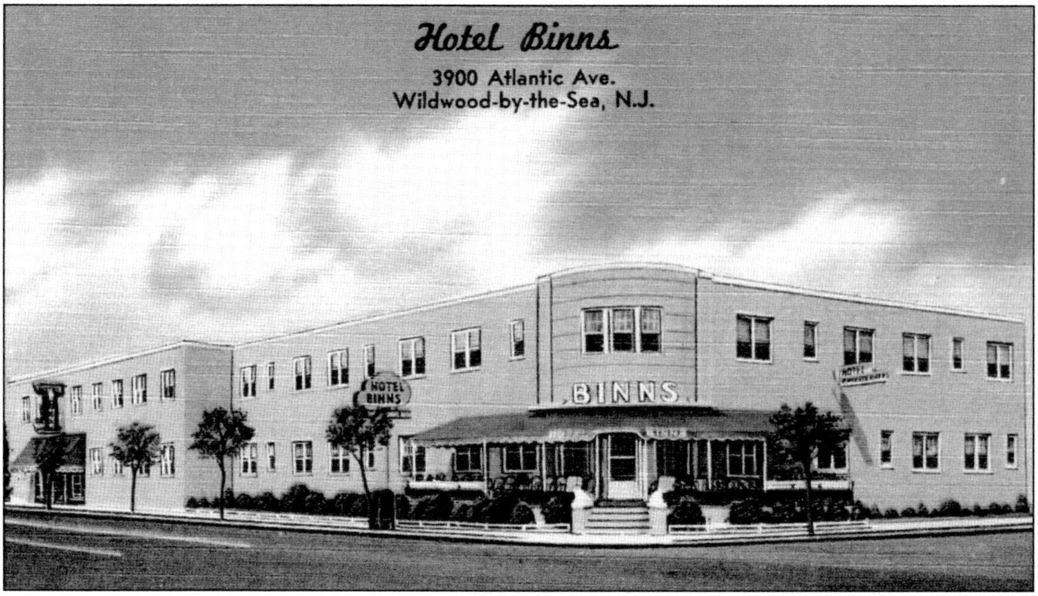

The Hotel Binns is seen in this postcard from the 1940s. Although the facade looks quite different today, the facility still operates as the Binns Motor Inn. Along with a later expansion, the full complex is located at 3900 Atlantic Avenue.

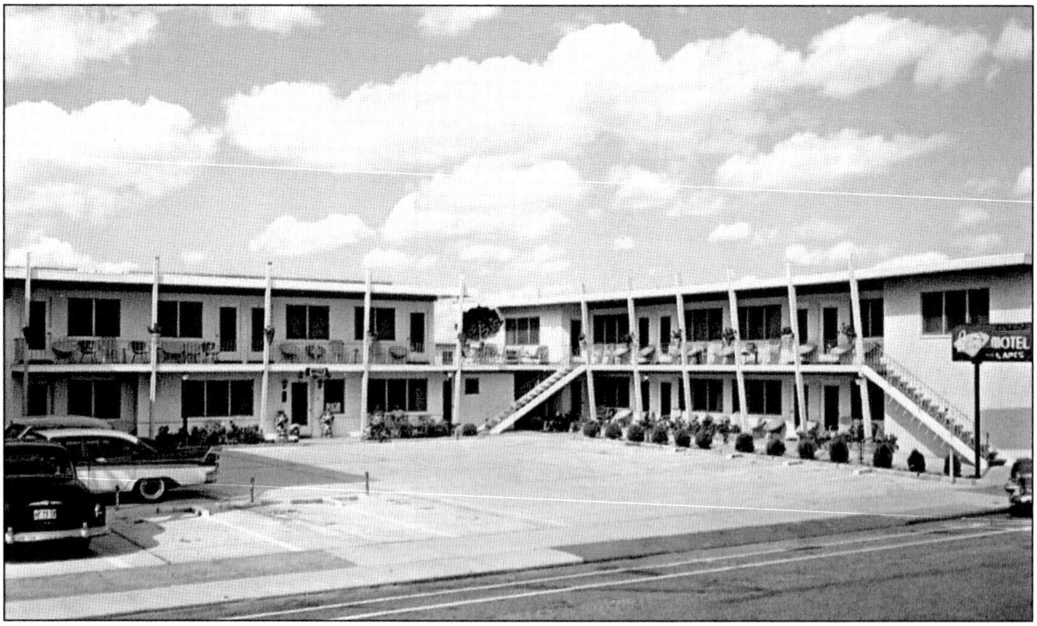

The Bonito Motel is seen in this postcard from the 1950s, located at 236 East Spicer Avenue. The rear of the card proudly touts an "all electric kitchen" as one of its main amenities. Today the Bonito Motel still remains, albeit with an expansion, and continues to rent rooms to visitors and tourists.

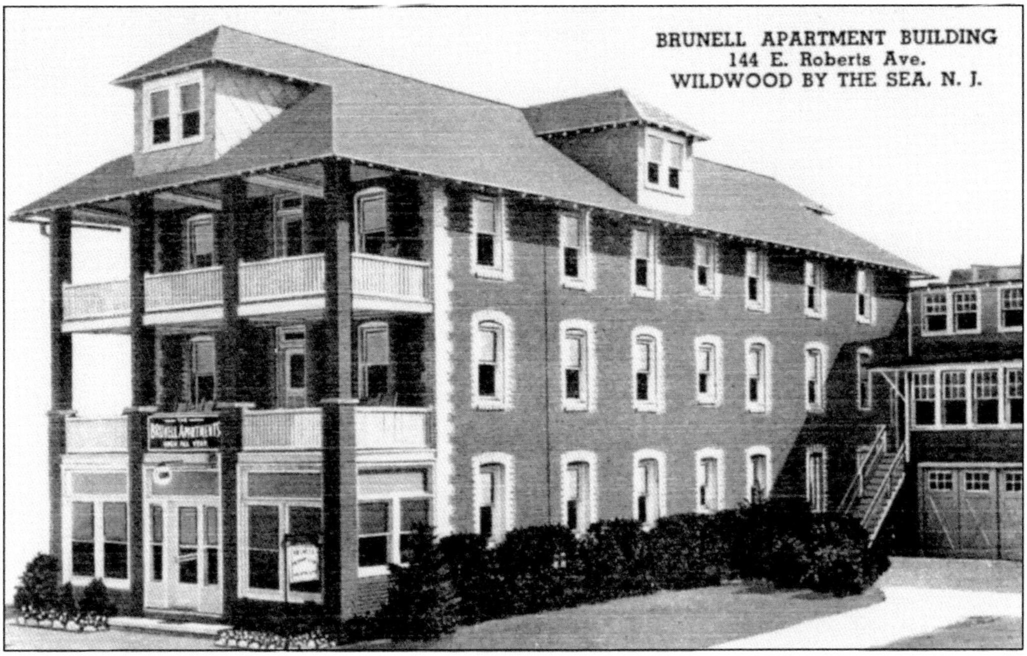

The Brunell Apartment Building was located at 144 East Roberts Avenue, as seen in this postcard from the 1940s. Amazingly the brick building with upper level porches remains today and looks much the same as it did more than 60 years ago. Even the small garage and apartments seen at the right side of the card have survived over the years and are still visible along Roberts Avenue.

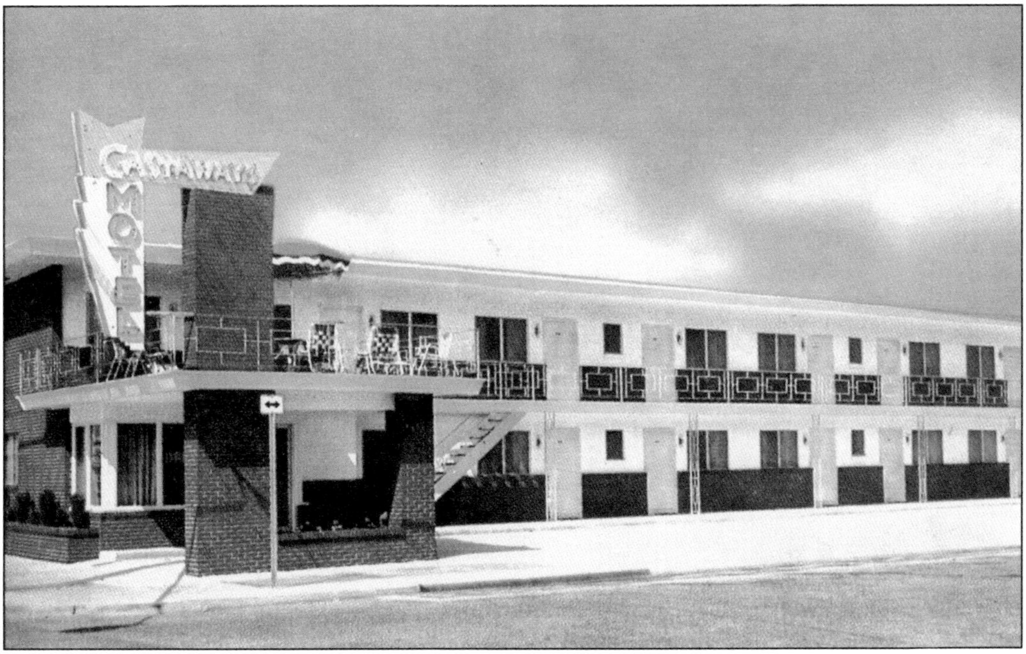

The Castaways Motel is located at 3700 Atlantic Avenue, dwarfed by its larger neighbor, the Brittany Motel next door. Although the building has received some modifications over the years, it looks much today as it did when this postcard was produced in the 1950s. It continues to function with its original intended use.

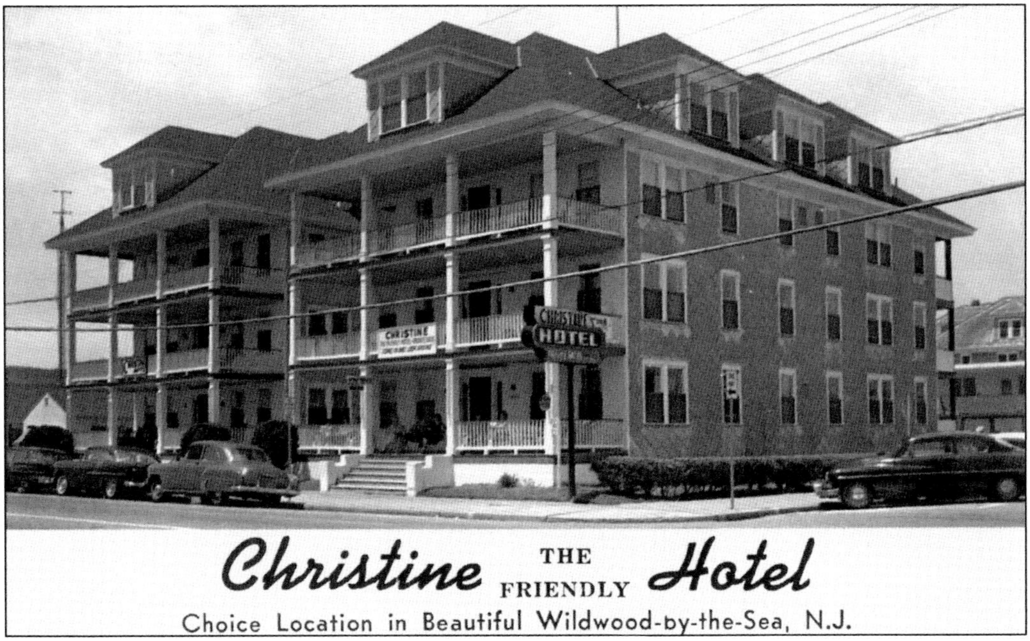

This view of the Christine Hotel from the 1950s shows billing as the "friendly hotel" in its location at 4300 Atlantic Avenue. Despite proximity to the beach, the structure was out-of-date by current standards. Today brand new condominiums stand in its place along Atlantic Avenue.

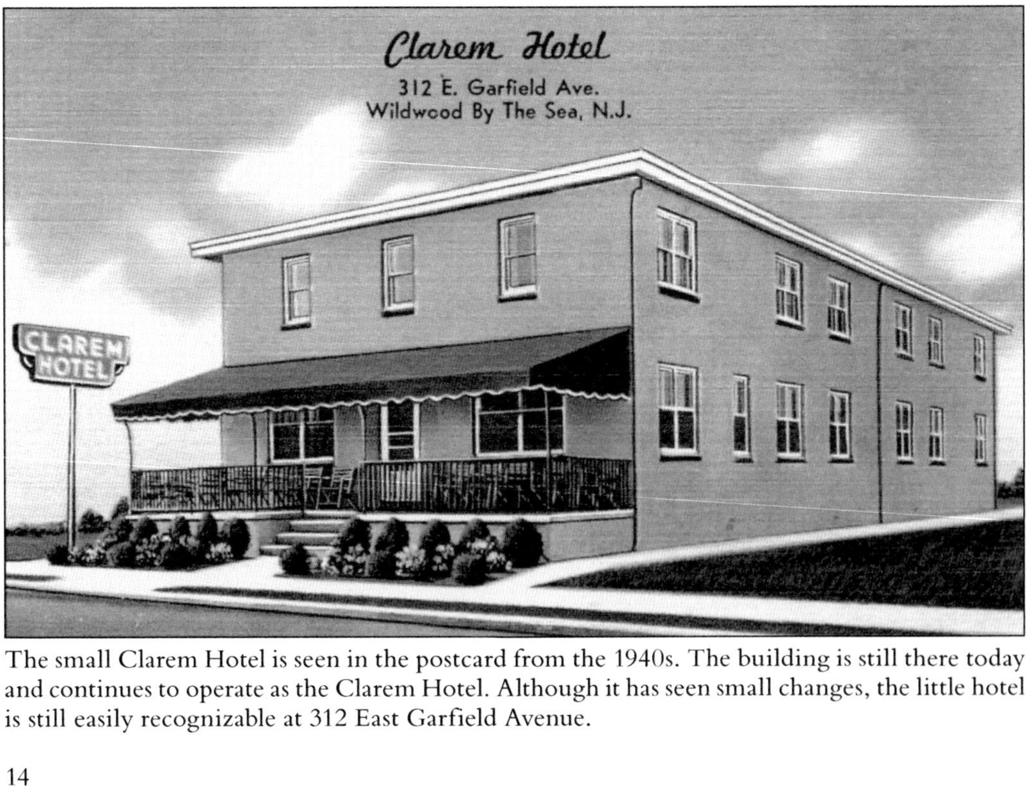

The small Clarem Hotel is seen in the postcard from the 1940s. The building is still there today and continues to operate as the Clarem Hotel. Although it has seen small changes, the little hotel is still easily recognizable at 312 East Garfield Avenue.

The Colwyn Apartments was located at 228 East Spencer Avenue and are seen in this postcard from the 1950s. Although the awnings have been removed, this structure has survived in the form of the Crescent Wind Apartments and still looks remarkably similar to the way it did more than 50 years ago.

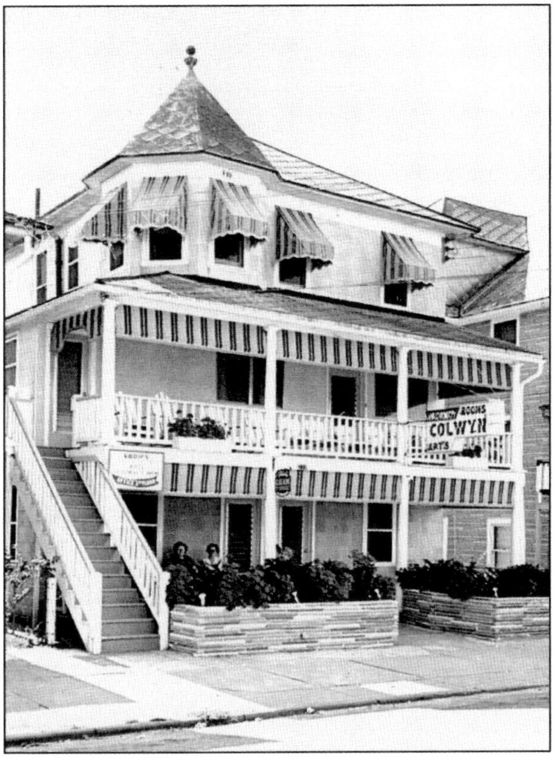

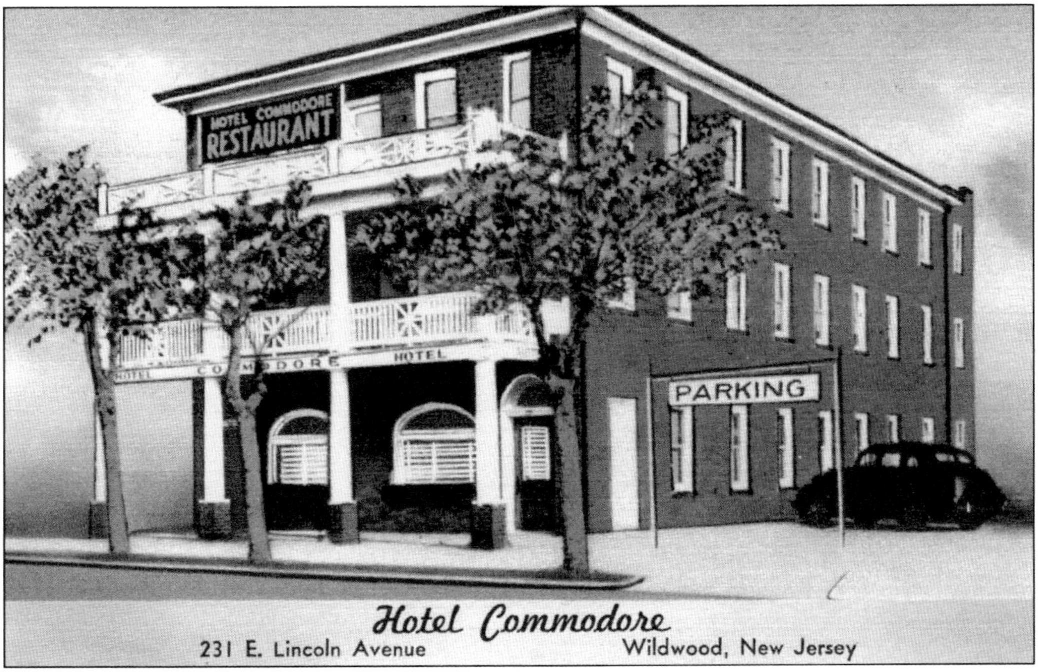

The Hotel Commodore was located at 231 East Lincoln Avenue in downtown Wildwood. Several years after this postcard was produced, the upper-level porches were removed and the hotel was rebranded as the Beach Hotel. Although the brick facade was covered with stucco long ago, the structure still remains today as the Beach Hotel.

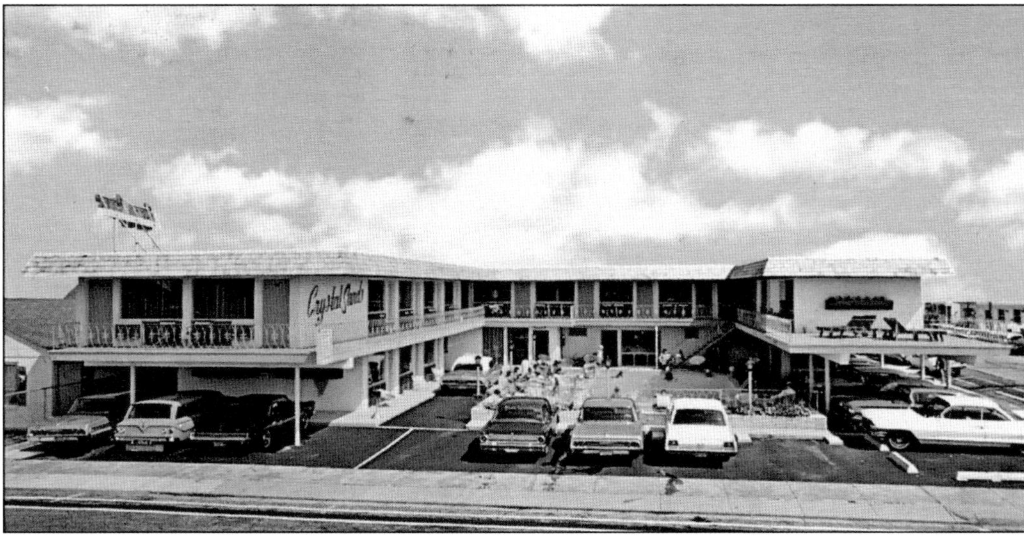

The Crystal Sands Motel is seen in this postcard from the early 1960s. The building continues to operate today as the Crystal Sands Motel from its location along Atlantic Avenue at Hand Avenue. One of many motels on this stretch of Atlantic Avenue, the Crystal Sands Motel has survived the test of time and has managed to retain much of its original structure.

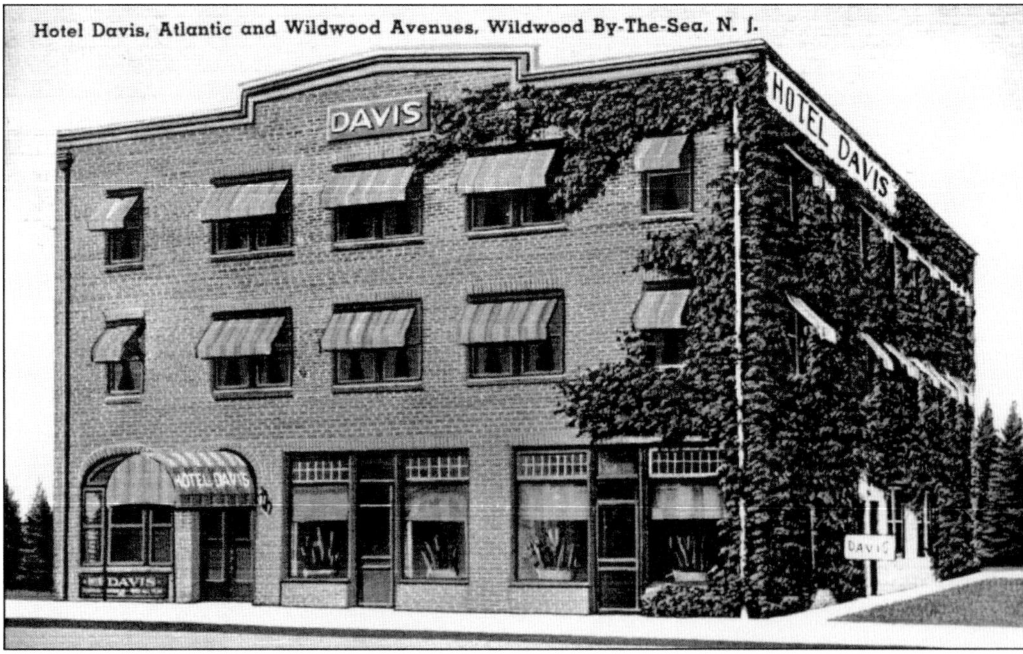

The Hotel Davis is seen in this postcard from the 1940s. The building was located at the intersection of Wildwood and Atlantic Avenues. The vine-covered building would last decades before giving way to time and progress at this busy intersection. In its place are newer motels and restaurants.

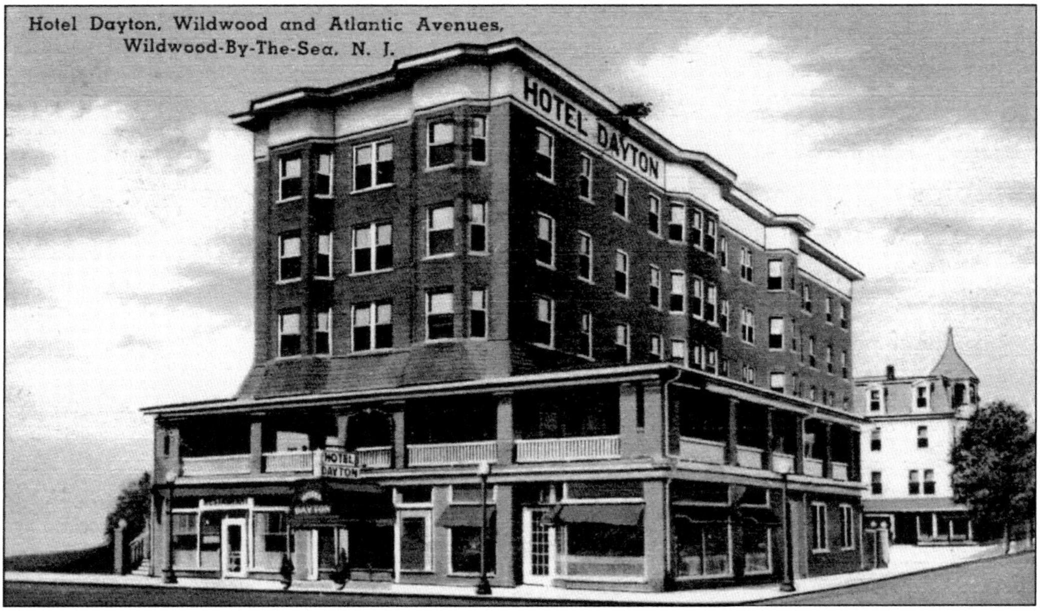

The Hotel Dayton was a five-story structure located at the intersection of Wildwood and Atlantic Avenues when this postcard was produced in the 1940s. Although it boasted many rooms and some ground floor shops, the Hotel Dayton had been surpassed by more modern offerings and is just a memory today.

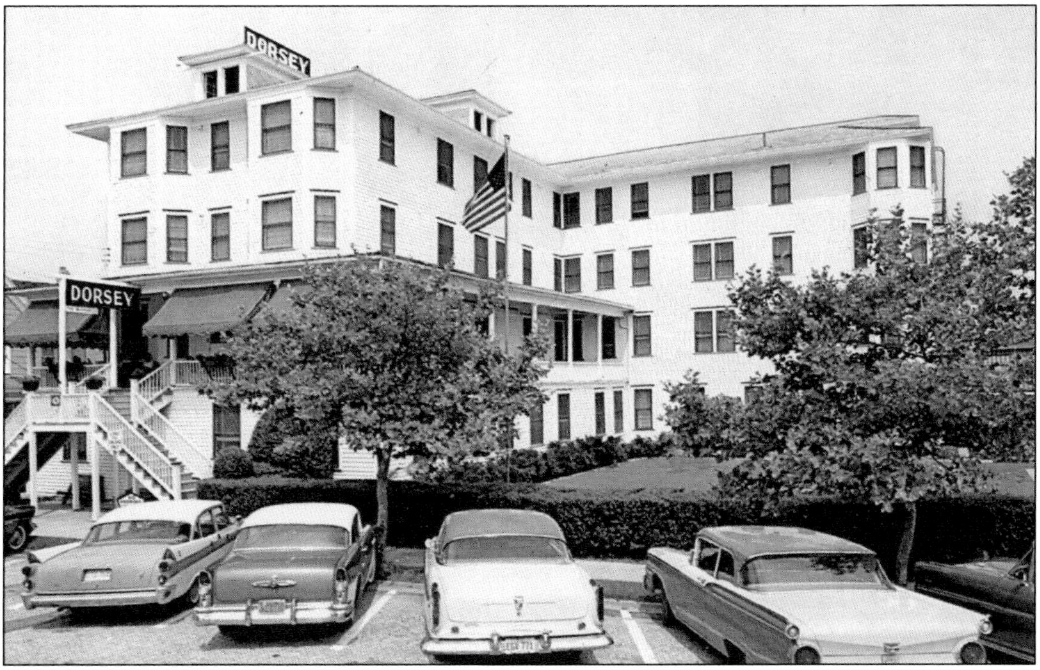

The Hotel Dorsey was located at 209 East Montgomery Avenue, near Pacific Avenue. The rear of this 1950s-era postcard touts rooms with "private toilet" and "running water." It also promises total relaxation and rest by "prohibiting excess noise at night." Despite such measures, the Hotel Dorsey had become a relic of the past. Today modern townhouses sit in its place along Montgomery Avenue.

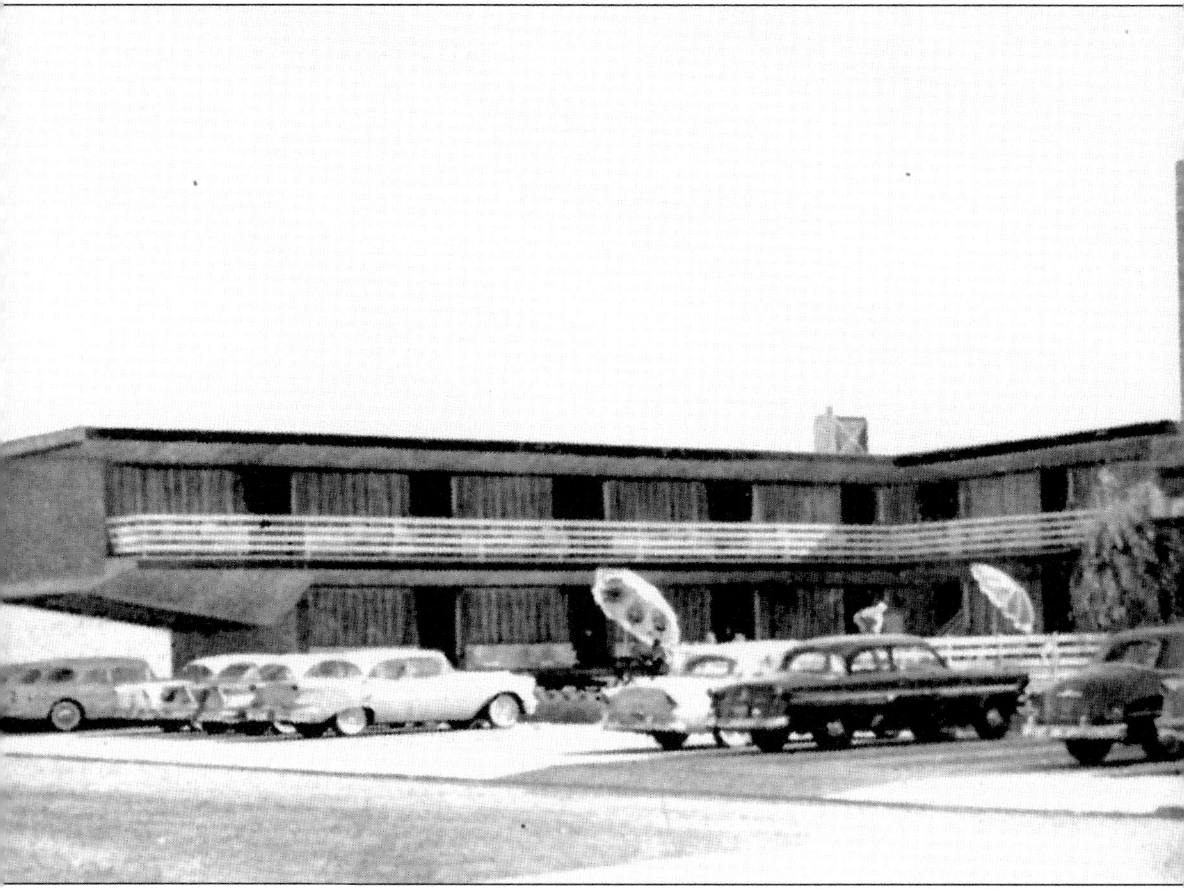

The Eden Roc Motel is seen in this view from the 1950s, shortly after its grand opening. If not modeled upon, then it was certainly inspired by the famous Eden Roc Hotel located in Miami Beach. This stunning example of 1950s architecture is an absolute gem located at the intersection of Atlantic and Bennett Avenues. The motel advertised air conditioning, television, and a swimming

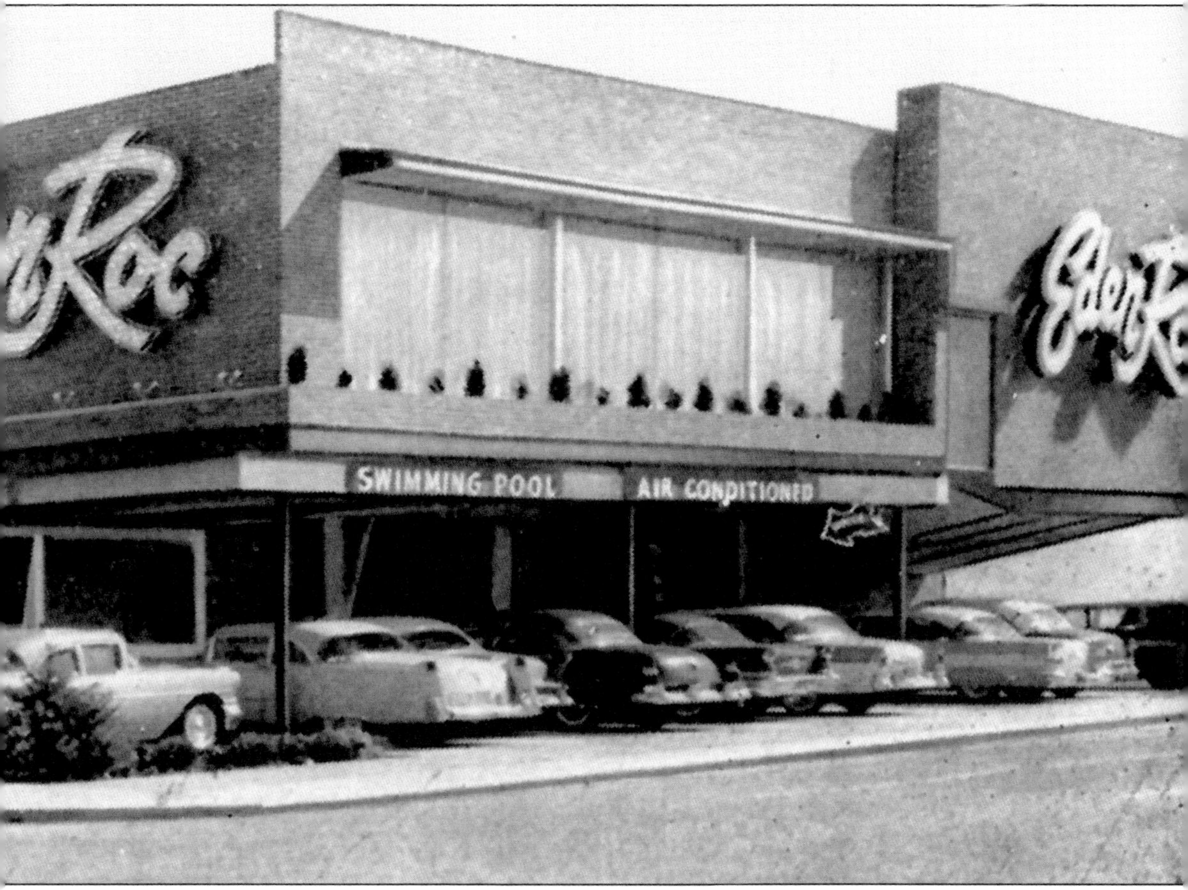

pool among its amenities. In later years, a coffee shop was added to the ground floor. Despite a great location and attractive look, the Eden Roc Motel has fallen on harder times. As of 2007, the structure is for sale. Sadly the sign suggests a "redevelopment opportunity." The Eden Roc Motel's days may very well be numbered.

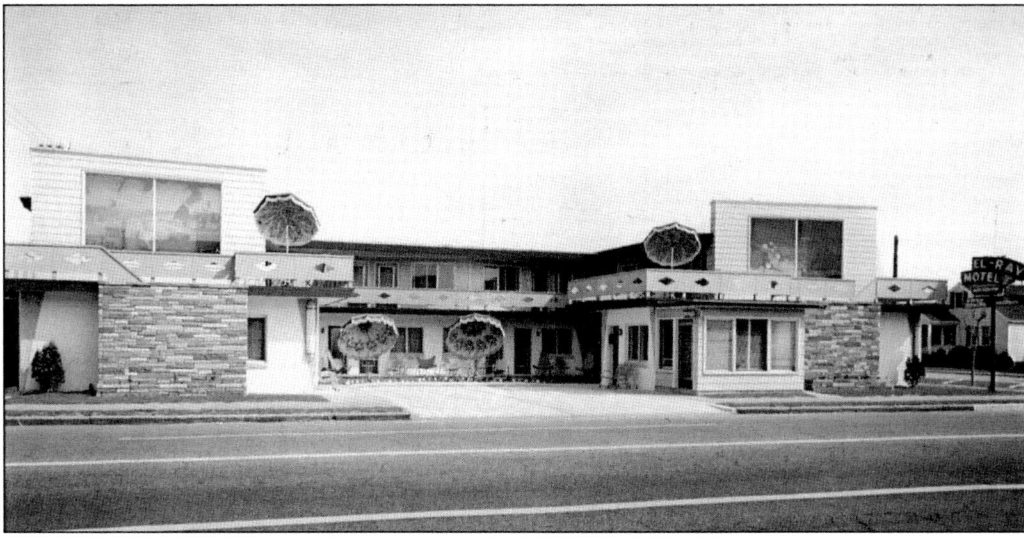

The El-Ray Motel is seen in this view from the 1950s, located at 4711 Atlantic Avenue. The rear of the postcard entices visitors to its location by exclaiming that Wildwood's beaches are the "safest and finest bathing beaches in the world." Although that proclamation might have been a bit of a stretch by aiming for global status, there is no denying that Wildwood has great beaches. The El-Ray Motel remains in place today and continues to operate as a motel.

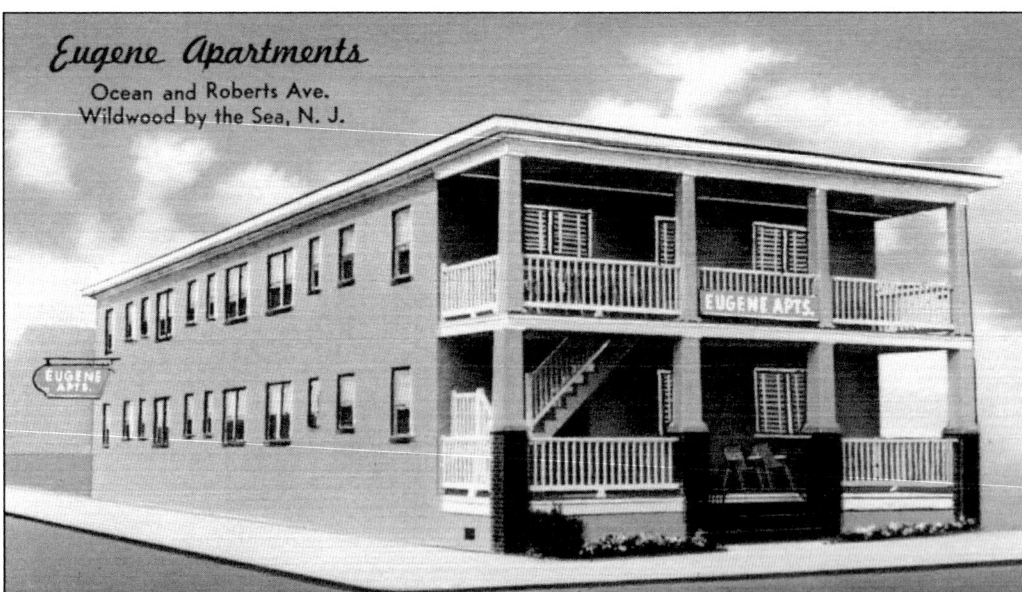

The Eugene Apartments was located along Ocean Avenue at Roberts Avenue, as seen in this postcard from the 1950s. The attractive little building would carry on for decades after this postcard was produced but has since been demolished.

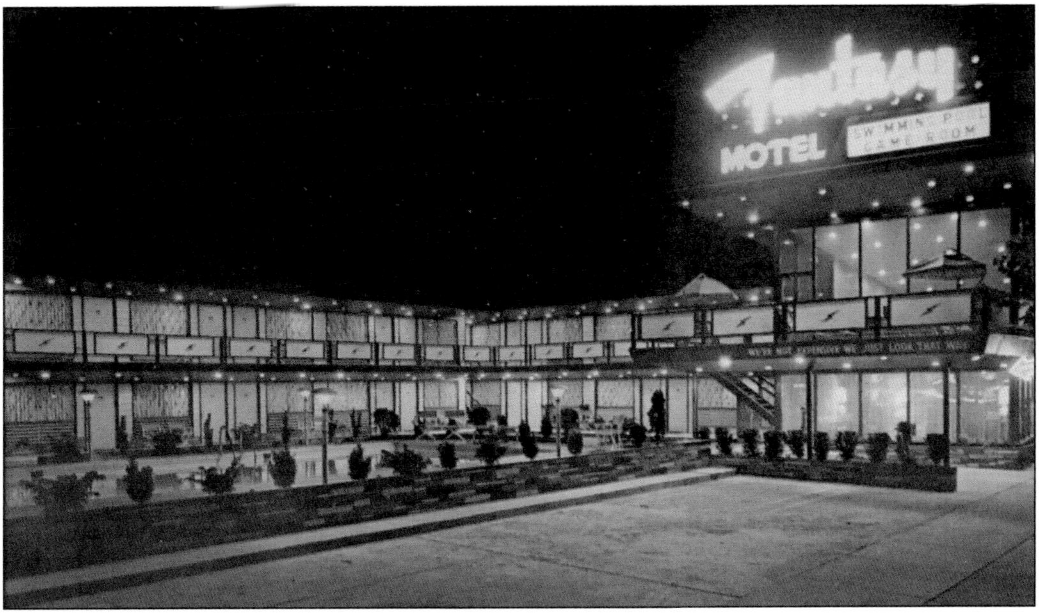

The Fantasy Motel was located at 131 West Rio Grande Avenue, along the principle thoroughfare entering Wildwood. This night-view postcard shows the motel as it appeared in the 1950s, once "featuring 21 of Wildwood's most ultra-modern motel units." By the late 1990s, the Fantasy Motel had certainly seen better days. Today the motel is gone, having been replaced with a parking lot for the adjacent Harley-Davidson Motorcycle dealership.

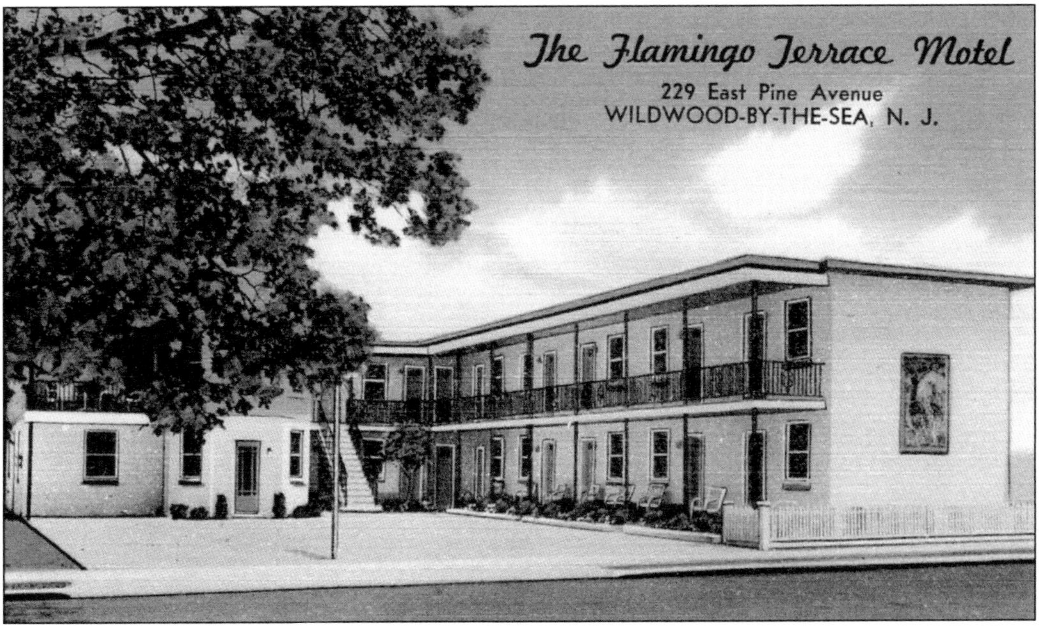

The Flamingo Terrace Motel was located at 229 East Pine Avenue and would operate in that capacity for many years before being demolished to make way for new residences. This postcard from the 1950s shows the modest motel as seen from Pine Avenue.

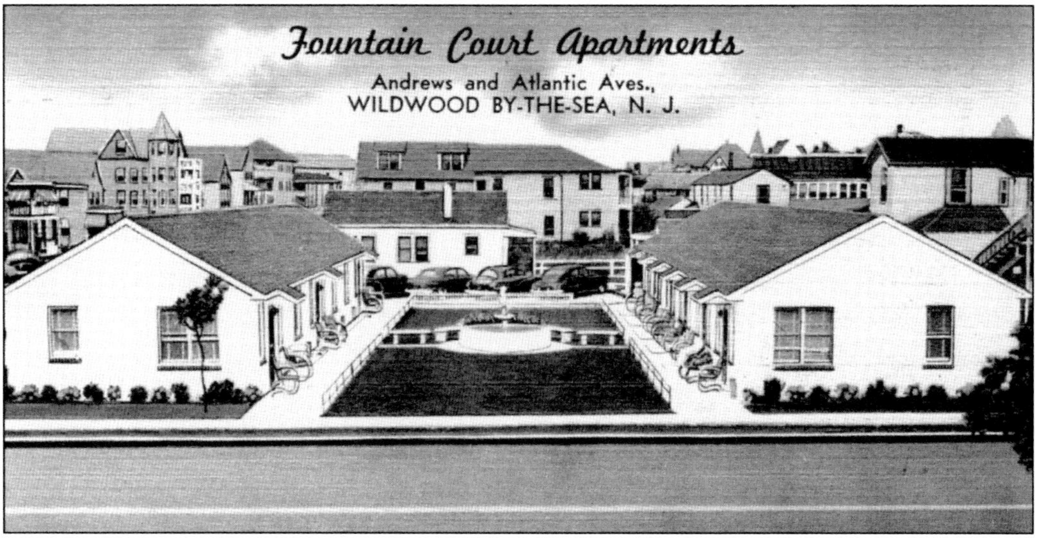

Originally known as the Fountain Court Apartments, this corner of Andrews and Atlantic Avenues has been home to the Fountain Motel for decades. The postcard at the top of the page was produced in the late 1940s, showing the Fountain Court Apartments as a pair of one-story buildings facing each other across a courtyard. As seen in this view, the mostly grass courtyard is adorned with the namesake fountain. Fast-forward just a few short years, and the Fountain Court Apartments had been remade and rechristened as the Fountain Motel. Subsequent to this conversion, the motel could now offer 24 modern units, each with private bath and television. The author and his family spent many summer vacations in Wildwood, often staying at the Fountain Motel. Although the building looks very similar today, a swimming pool has been added to the property and the classic 1950s-era sign has been removed.

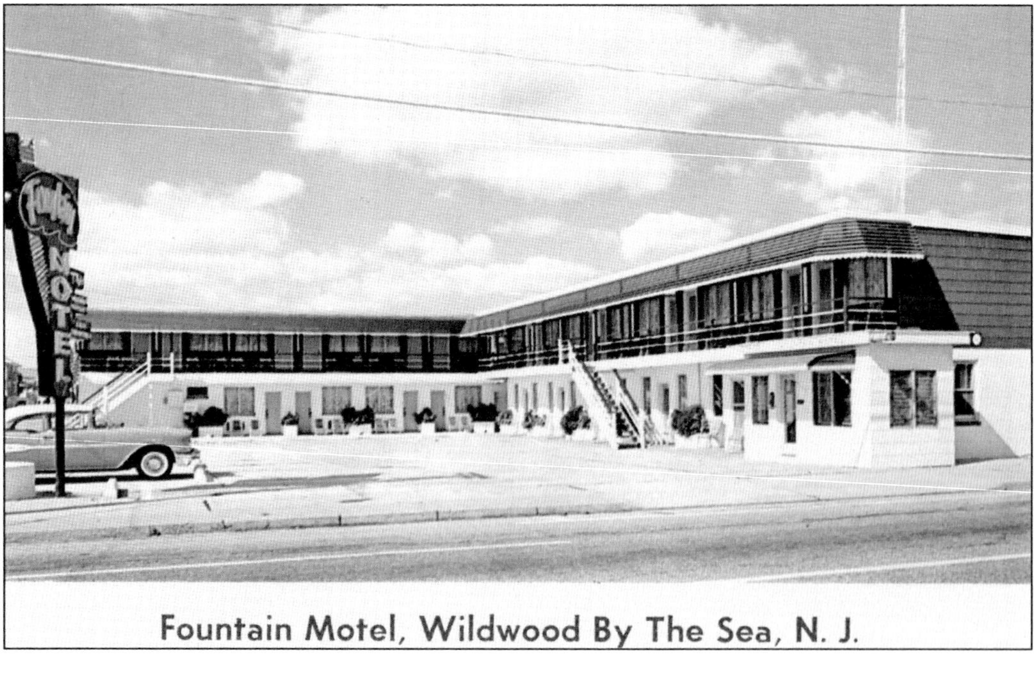

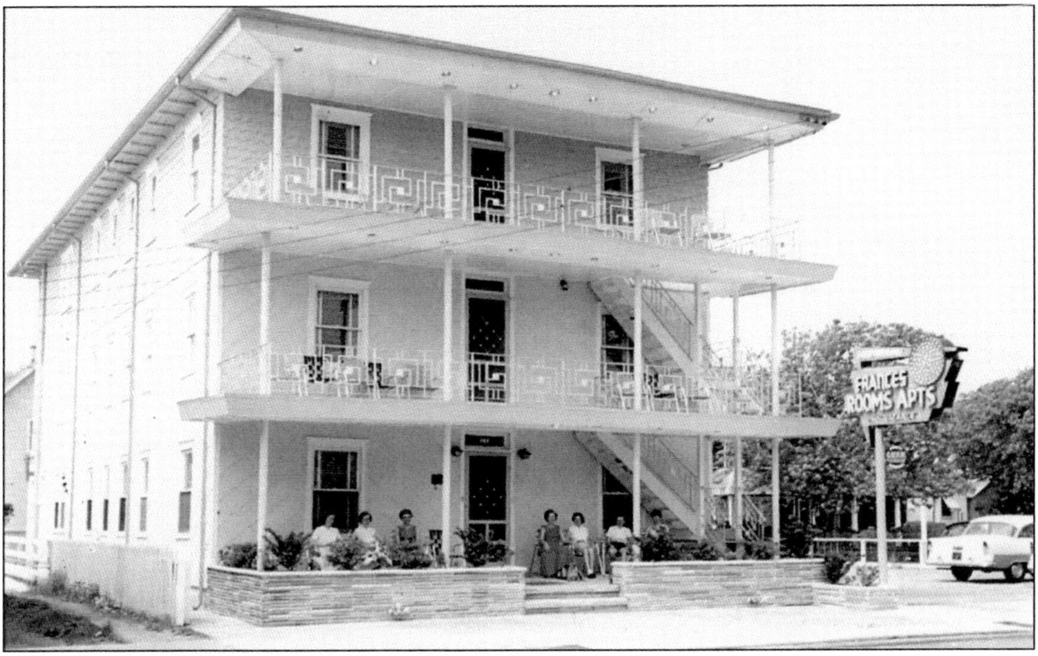

The Frances Apartments was located at 146 East Spencer Avenue as seen in this postcard from the 1950s. Despite an elapse of more than five decades, the building is still painted the same color and looks much the same today as it did then. However, the old sign has been removed from the front, and it now functions as more of a traditional apartment house.

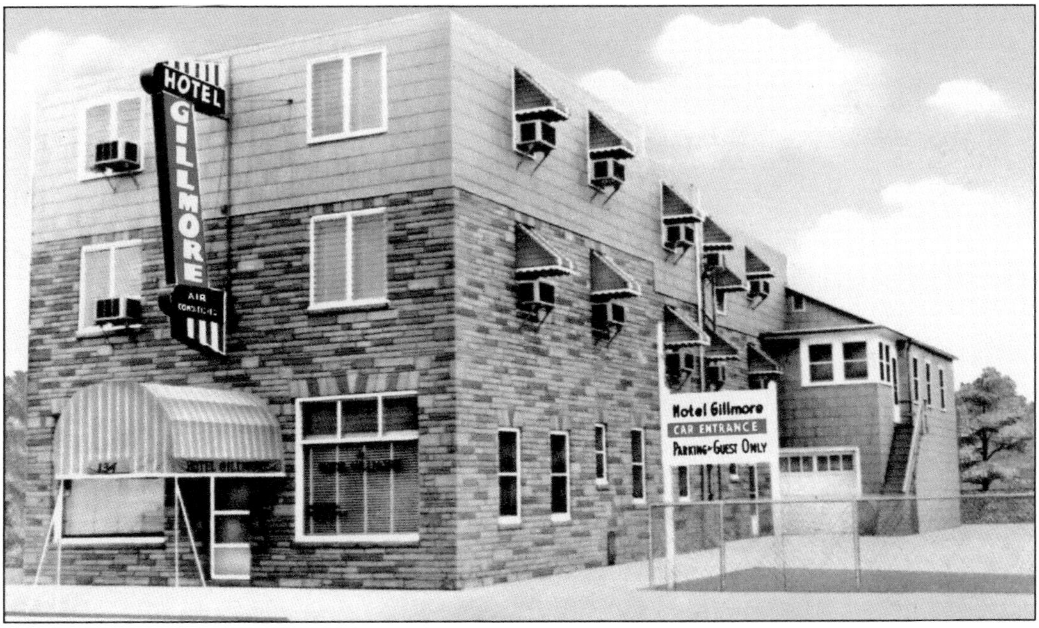

The Hotel Gillmore is located at 134 East Schellenger Avenue and seen in this postcard from the 1950s. Today the building still functions as the Hotel Gillmore, and the presence of the old sign still looms over Schellenger Avenue below. Remarkably the Hotel Gillmore's exterior has changed very little over the last five decades.

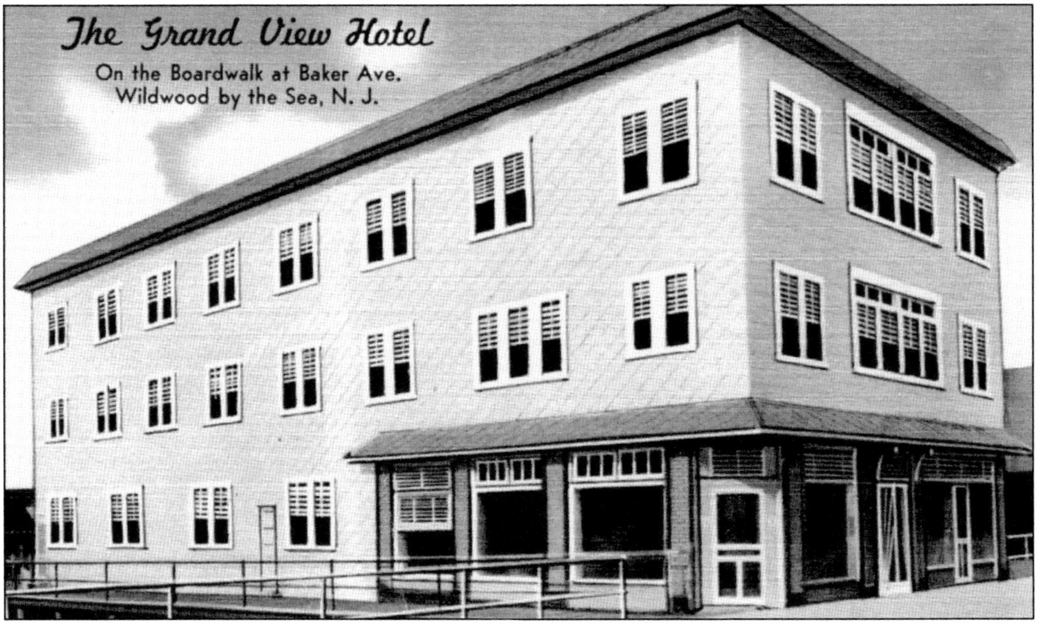

The Grand View Hotel was once located on the boardwalk at Baker Avenue. This postcard from the 1940s shows a sparsely decorated building that must have had phenomenal ocean views from its perched vantage point along the boardwalk. Today the building remains in place but no longer operates as a hotel. The ground floor contains a store appropriately named the Grandview Gift Shop. Additionally the building has been given a layer of more modern siding to its exterior.

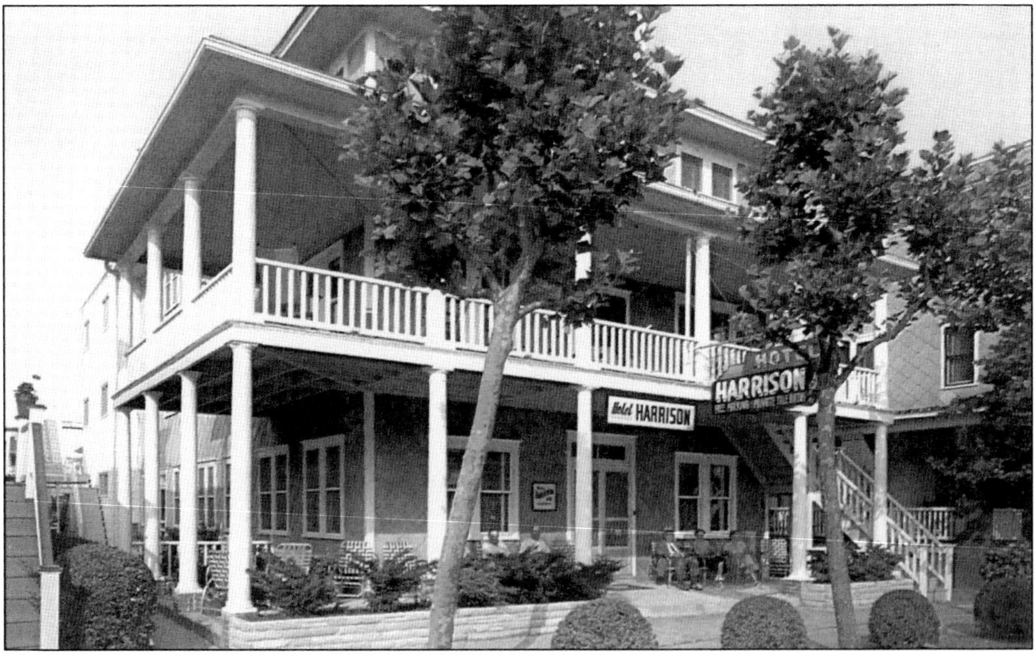

This postcard from the 1950s shows the Harrison Hotel located at 310 East Pine Avenue. The rear of the postcard notes that the hotel was only a meager 200 feet from the beach and featured 44 units, each with private bath. Today the Harrison Hotel is gone. The hotel's former site now hosts a swimming pool next to the Doris Vernon Hotel.

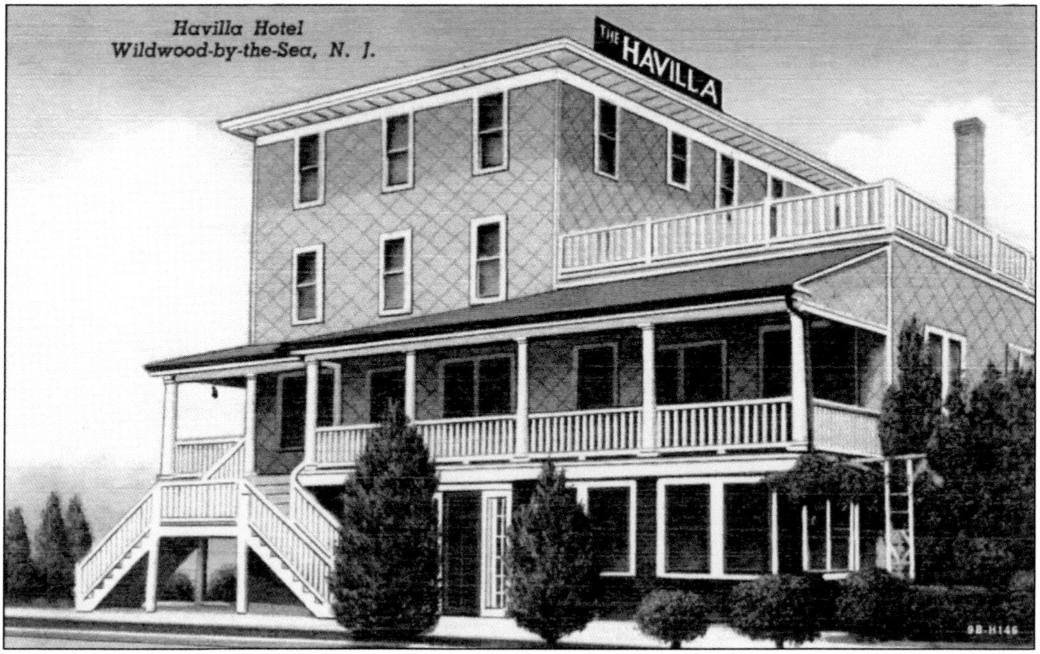

The Havilla Hotel is seen in this postcard from the 1940s. This four-story building was located at 233 East Burk Avenue in downtown Wildwood. The Havilla Hotel was just one of many similarly designed buildings in the immediate area. Today the Havilla Hotel's former site is now a parking lot.

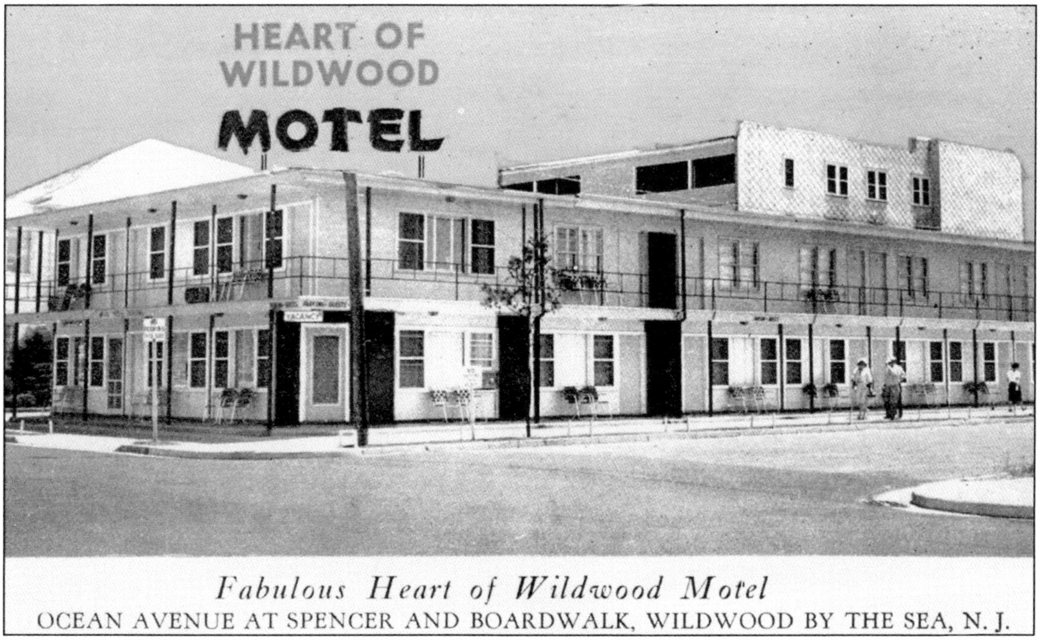

The Heart of Wildwood Motel is located at 3915 Ocean Avenue, at Spencer Avenue. This postcard from the 1950s shows the motel before the full third story was added on to it. Despite several interior and exterior modifications over the years, the main entrance remains directly at the corner. Today the facility still operates as a motel.

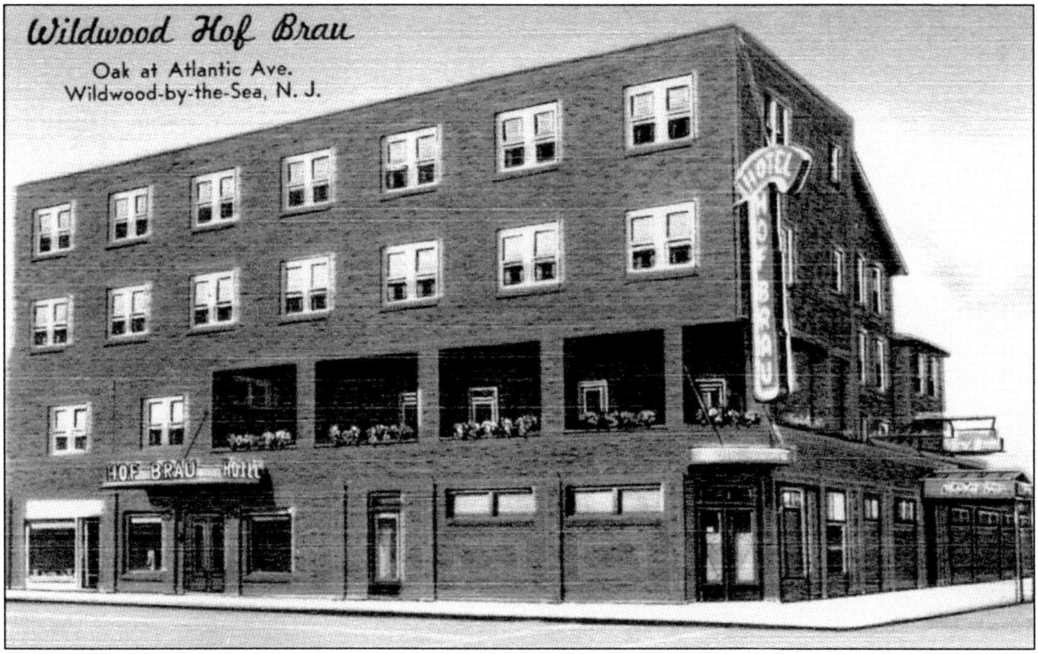

The Hotel Hof Brau was located at the corner of Oak and Atlantic Avenues, as seen in this postcard from the 1940s. The imposing four-story brick building had a vertical sign hanging over the corner entrance. Later the ground floor would become home to Valentino's Restaurant. Today the Hotel Hof Brau is but a memory of the past.

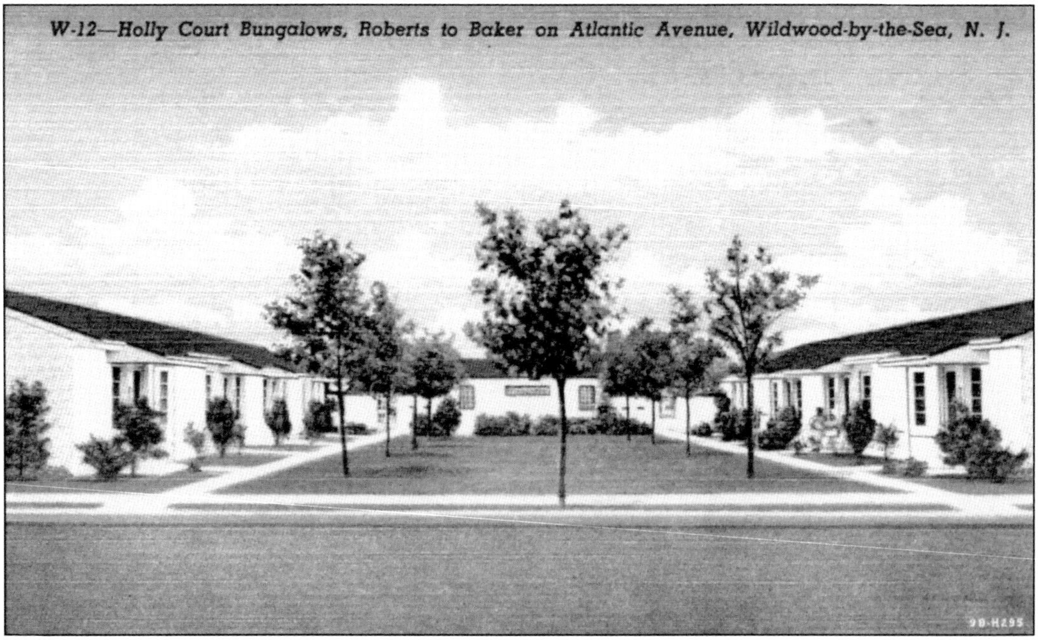

The Holly Court Bungalows were located along Atlantic Avenue, between Roberts and Baker Avenues. This postcard from the 1950s shows the quaint buildings surrounding a tree-lined courtyard. Today this area of Atlantic Avenue has seen copious commercial development, and the Holly Court Bungalows have become a thing of the past.

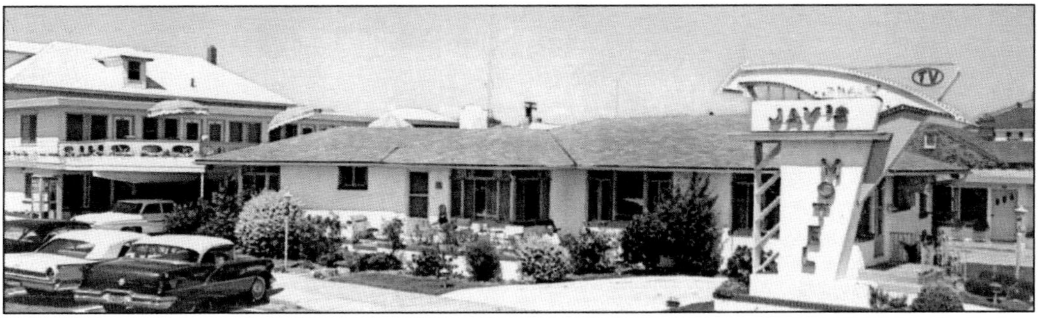

Jay's Motel was located at 5210 Atlantic Avenue, as viewed in this postcard from the 1950s. The great 1950s-era sign partially obscures one of the 24 "modern" motel units that Jay's Motel offered. Today the motel is gone, replaced by the somewhat ubiquitous condominiums that seem to be everywhere in Wildwood today.

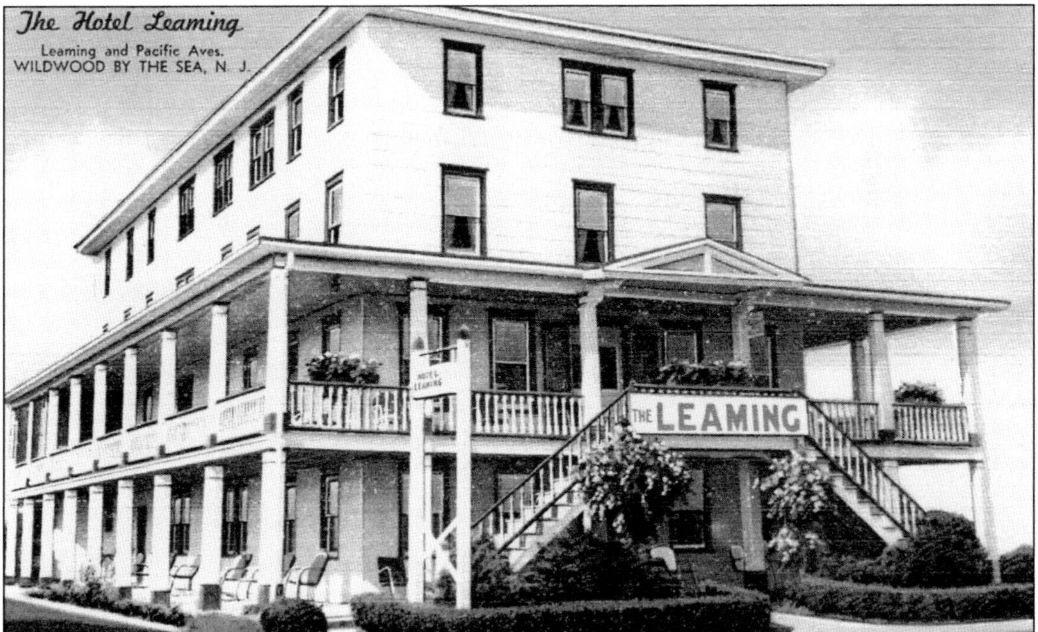

The Hotel Leaming was located appropriately enough at the intersection of Leaming and Pacific Avenues. This postcard from the 1940s shows the four-story building with a dual staircase entrance decorated by various types of foliage. Today the Hotel Leaming is but a memory of the past.

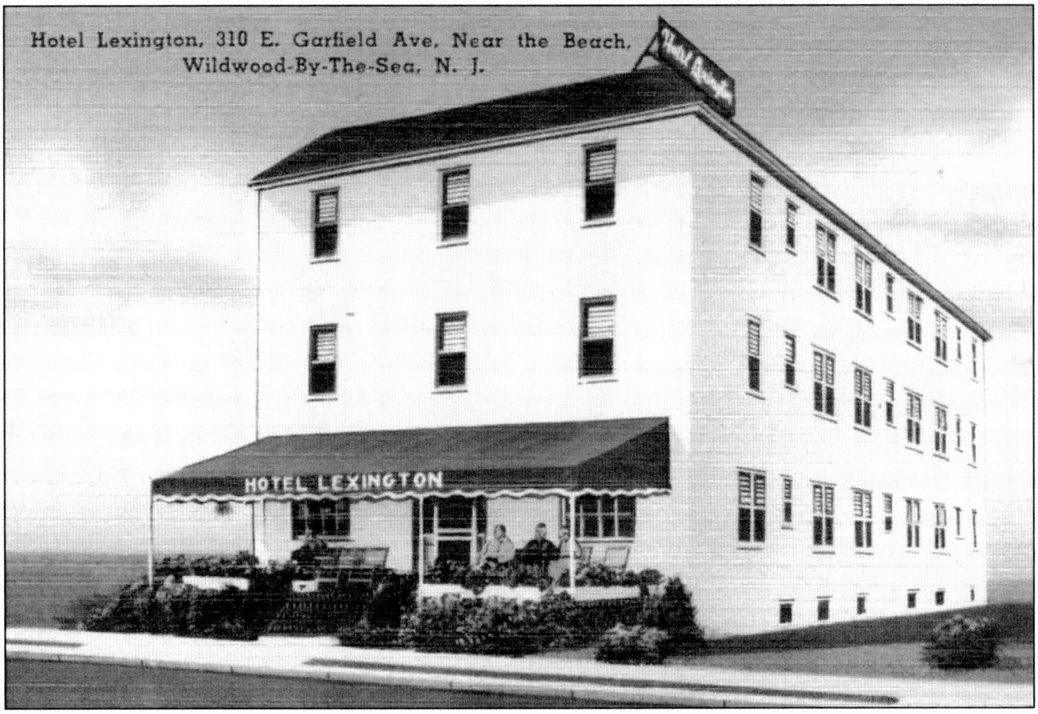

The Hotel Lexington was originally known as the Hotel Lessington and located at 310 East Garfield Avenue. Today the building remains but is now operated under the name of Key West Hotel. Despite several exterior modifications over the years, the building is still easily recognizable.

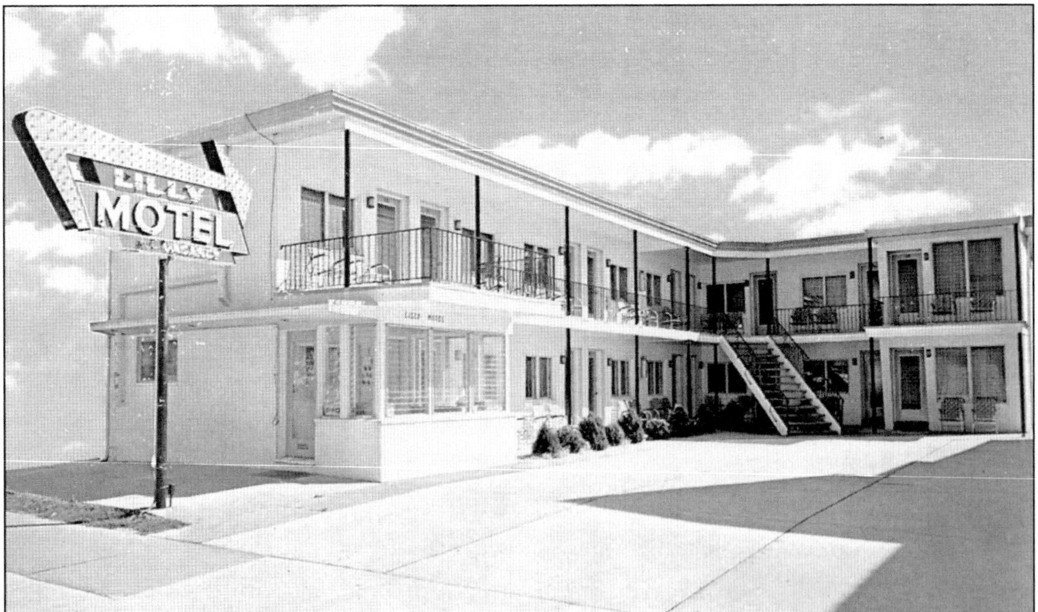

The Lilly Motel was located at 228 East Magnolia Avenue and is seen in this postcard from the late 1950s. The back of the card promises "modest rates," along with private baths. Today the building still exists but is now home to the Luther Inn Retreat Center, a religious organization.

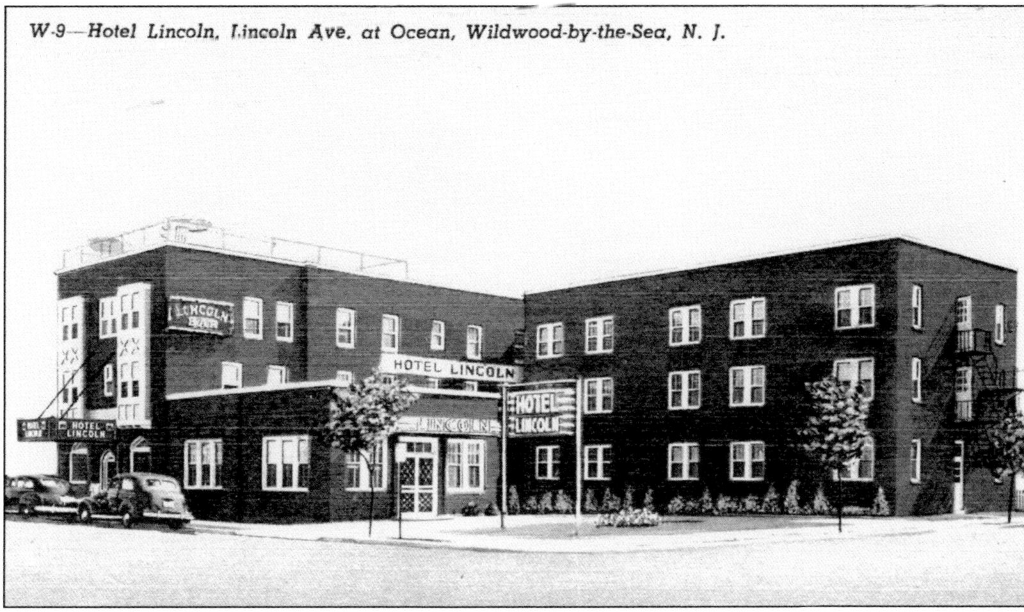

This postcard shows the Hotel Lincoln, aptly located at Lincoln Avenue and Ocean Avenue. This moderately sized, three-story brick hotel dominated the corner and featured the popular Mirror Room bar in its day. Despite its popularity years ago, the Hotel Lincoln is long gone and has become one of many Wildwood hotels that are no more.

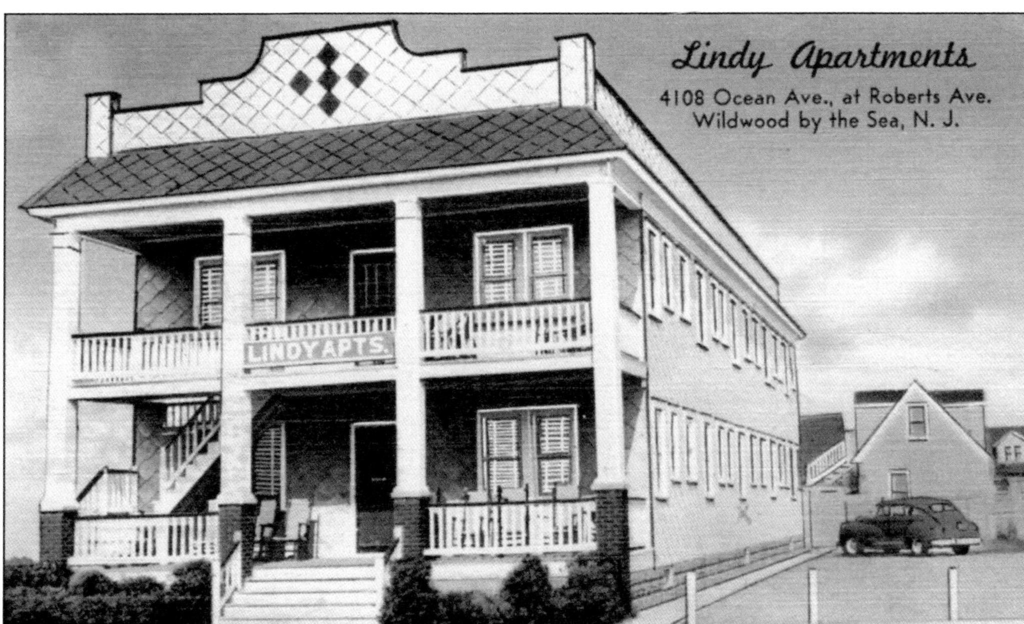

The Lindy Apartments was located at 4108 Ocean Avenue at Roberts Avenue, as seen in this postcard from the late 1940s. The small building would seem quite out of place today along this block of Ocean Avenue that is dominated by larger, more modern motels. As such, the Lindy Apartments ceased to be long ago.

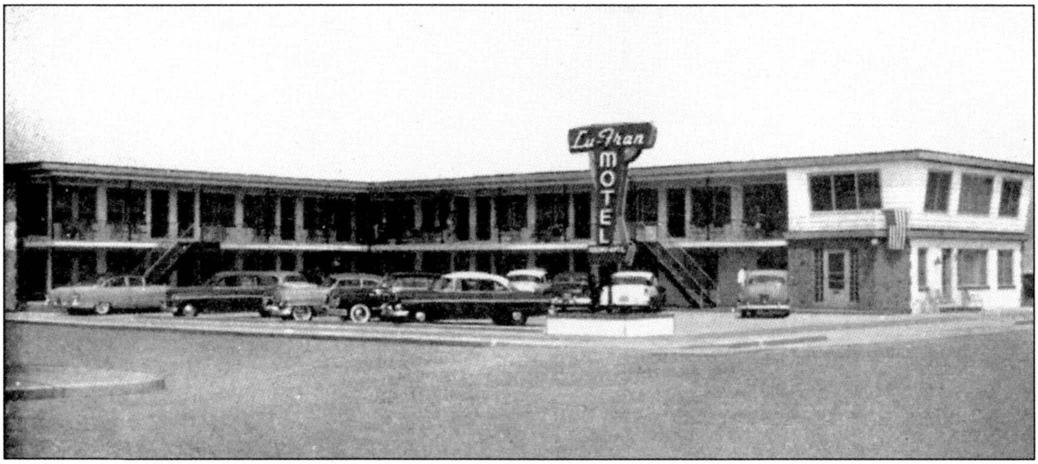

The Lu-Fran Motel is seen in this view from the early 1950s in its location at 5106 Ocean Avenue at Bennett Avenue. The motel is still in business today and has seen a portion of the parking lot turned into a swimming pool. Fortunately the motel's owners have resisted the notion of selling the motel for redevelopment in an area that has seen many other such motels demolished.

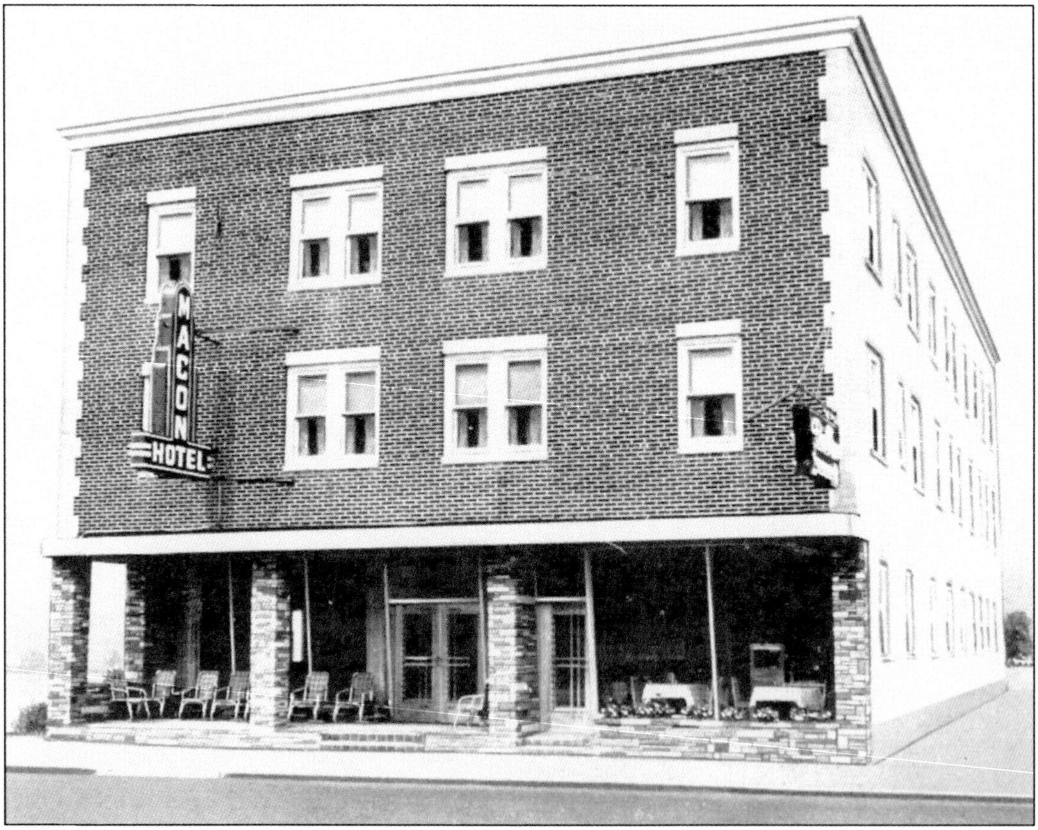

The Hotel Macon was located at 315 East Wildwood Avenue, as seen in this postcard from the 1950s. The hotel offered only some rooms with private baths, something that would be considered a standard necessity in today's world. Today modern townhouses sit on the former site of the Hotel Macon.

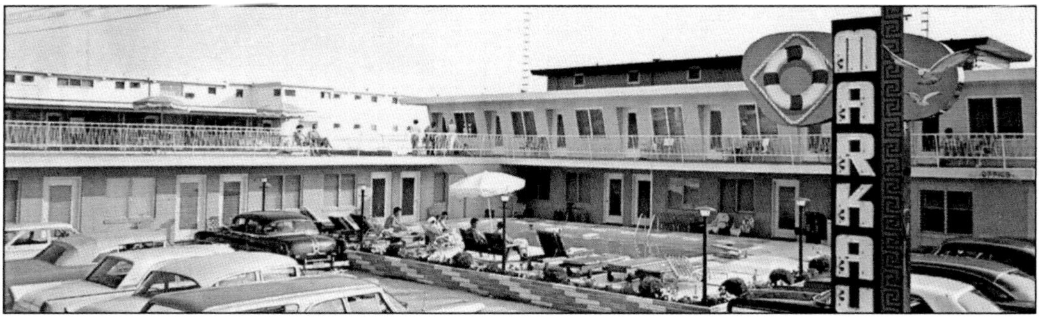

The Markay Motel was located at 3701 Atlantic Avenue and is seen in this postcard from the 1950s. The motel featured a swimming pool and off-street parking. As development and progress presses forward in the Wildwoods today, the Markay Motel is one of many that have not survived into the 21st century.

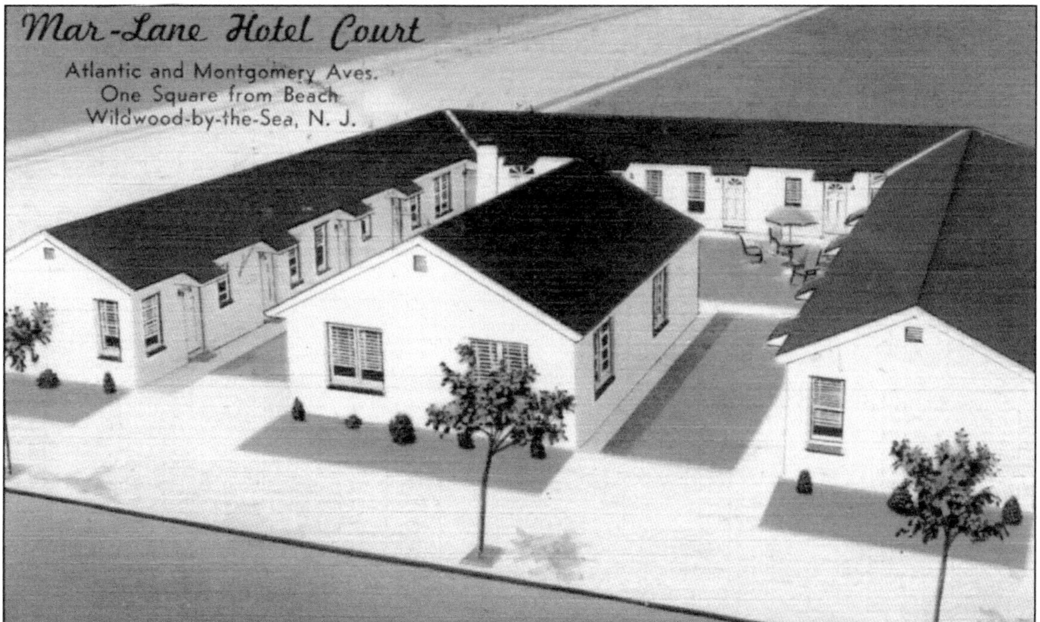

The Mar-Lane Hotel Court has been simply renamed MarLane and still offers lodging more than 50 years after this postcard was produced. The facility continues to be located at Atlantic and Montgomery Avenues but has been modified significantly over the years.

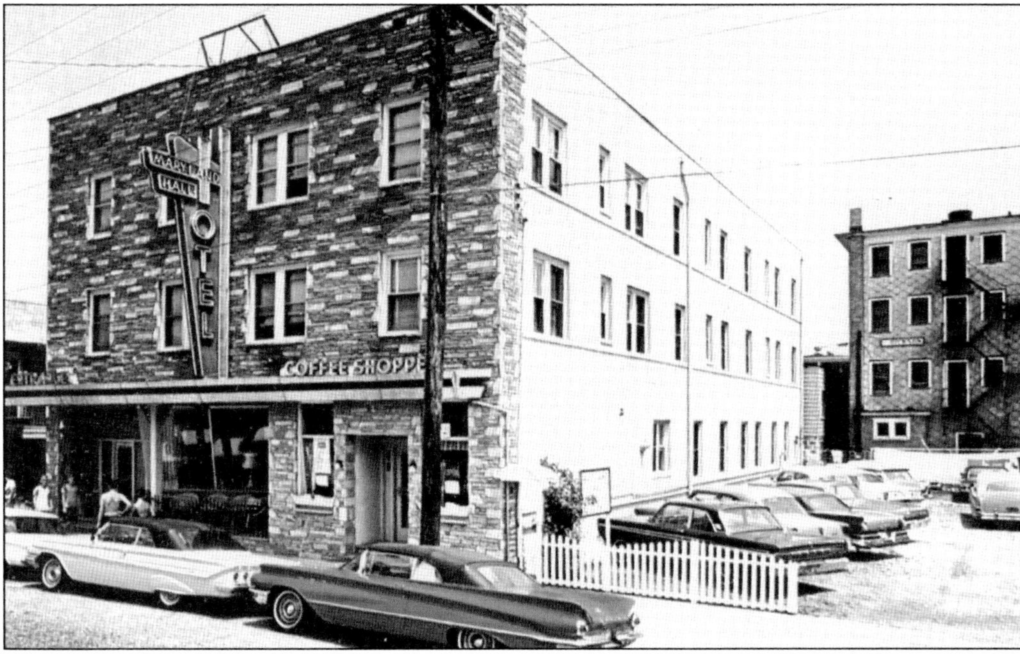

The Maryland Hall Hotel was located at 327–329 East Wildwood Avenue. Seen in a postcard from the 1950s, the hotel would serve tourists for decades. It featured an on-premises coffee shop and was only steps from the famous three-mile boardwalk. Today modern townhouses sit in its place on East Wildwood Avenue.

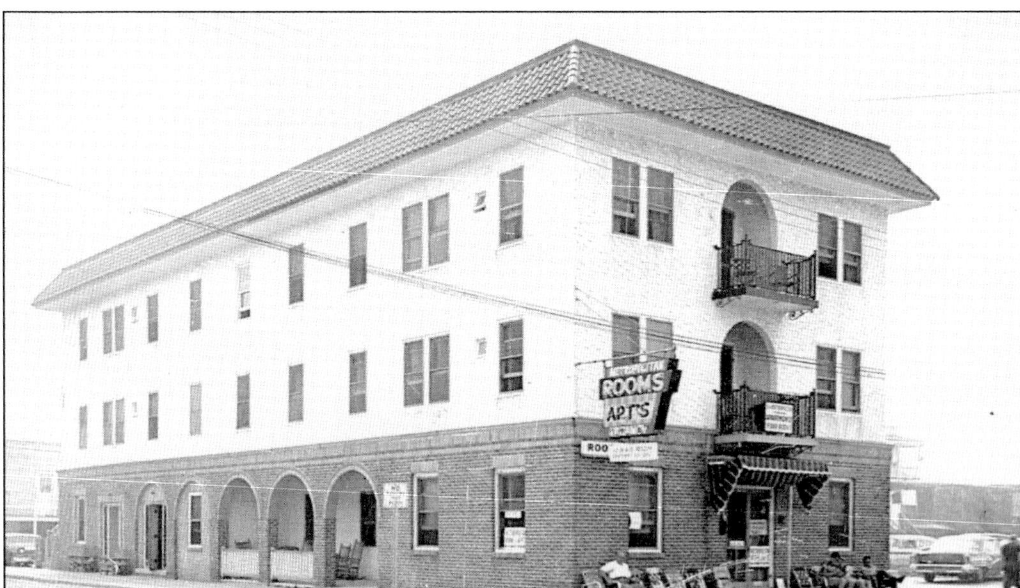

The Metropolitan Hotel and Apartments is seen in this postcard from the 1950s. The rear of the card provides two addresses for the dual facility at 4301 and 4211 Ocean Avenue. The information given on the postcard also boasts of the hotel's proximity to the beach. Today the hotel and apartments are gone, a memory of Wildwood's past.

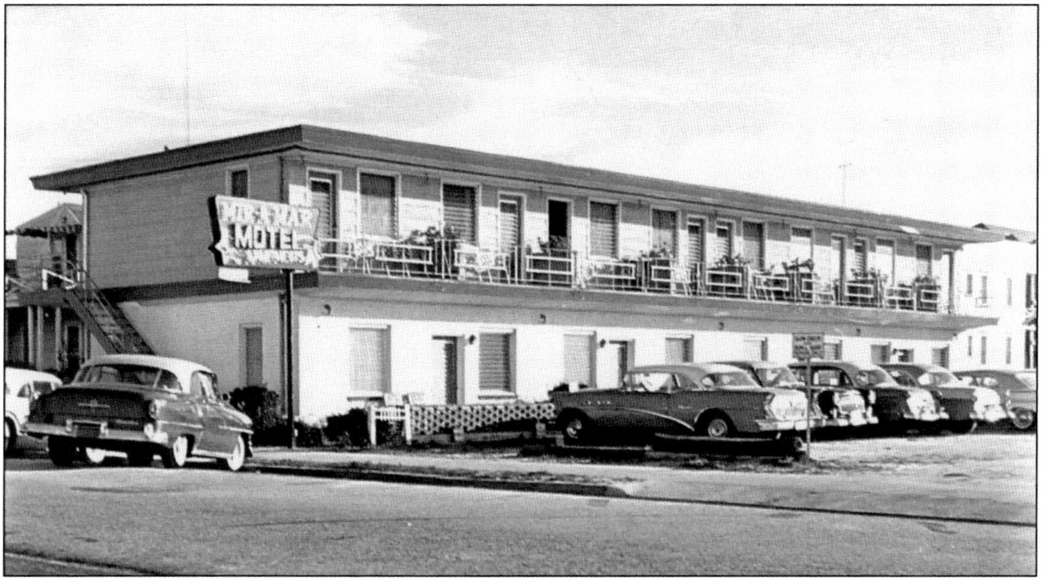

The Mir-A-Mar Motel had the dual address of 307 East Taylor Avenue and 306 East Andrews Avenue, two streets that run parallel to each other. The small but comfortable motel is yet another in a long list of Wildwood motels that have been lost to time and progress.

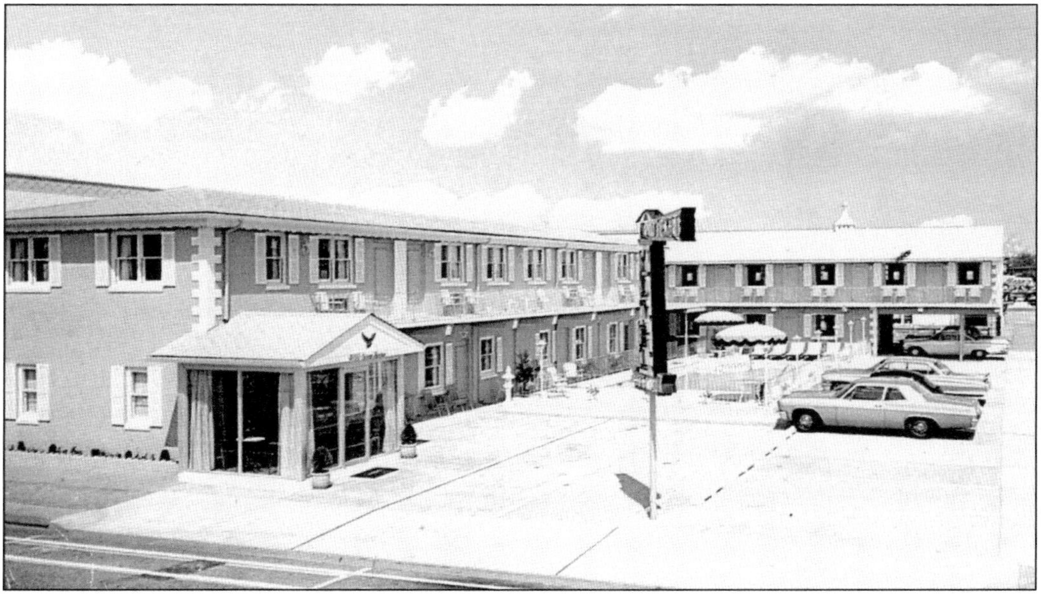

The Nantucket Motel is located at 4100 Ocean Avenue and boasts standard rooms as well as efficiency units. This postcard from the 1960s shows the motel from Ocean Avenue with a view of the swimming pool. Today the building has been painted yellow and still operates as a motel.

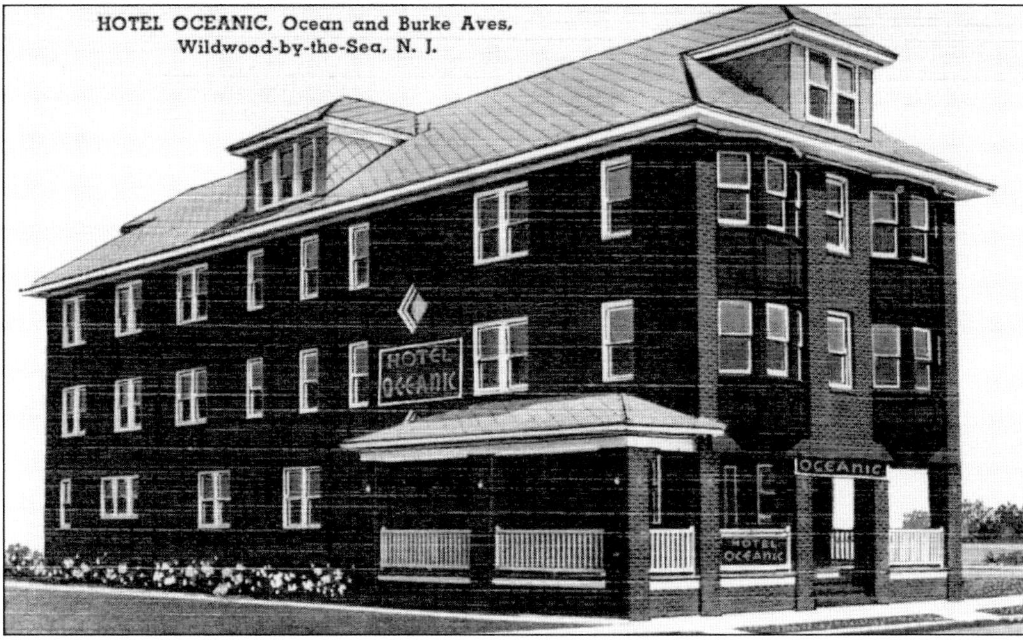

The Hotel Oceanic is located along Ocean Avenue at Burk Avenue. The 1940s-era postcard at the top of the page shows the original building, a four-story brick structure with commanding views of the ocean. Given the popularity of the hotel and its magnificent location, a larger and more modern hotel was constructed adjacent to the original building and can be seen in the postcard at the bottom of the page. Despite this addition to the property, the original hotel building can still be seen on the left side of this 1950s-era postcard. Although the newer building remains in place today, the original hotel was replaced with a more modern building years ago. At the time of this writing, an enormous banner hanging from the building proclaims the Hotel Oceanic as the future site of "condotels," a new concept that represents a hybrid in terms of rental and ownership.

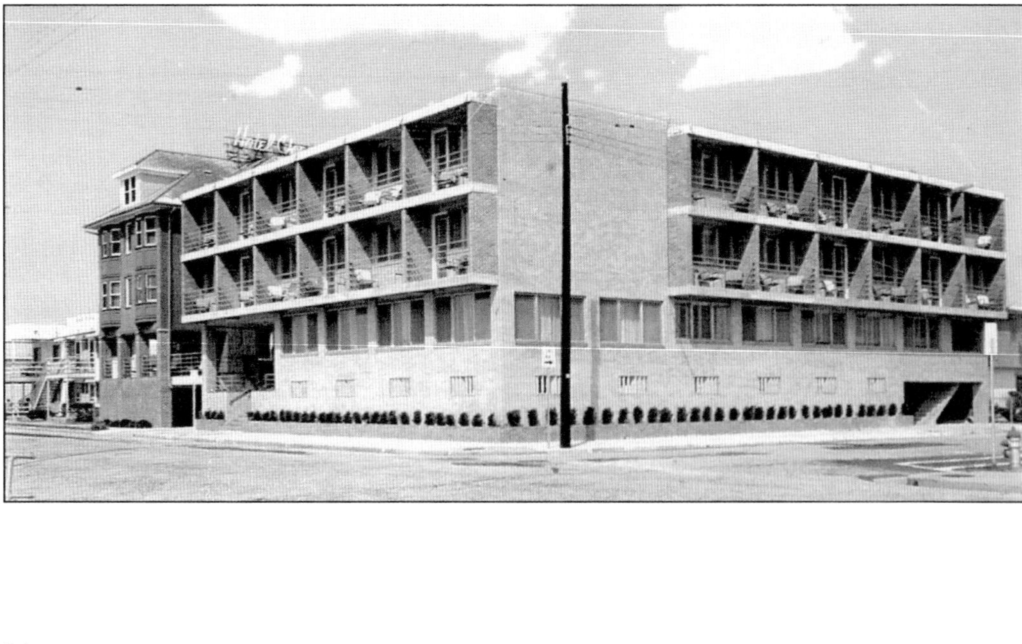

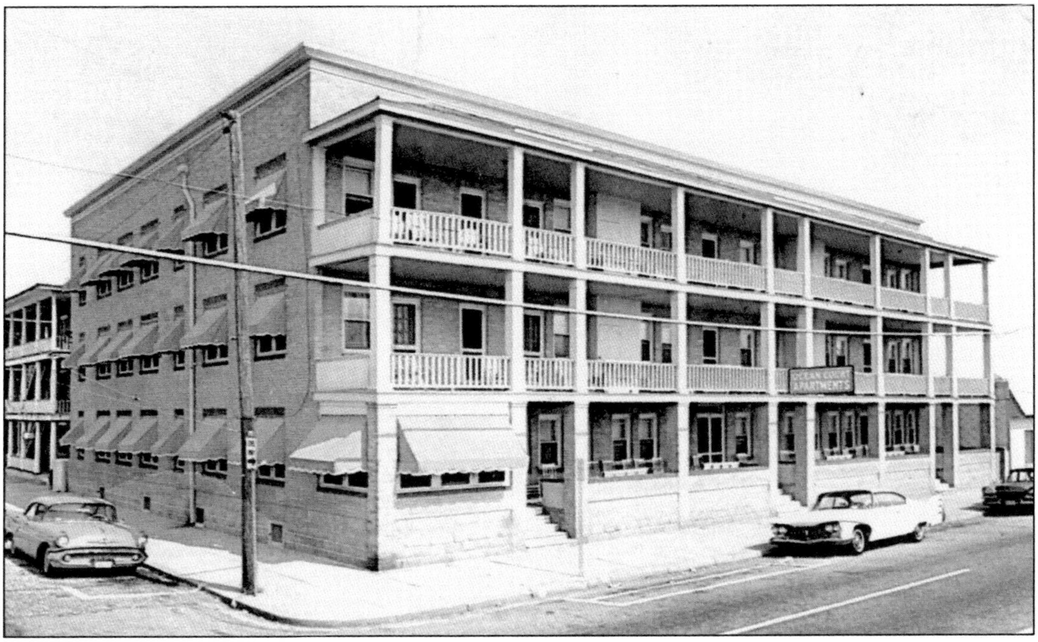

The Ocean Court Apartments was located at Davis and Atlantic Avenues, as seen in this postcard from the 1950s. The three-story brick building featured 36 "modern" and "furnished" apartments. The rear of the card touts the presence of an "Electrolux Refrigerator" in every room. Today the Ocean Court Apartments is just a memory.

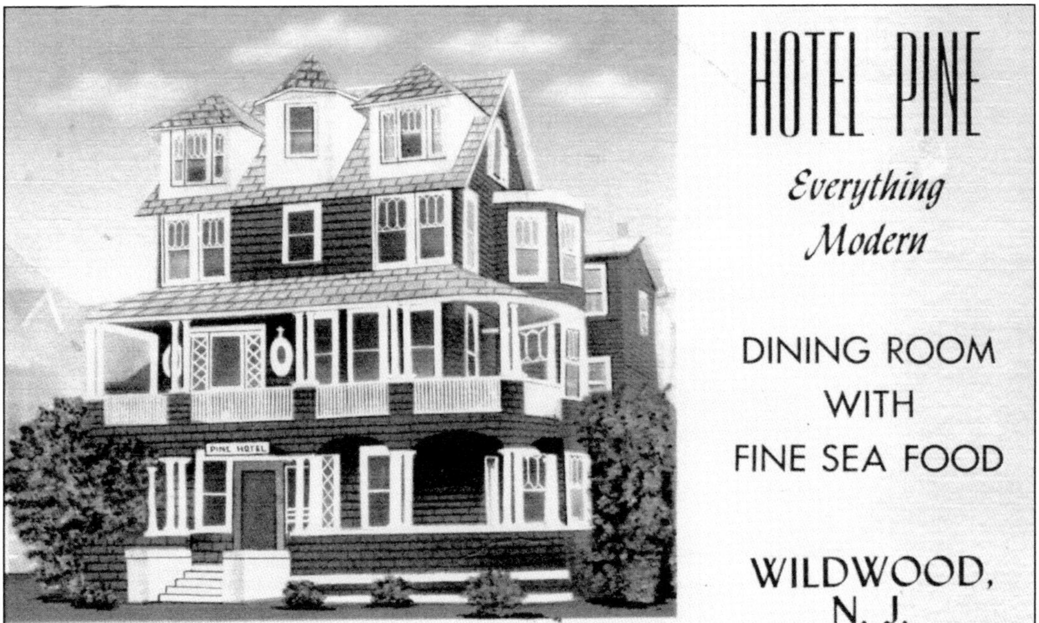

This postcard from the 1940s shows the Hotel Pine located at 221 East Pine Avenue. The front of the card proudly mentions that the dining room features "fine sea food." Today the small Hotel Pine no longer exists. The former site is now home to several modern residences.

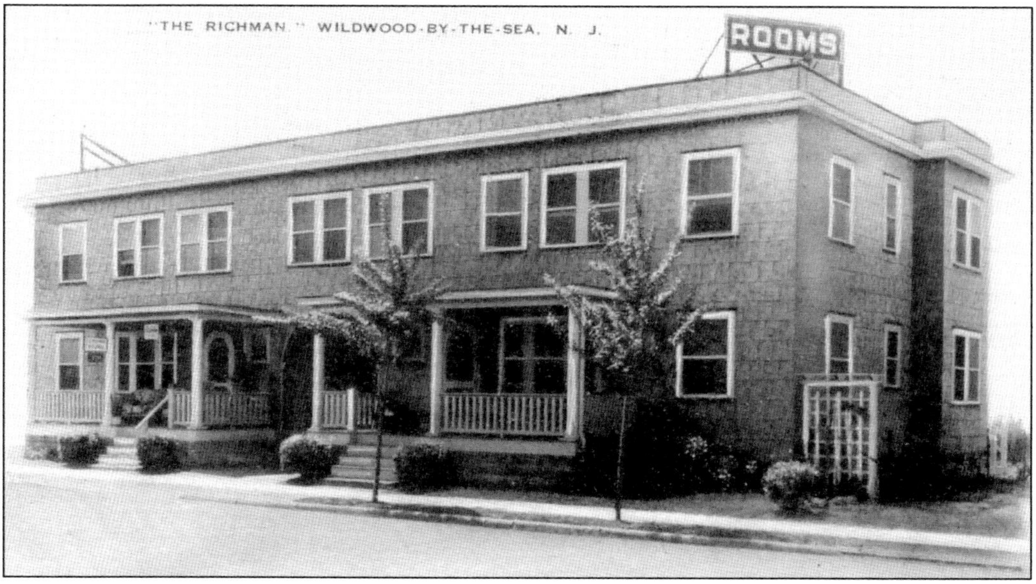

A postcard from the 1940s shows the Richman, located at 318 East Poplar Avenue. The rear of the card notes that the hotel features "unusual furnished rooms." Today the building remains in its place, although it no longer functions as a hotel.

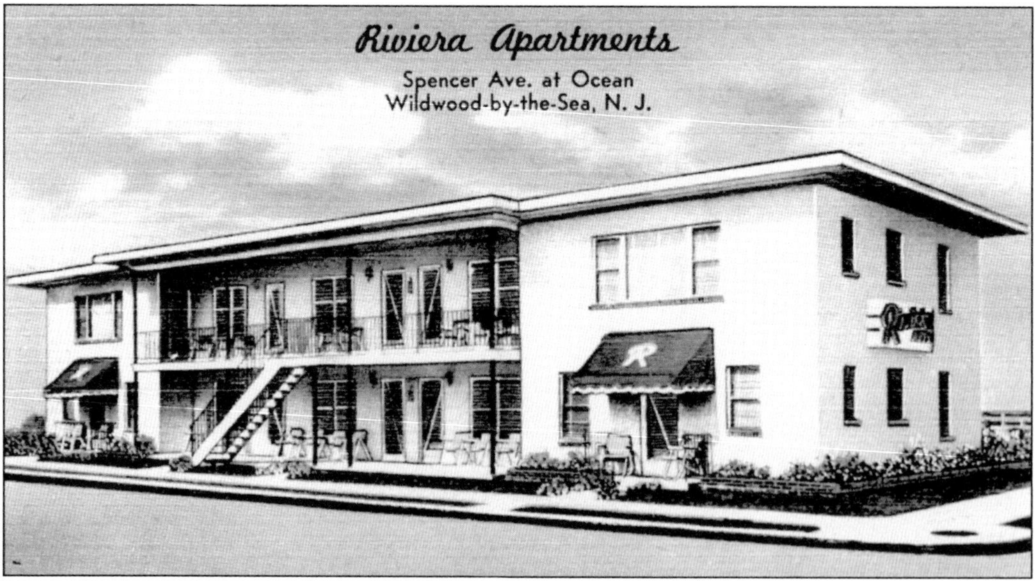

This postcard from the 1940s shows the Riviera Apartments, located at the corner of Spencer and Ocean Avenues. The modest motel has received significant modification over the years, but the original structure has managed to stay intact. Today it is known as the Riviera Resort Motel.

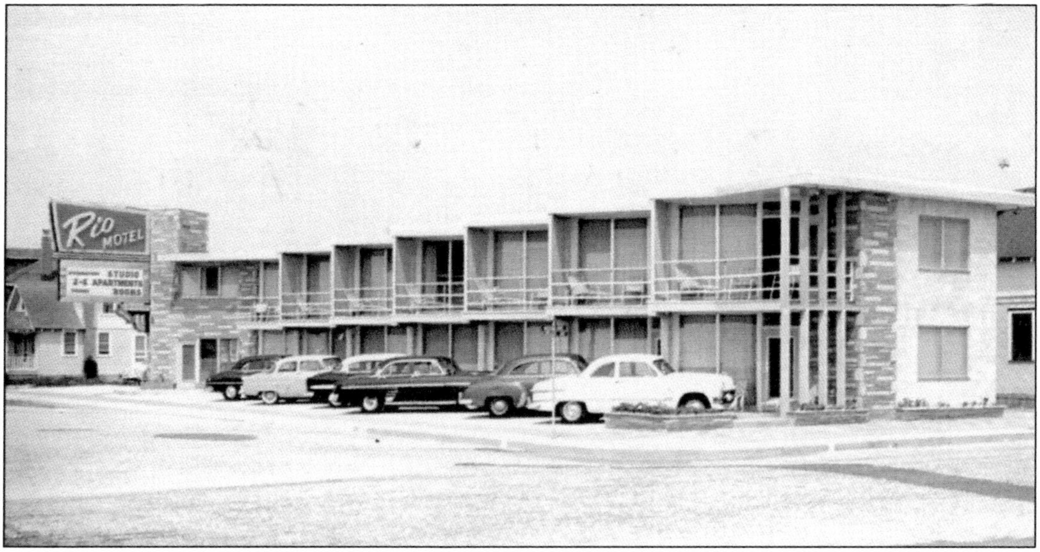

The expansive complex that was the Rio Motel was located at the corner of Rio Grande and Ocean Avenues in one of Wildwood's most prime lots. The postcard at the top of the page was created in the 1950s and shows several cars parked outside of rooms that faced Rio Grande Avenue. The motel would receive several modifications over the coming years, resulting in the addition of many rooms with great ocean views. The view at the bottom of the page was produced in the 1960s and shows the pool deck that looked out over the ocean. Sadly this truly classic Wildwood motel was demolished to make way for redevelopment. At the time of this writing, the large lot remains empty amid a softening real estate market in Wildwood.

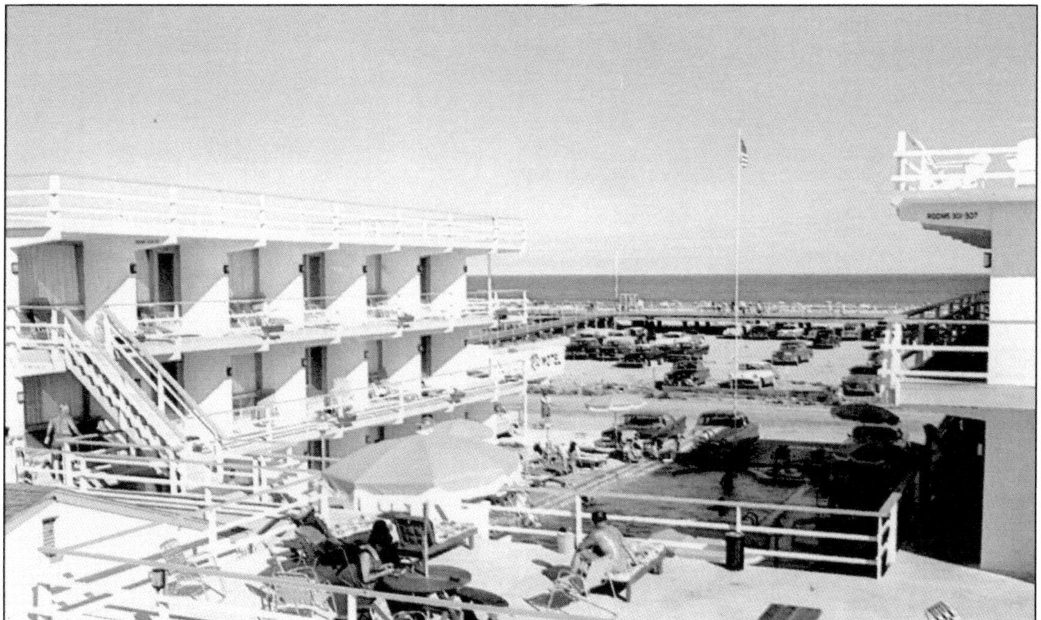

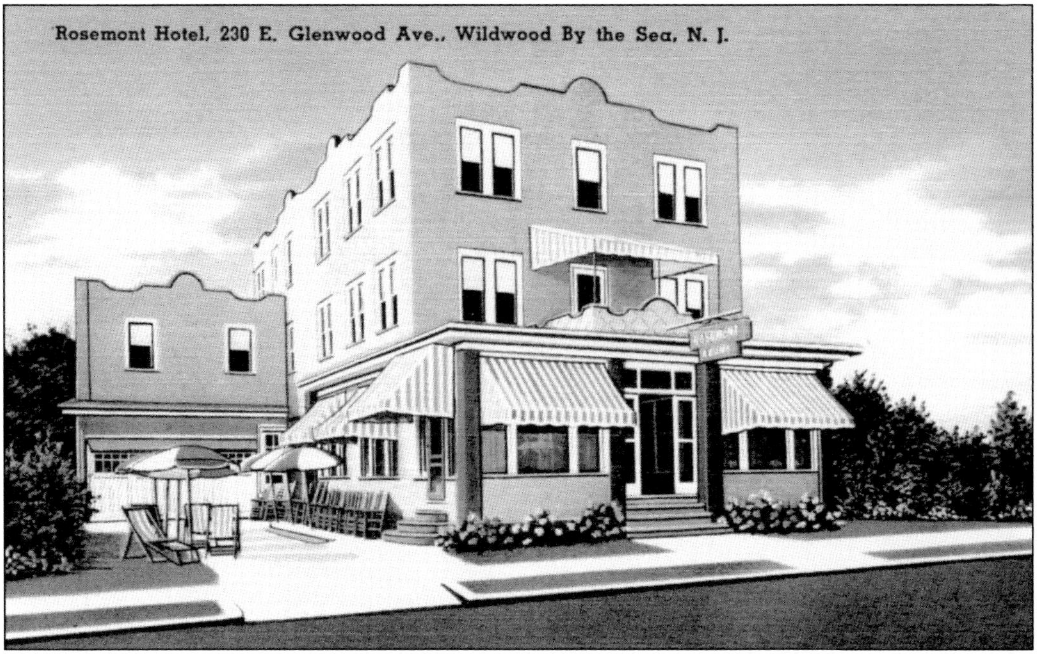

This postcard from the 1940s shows the Rosemont Hotel located at 230 East Glenwood Avenue. The modest three-story hotel boasted comfortable accommodations and a sitting area outside. Outdated by today's modern standards, the former site of the Rosemont Hotel is now home to new townhouses.

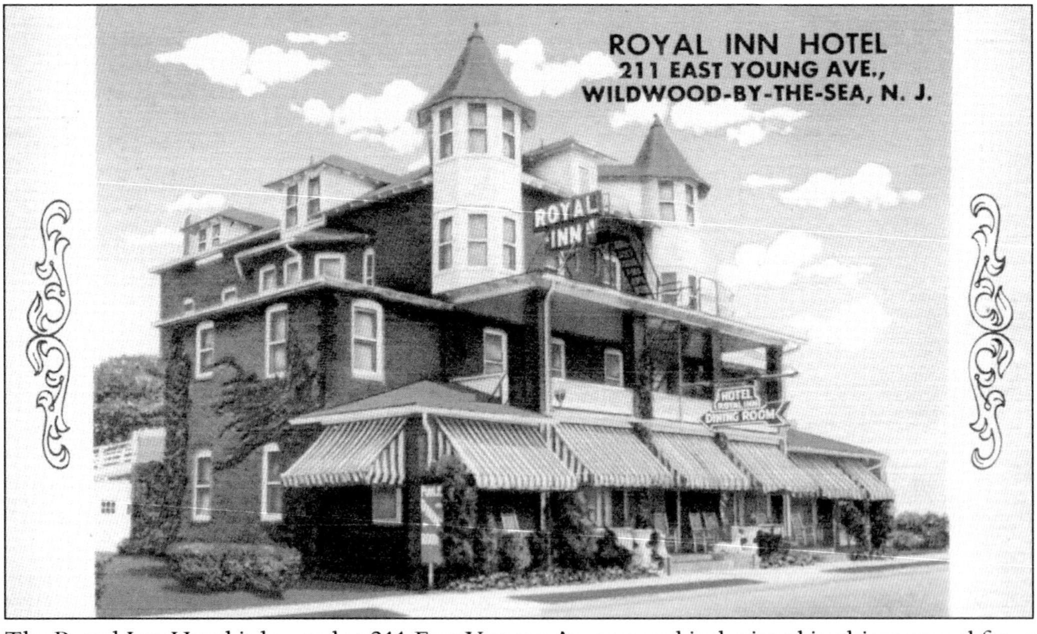

The Royal Inn Hotel is located at 211 East Youngs Avenue and is depicted in this postcard from the 1940s. Although still operating as a hotel, the Royal Inn Hotel has seen far better days. Since this image was produced, the twin spires that crowned the top of the building have been removed and capped. The hotel also no longer offers an on-site restaurant as it once did. Despite these changes, the building is still easily recognizable today.

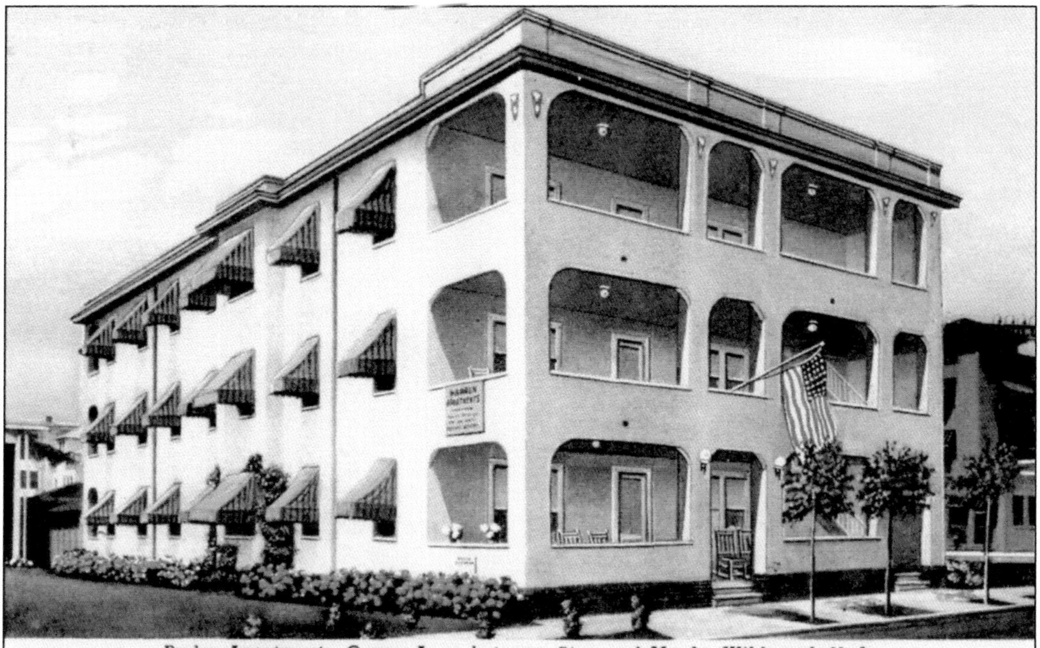

Ryder Apartments, Ocean Ave., between Pine and Maple, Wildwood, N. J.

The Ryder Apartments was located on Ocean Avenue, between Pine and Maple Avenues. This postcard shows the building as it appeared in the 1940s. Today the three-story building has been relegated to the ever-expanding list of long-gone hotels, motels, and apartment houses.

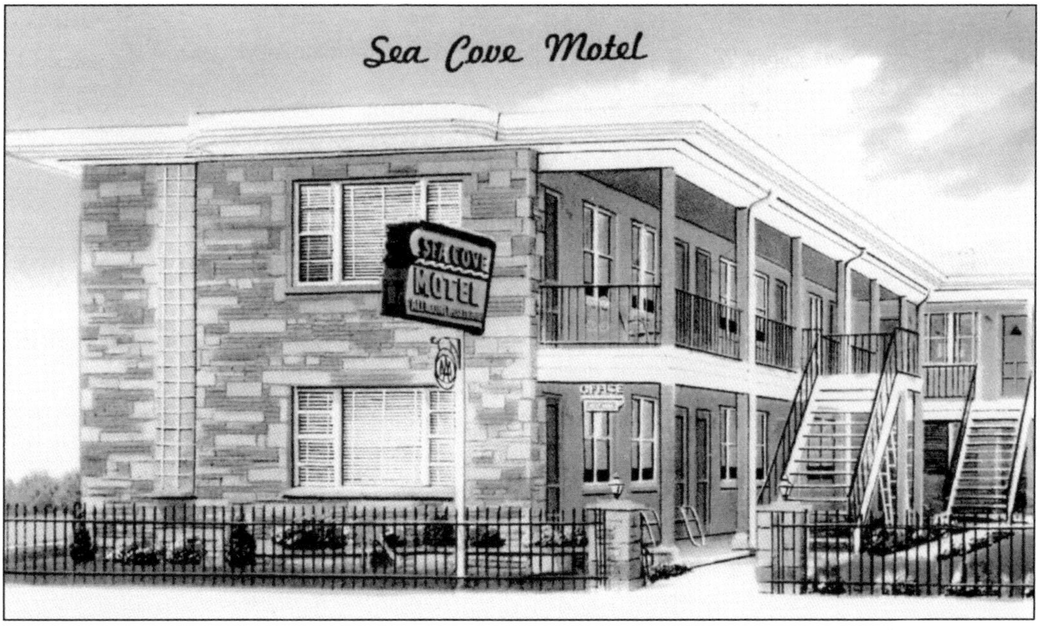

This postcard shows an artist's rendering of the Sea Cove Motel as it appeared in the 1940s. The motel was located at 323–325 East Wildwood Avenue. One unique feature noted on the rear of the card was the presence of walk-in closets in each room. Today the Sea Cove Motel is gone, replaced by modern residences.

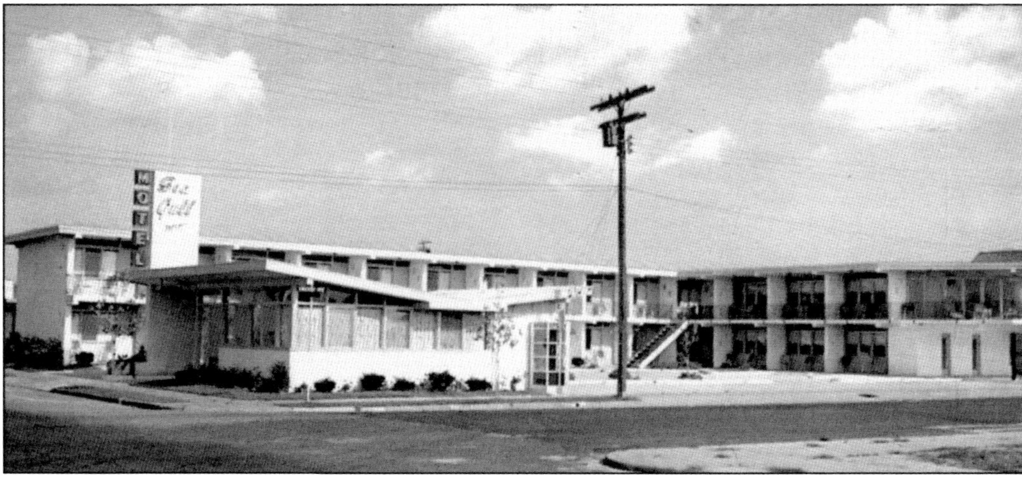

The Sea Gull Motel began its life as the Sea Gull Lodge and is located at 5305 Atlantic Avenue at Cresse Avenue. This view shows the motel as it appeared in the late 1950s. Today the Sea Gull Motel is still in operation and continues to welcome visitors. Several additions over the years have increased the lodging capacity at the Sea Gull Motel.

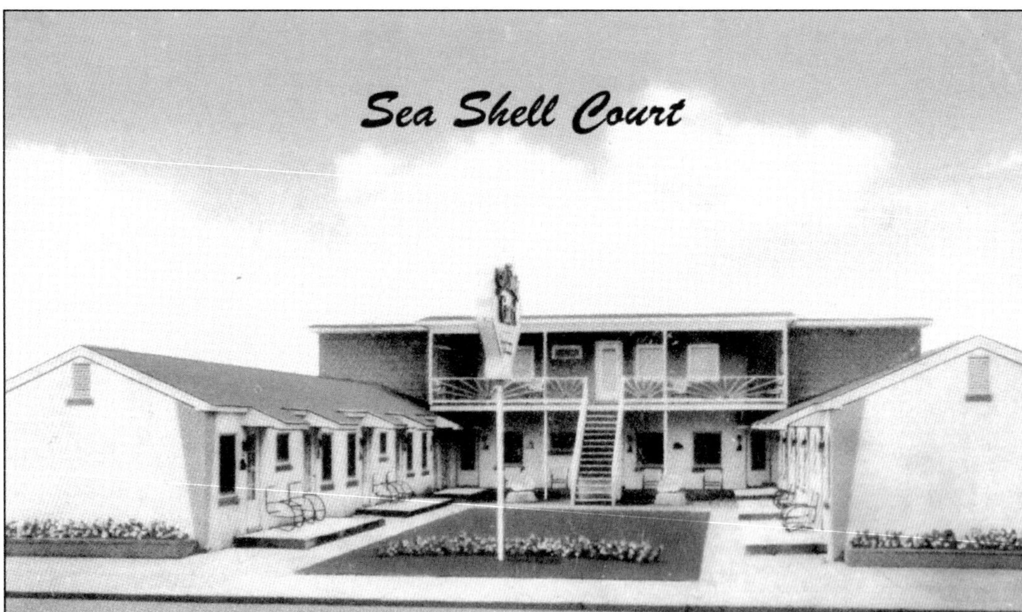

This postcard from the 1950s shows the Sea Shell Court, located at 246–248 East Rio Grande Avenue, near Atlantic Avenue. Since this postcard was produced, the grass courtyard has been replaced with a swimming pool. Fortunately the Sea Shell Court has withstood the test of time and still operates as a motel to this day.

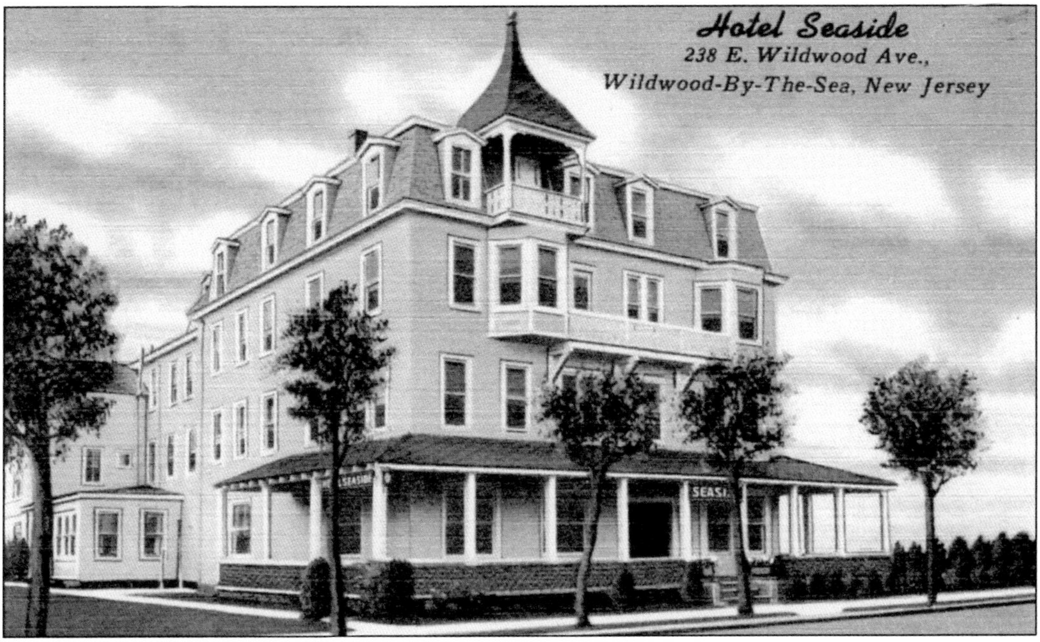

The Hotel Seaside is seen in this postcard from the 1940s in its location at 238 East Wildwood Avenue. The Victorian structure is reminiscent of those buildings found more commonly in nearby Cape May. Today the former site of the hotel now plays host to newer motels and nondescript parking lots.

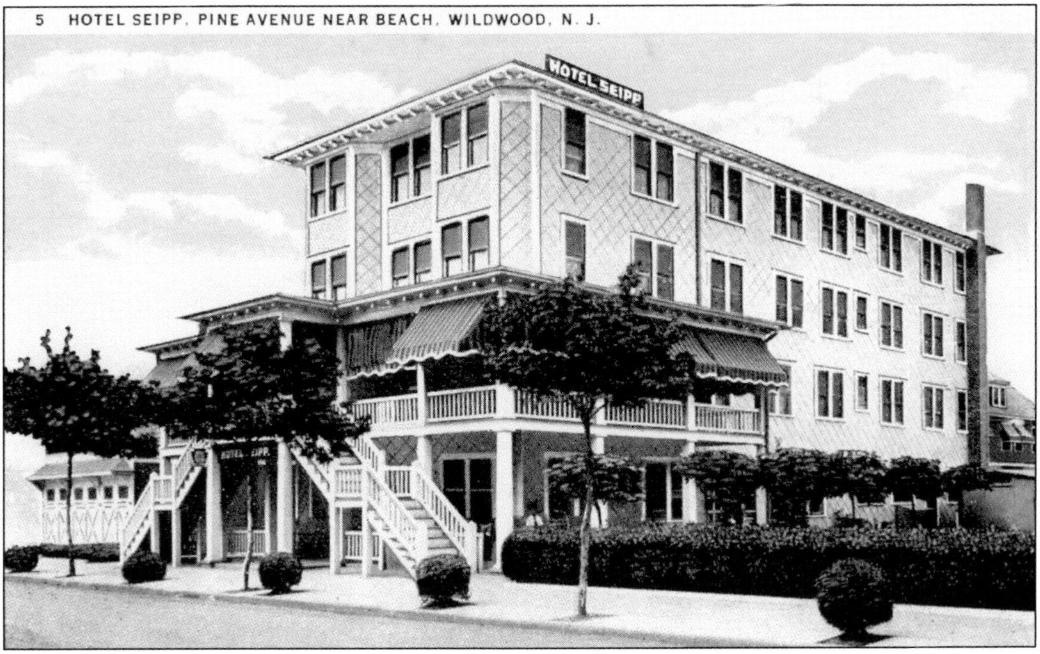

The Hotel Seipp is seen in this postcard from the 1930s and was located on Pine Avenue near the beach in Wildwood. The four-story building was constructed in a style that was typical of its day for hotels in Wildwood. Today the Hotel Seipp is just a memory amid a sea of development in the Wildwoods.

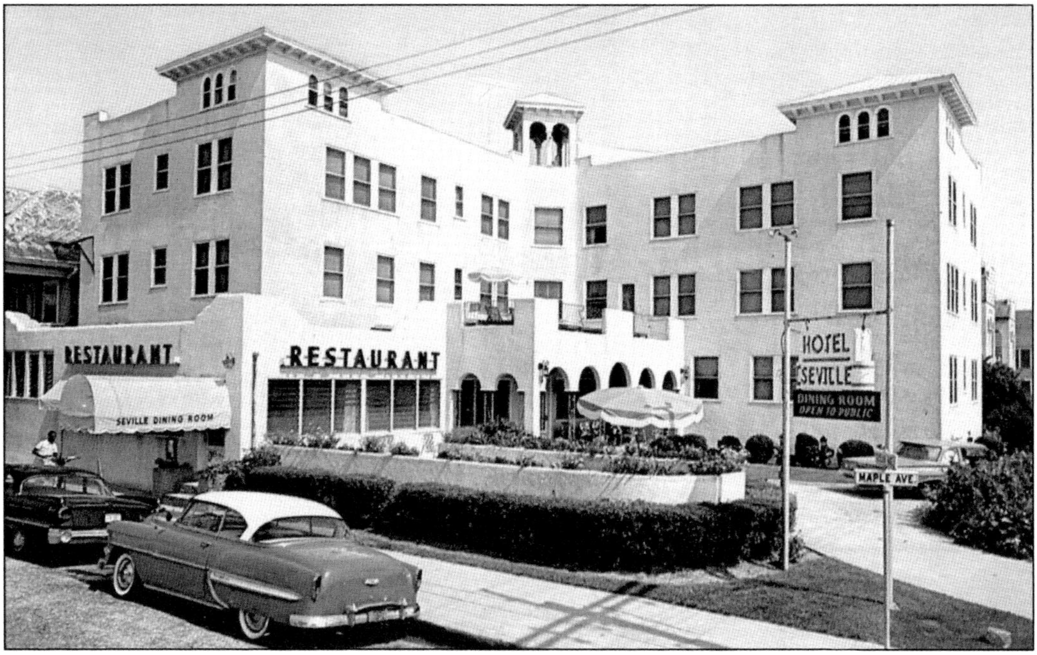

This postcard from the 1950s shows the Hotel Seville, located on the ocean at Maple Avenue. The rear of the card boasted that the hotel was only 50 feet from the beach. This imposing structure was painted pink and featured an on-premises restaurant. Today the Hotel Seville is long gone. The hotel's former neighborhood is now home to a multitude of businesses and residences.

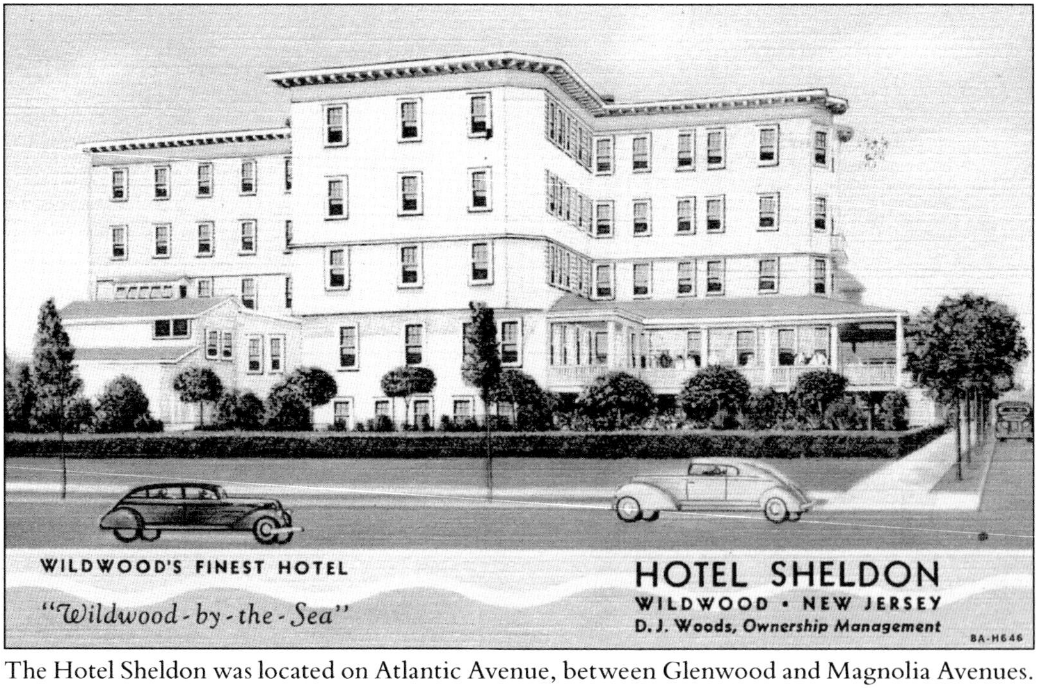

The Hotel Sheldon was located on Atlantic Avenue, between Glenwood and Magnolia Avenues. This postcard from the 1940s shows the large hotel and adjacent garden. Eventually the hotel would be replaced by a parking lot for the St. Ann's Catholic Church located across the street.

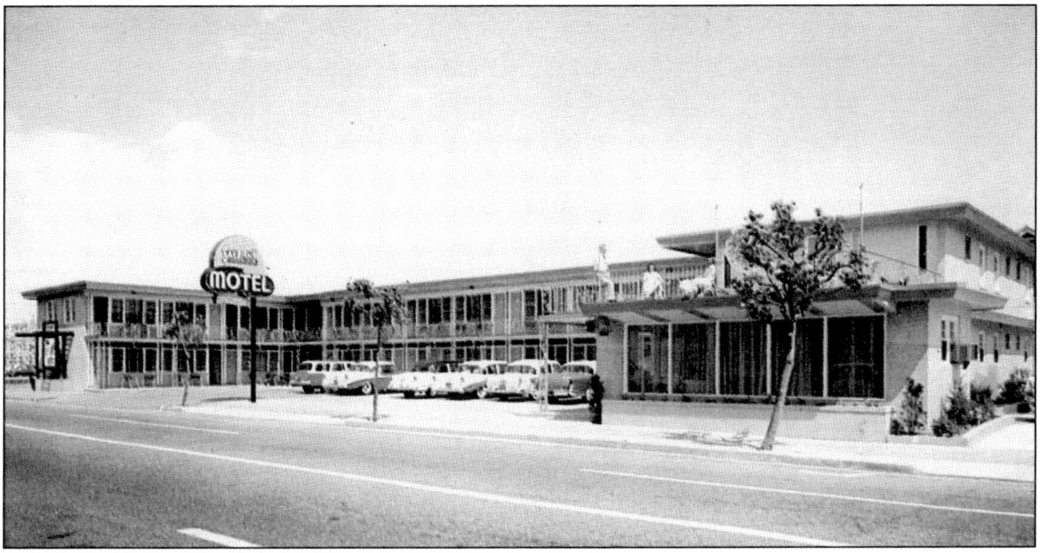

This postcard from the 1950s shows the Skylark Motel, located at 3917 Atlantic Avenue. This motel has enjoyed a long and successful presence among Wildwood's coterie of motels. Today the Skylark Motel still operates from its location at Atlantic and Spencer Avenues.

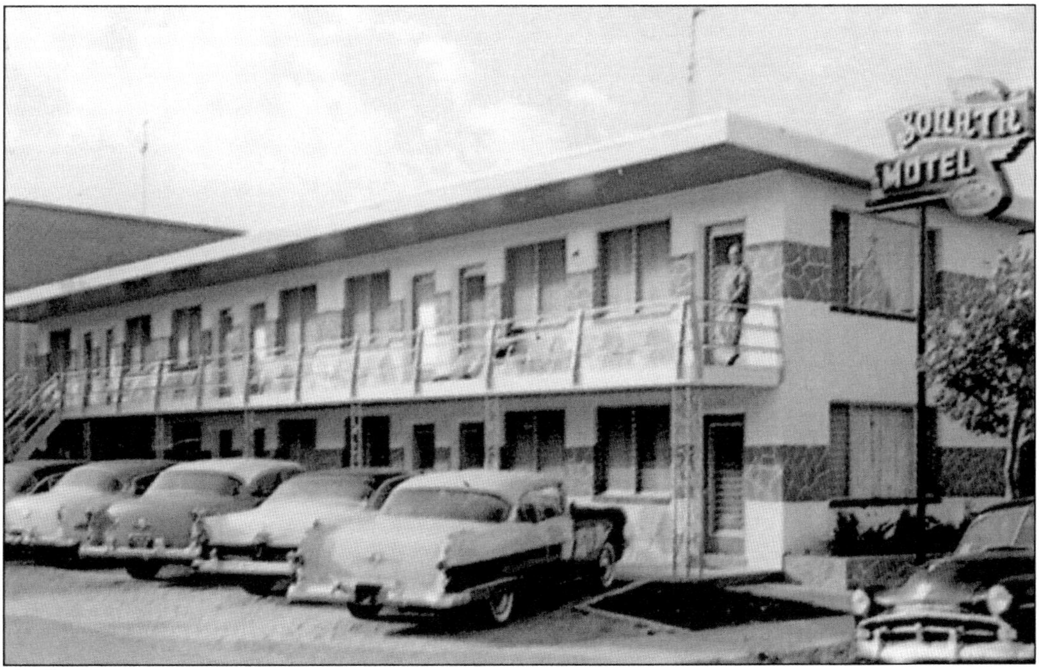

The Sonata Motel is seen in this postcard from the 1950s. The Sonata Motel was located at 2703 Atlantic Avenue, and according to the card, it featured "room controlled music." Today the Sonata Motel is gone and has been replaced by condominiums that have been appropriately named the Sonata Condominiums.

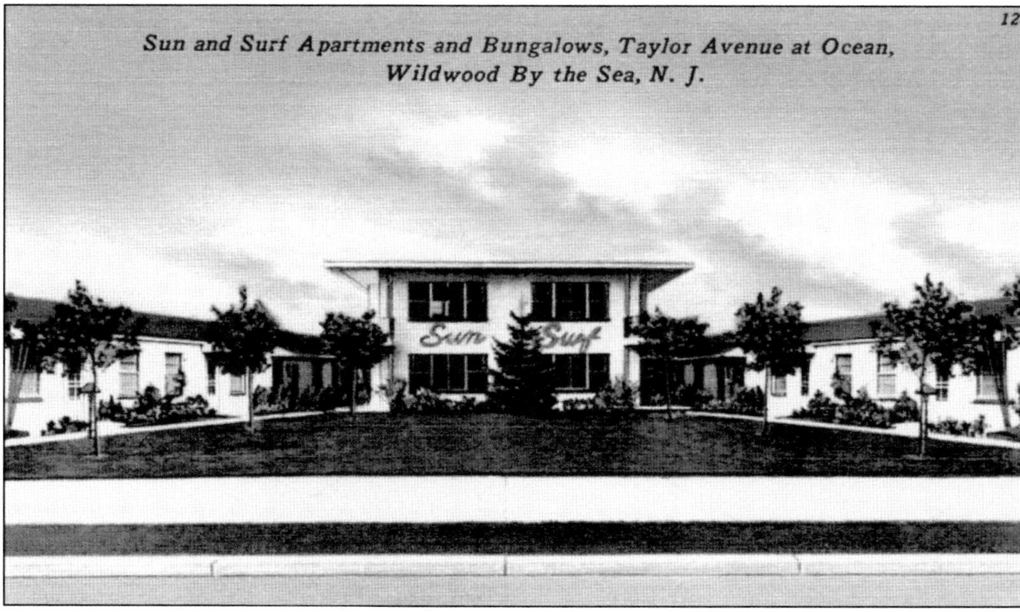

The Sun and Surf Apartments and Bungalows were located along Taylor Avenue, between Ocean and Atlantic Avenues. This view from the early 1950s shows the modest structure and its expansive courtyard. Today the Sun and Surf Apartments and Bungalows building still exists, although the units have been converted to condominium ownership.

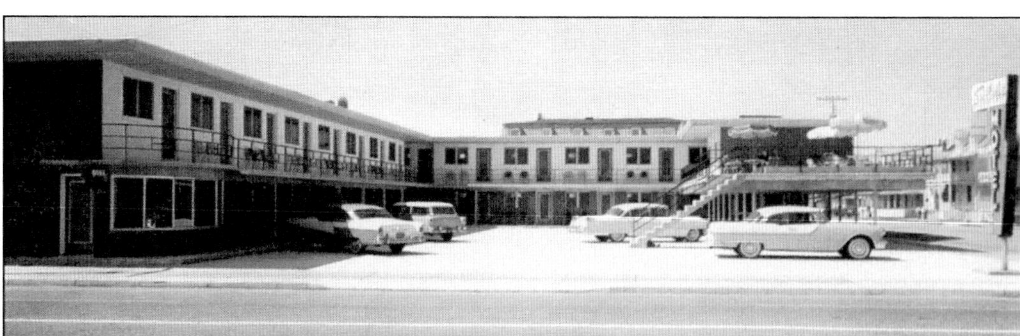

The Surf Comber Motel is located at 4800 Atlantic Avenue and is seen in this postcard from the late 1950s. At the time, the motel offered 32 units split between traditional motel rooms and efficiencies. Although the building is still there today, as of 2007, a large sign hanging on the property proposes a redevelopment of the site for commercial and residential use.

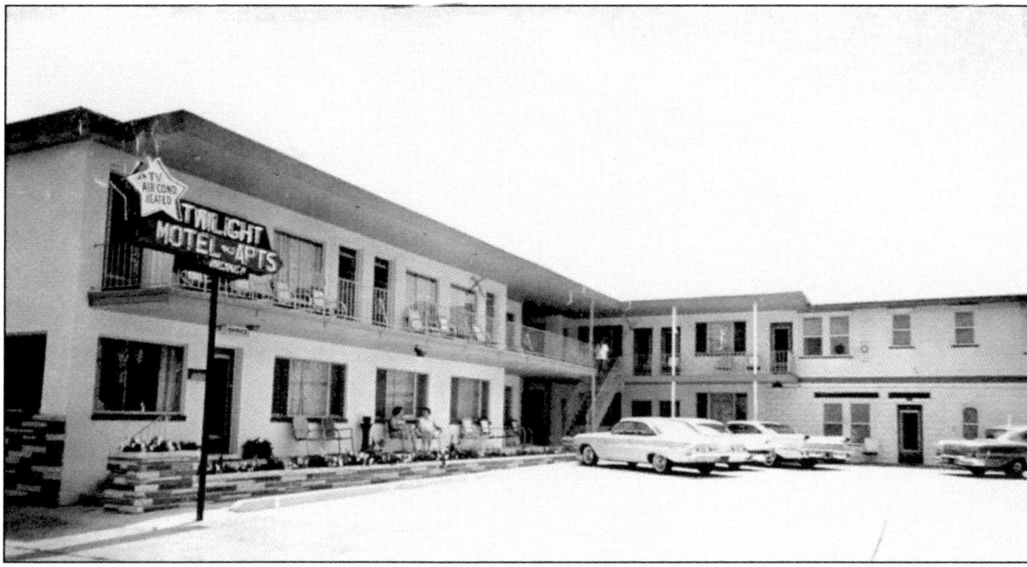

This postcard from the early 1960s shows the Twilight Motel located at 210 East Spicer Avenue. The rear of the card proudly states that the property is under "owner-management." Fortunately the Twilight Motel survives today with most of its original structure intact and continues to operate as a motel.

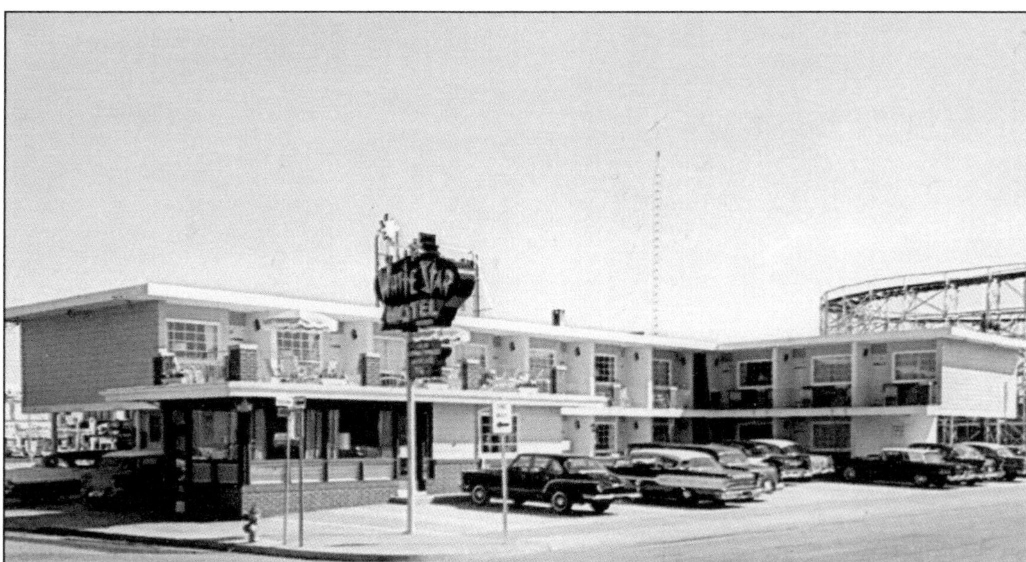

The White Star Motel is located at the intersection of Lincoln Avenue and Ocean Avenue. This postcard from the 1950s shows the motel with a roller coaster in the background, underscoring the location's proximity to the boardwalk and its amusements. The White Star Motel still operates as a motel today.

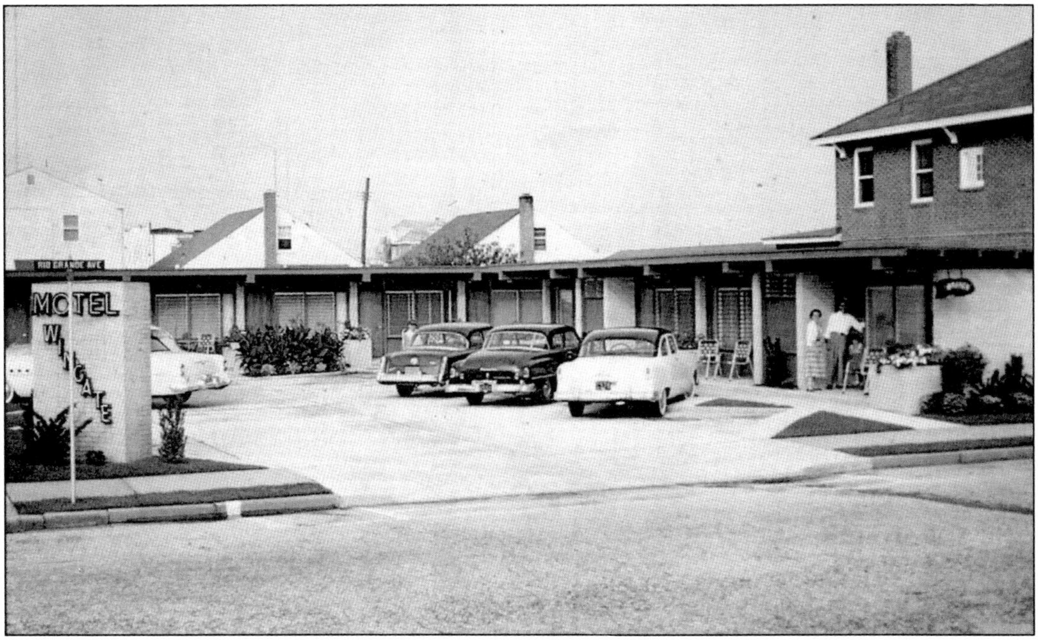

This postcard from the early 1960s shows the Wingate Motel, located at the corner of Rio Grande and Atlantic Avenues. Although it was originally just a one-story motel, a more modern three-story motel was added to the site several years later. The Wingate Motel is gone today and in its place a new motel called the Starlux has raised. The Starlux has been built in a style evocative of the 1950s.

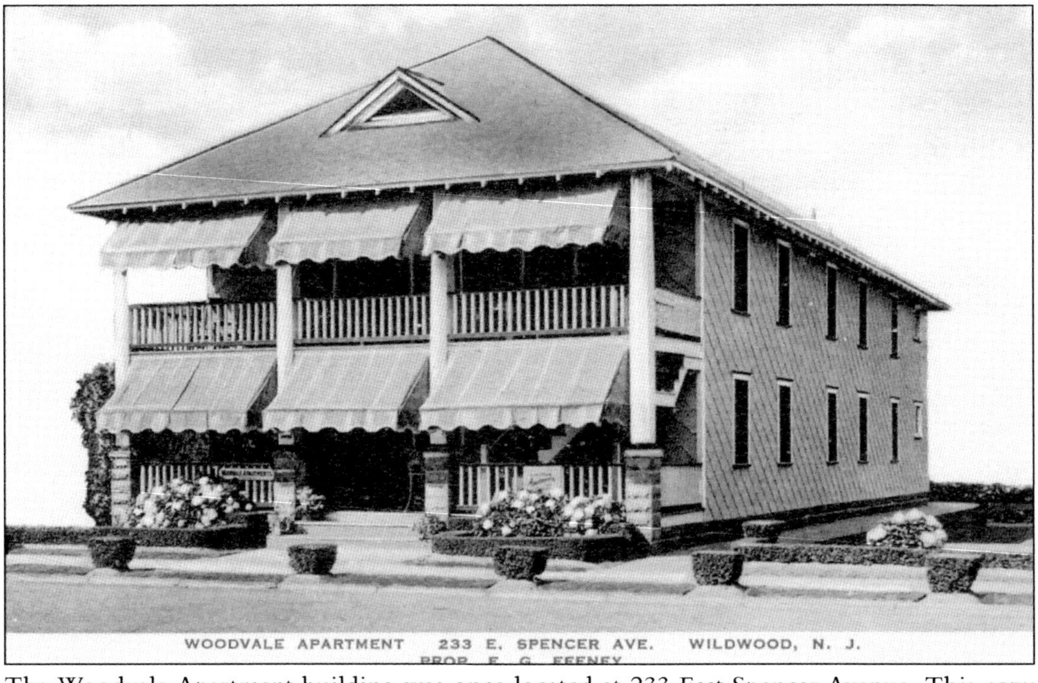

The Woodvale Apartment building was once located at 233 East Spencer Avenue. This cozy apartment house offered modest accommodations in its day. However, the little building was no match for the progress gripping Wildwood. Today the site is home to modern residences.

Two

Accommodations in Wildwood Crest

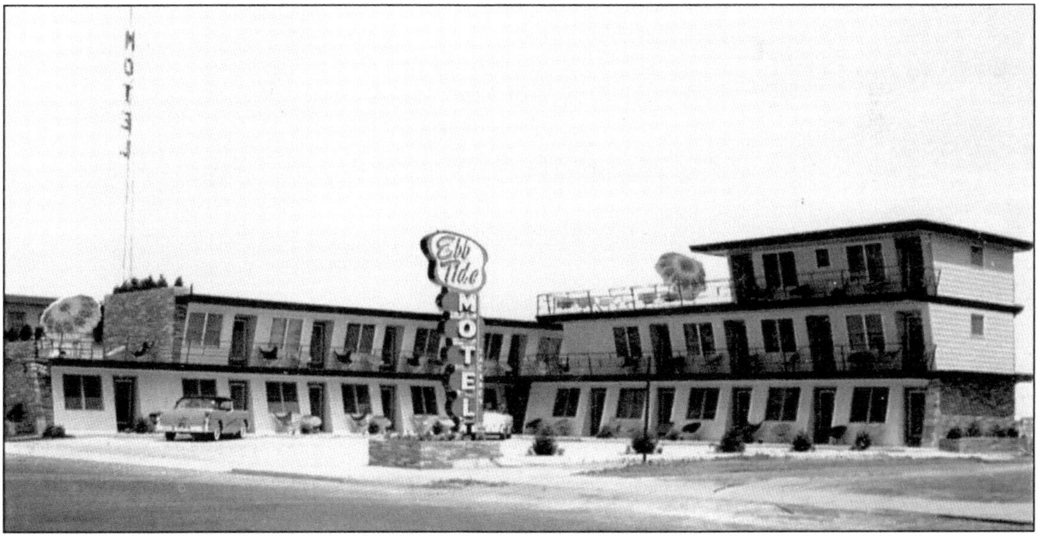

This postcard from the 1950s shows the Ebb Tide Motel, located at 5711 Atlantic Avenue. The rear of the card promotes the motel as "Wildwood's most modern, triple-deck motel." The Ebb Tide Motel would receive numerous additions and expansions over the coming years, but none would be enough to prevent the inevitable. The Ebb Tide Motel was demolished to make way for a new development of condominiums.

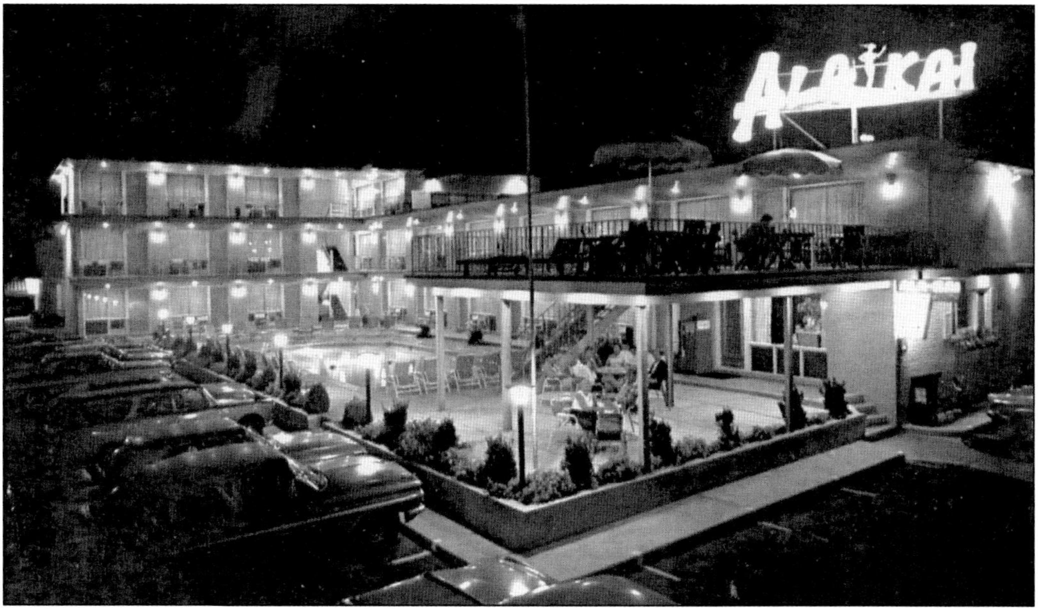

The Ala Kai Motel is located on the beach at Toledo and Atlantic Avenues. Although this card was produced in the early 1960s, the motel featured a heated pool at that time, among other "modern" amenities. Today the Ala Kai Motel continues to operate as a motel in Wildwood Crest.

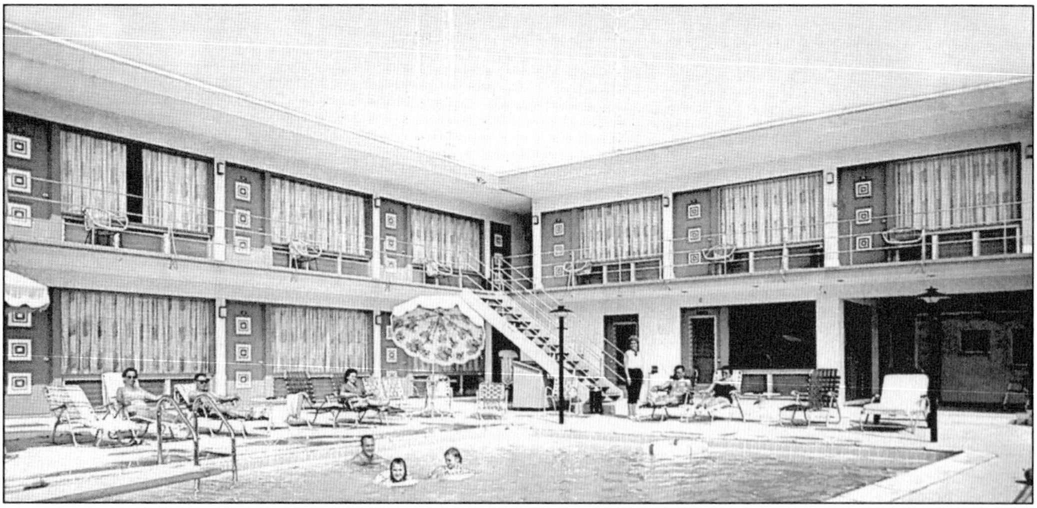

This postcard from the 1960s shows the Bali-hi Motel, located on the ocean at Louisville Avenue. The motel offered efficiency apartments for two to six persons according to the language on the rear of the card. Although the building remains today, it has been absorbed by a contiguous motel complex. At the time of this writing, the nondescript structure faces an uncertain future.

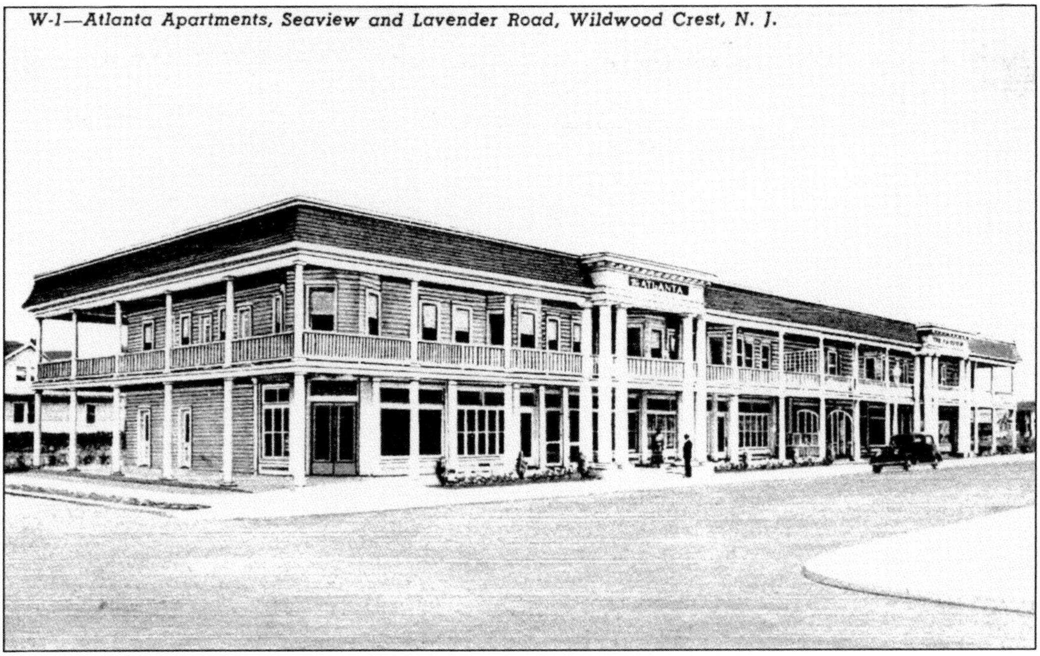

The Atlanta and Fairview Apartments is seen in these views from the 1940s and 1950s respectively. The Atlanta and Fairview Apartments occupied one building located along Seaview Avenue, between Lavender and Buttercup Roads. The two-story structure has survived for decades and remains in place today, although it has since been converted to condominium units and no longer operates in a traditional room rental capacity. Despite the removal of some of the more decorative architectural elements, the Atlanta and Fairview Apartments is still easily recognizable today.

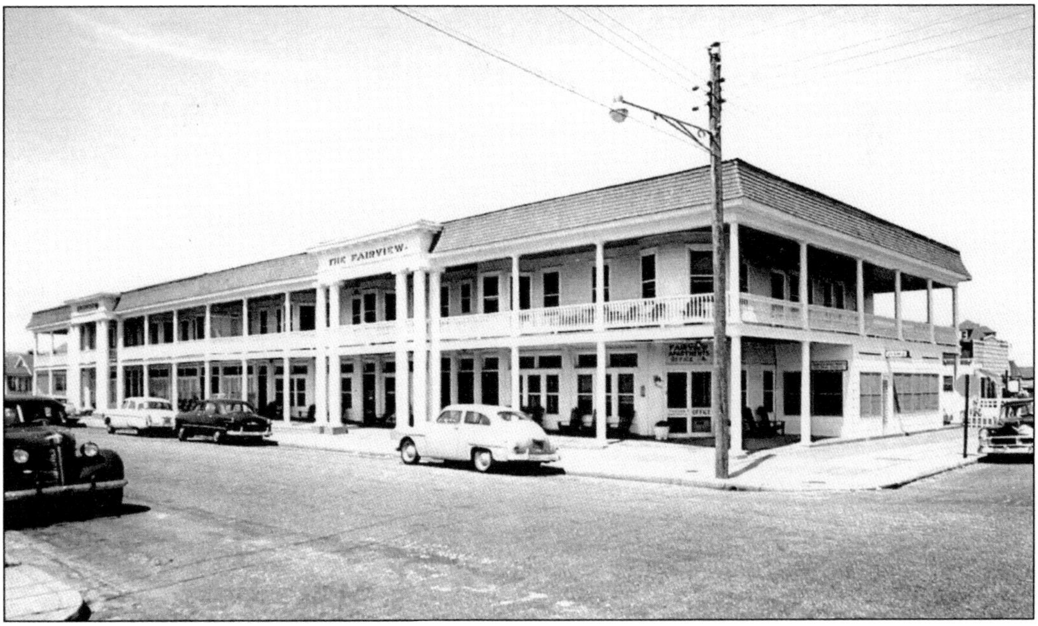

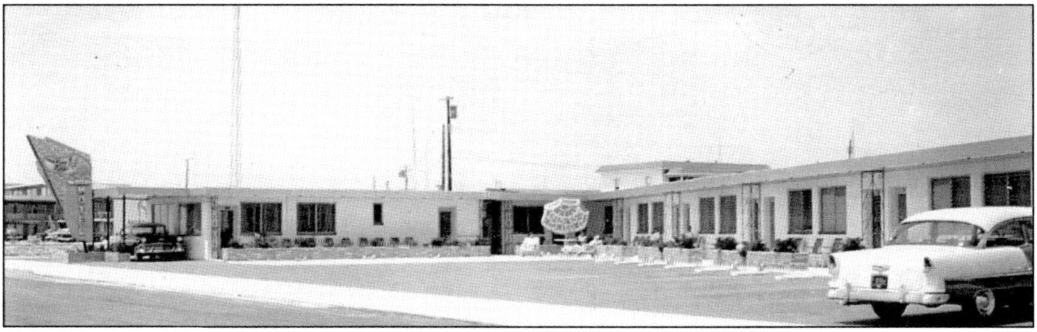

The Bel Air Motel is seen in this postcard from the 1950s. The motel is located at 5510 Ocean Avenue and still operates in its original intended capacity. The back of the card proudly boasts wall-to-wall carpeting among its many amenities. In the almost 50 years that have elapsed since this image was produced, the motel has received several modifications including an additional story.

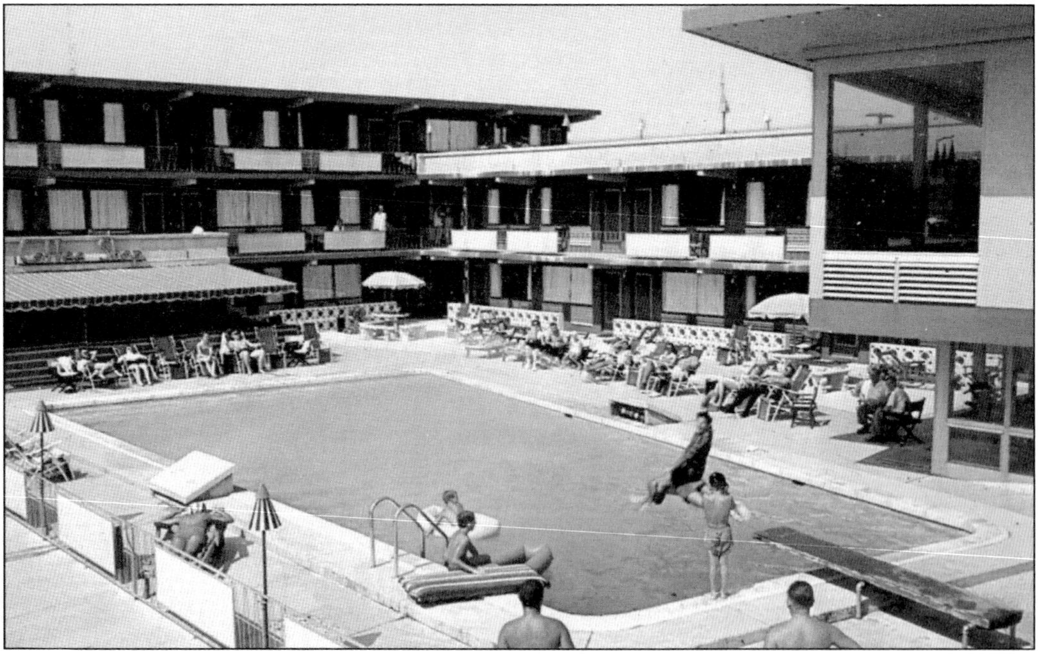

This postcard from the early 1960s shows the Carousel Motel located along Ocean Avenue, between Lavender and Heather Roads. In this view, the pool, several rooms, and the entrance to the coffee shop can be seen. Unfortunately, despite being one of the more uniquely designed motels in Wildwood Crest, the Carousel Motel was torn down to make way for redevelopment.

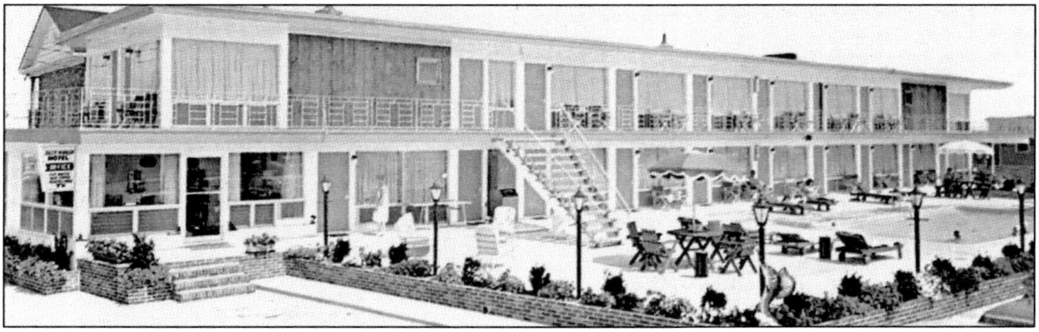

The Blue Marlin Motel is located at the intersection of Toledo and Atlantic Avenues. This postcard view shows how it looked in the early 1960s. The rear of the card advertises free ice, continental breakfast, and daily maid service among its offerings. Fortunately the Blue Marlin Motel still looks much the same today as it did then and continues to operate as a motel.

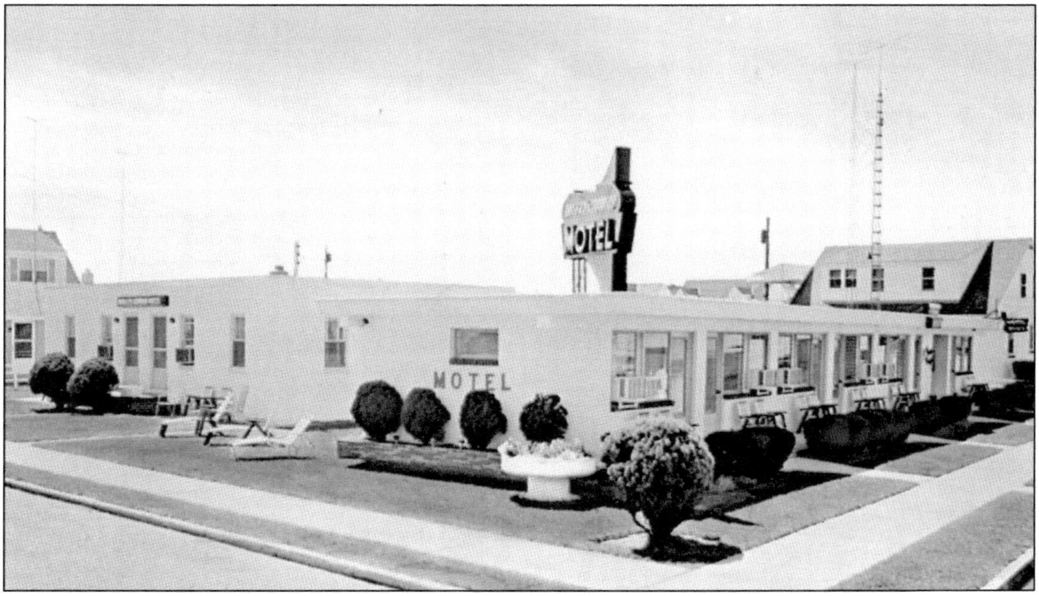

The Breezy Corner Motel and Apartments were located at 7901 Seaview Avenue, at Louisville Avenue. The structure is seen in this postcard from the 1960s, showing the one-story building situated on the corner. Unfortunately the small motel had become obsolete and was demolished. At the time of this writing, the former site is an empty lot awaiting redevelopment.

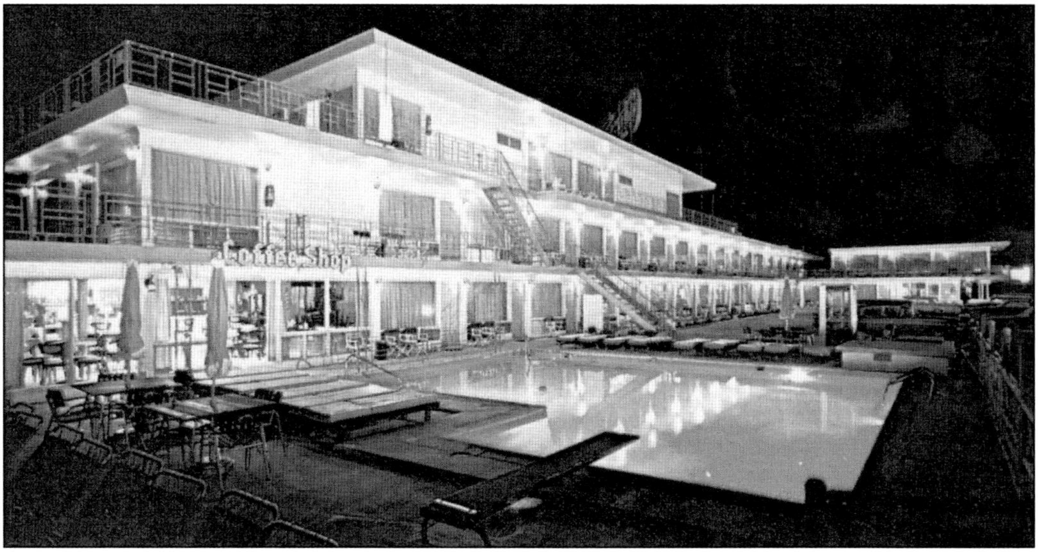

The Chalet Motel was located on the beach at Miami Avenue and is seen in this postcard from the 1960s. The motel offered an on-site coffee shop, shuffleboard, and in-room television. Unfortunately the Chalet Motel was torn down to make way for redevelopment among the highly sought after property in Wildwood Crest.

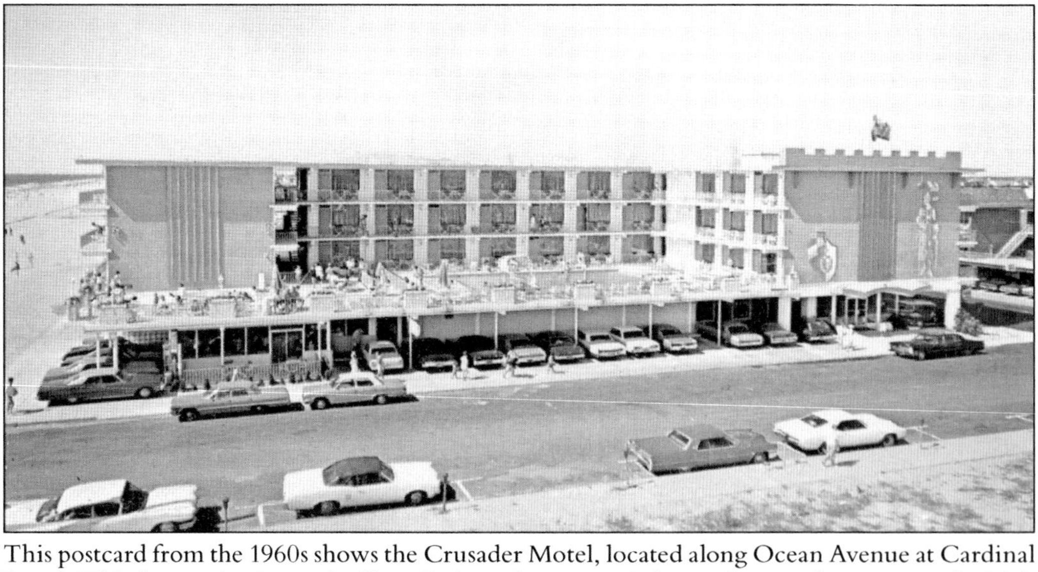

This postcard from the 1960s shows the Crusader Motel, located along Ocean Avenue at Cardinal Road. This larger sized motel offers distinct signage and decorative touches, some of which depict a gallant crusader. The motel is still in operation today and has managed to retain much of its original structure.

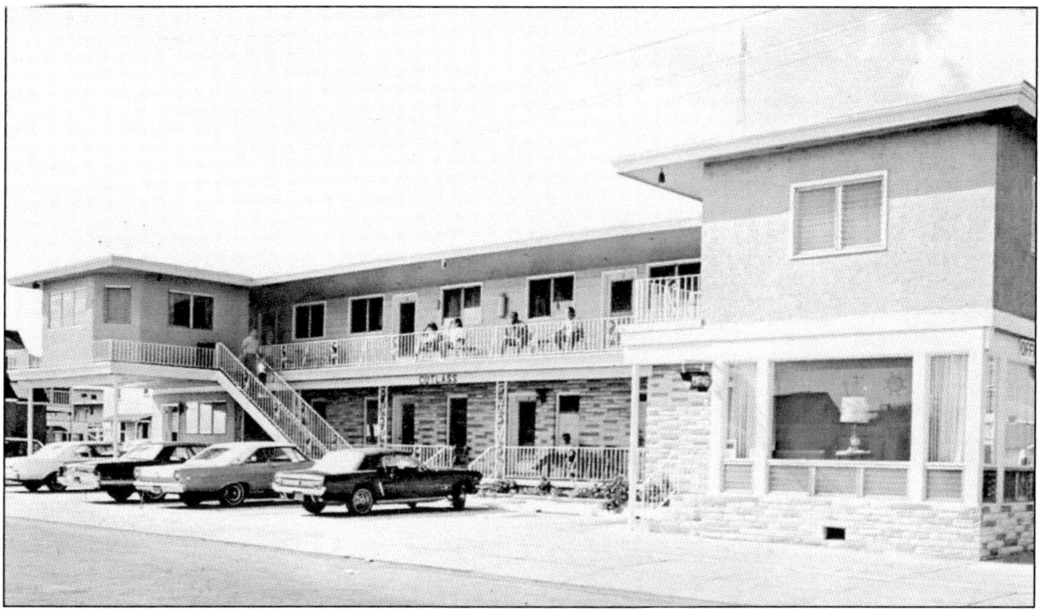

This view from the early 1960s shows the Cutlass Motel Apartments located at 5601 Seaview Avenue. The facility offered one-, two-, or three-bedroom units along with "completely equipped" kitchens. The building remains today, although the Cutlass Motel Apartments have been converted into the Buttercup Condominiums.

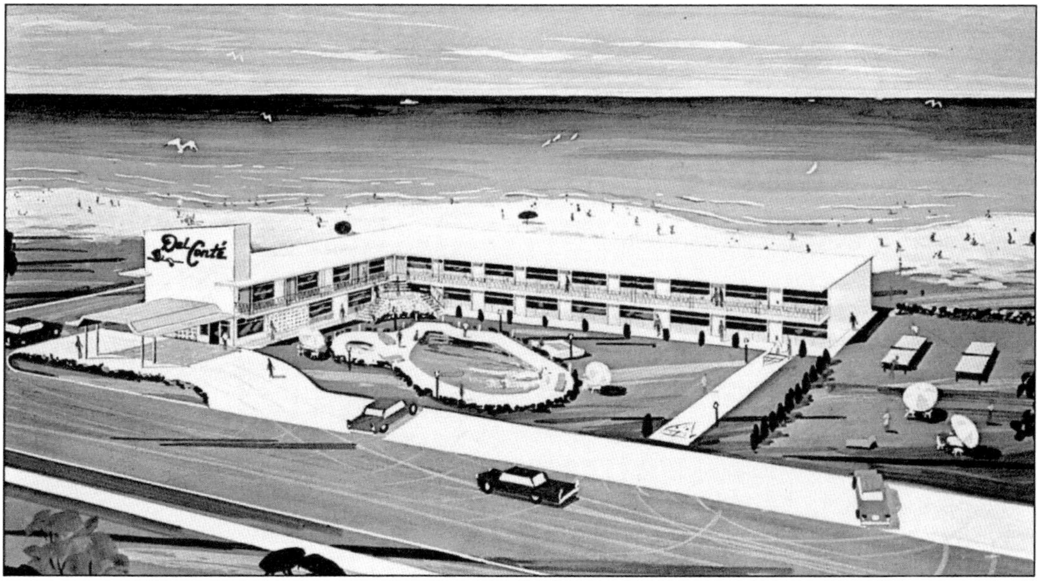

The Del Conte Resort Motel is seen in this postcard from the 1960s. The artist's rendering shows an aerial view of the property, with careful attention given to the facility's proximity to the beach. The motel was located at the intersection of Stanton Road and Ocean Avenue but has since given way to redevelopment.

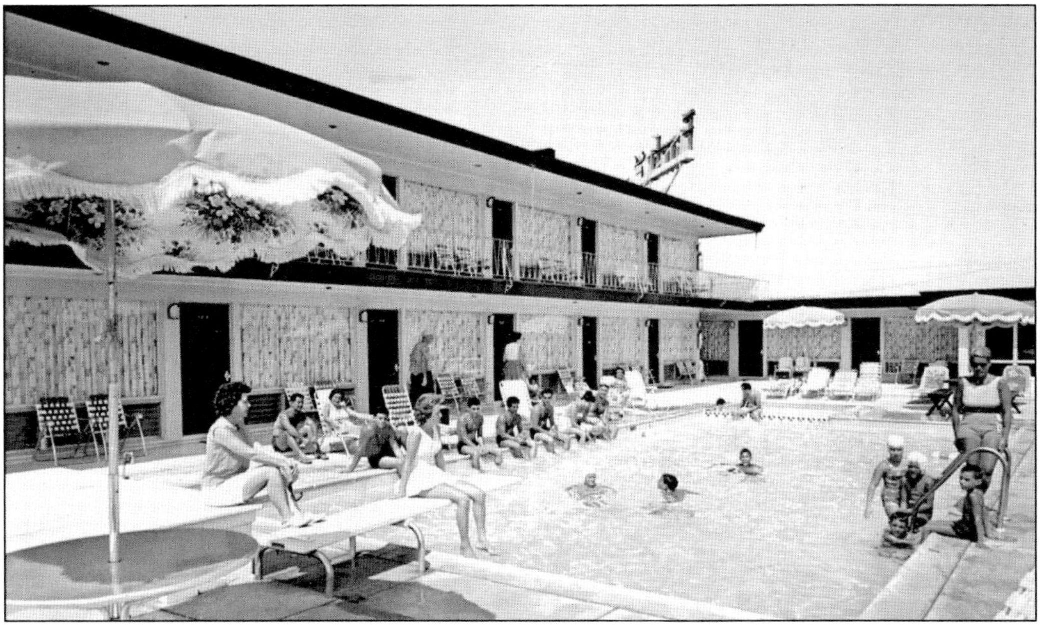

The Earle Resort Motel was located at the intersection of Hollywood and Seaview Avenues and is seen in this postcard from the early 1960s. The rear of the card advertises "automatic coffee machines in every unit," as well as "portable hairdryers." Unfortunately the Earle Resort Motel was demolished and replaced with condominiums.

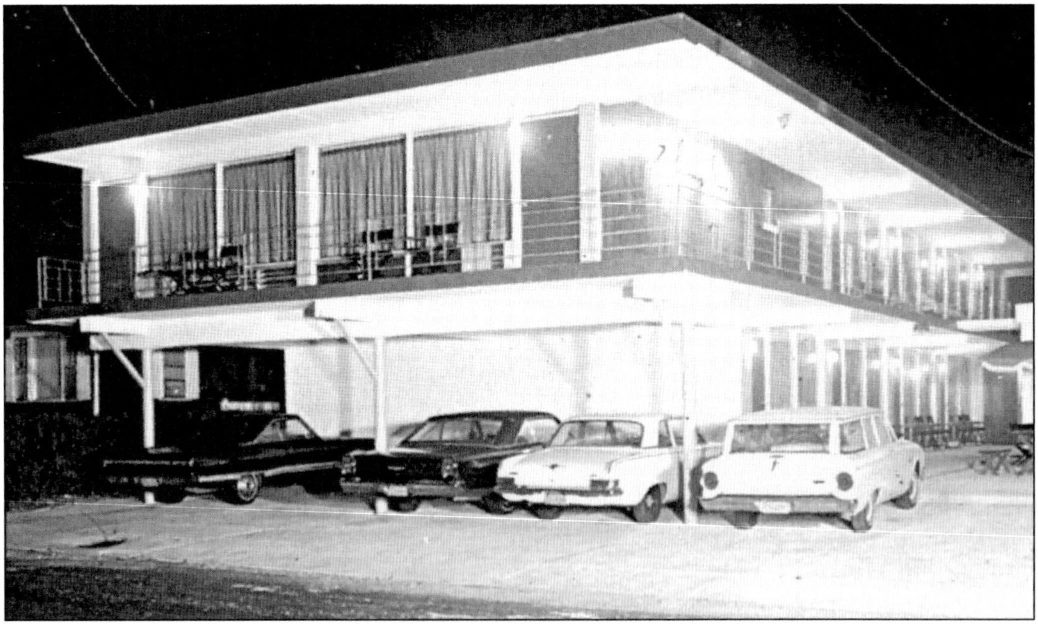

This postcard from the 1960s shows the Evening Star Motel, located at the corner of Pacific Avenue and Stockton Road. The rear of the card trumpeted the "soundproof" construction as well as the "Hi-Fi Music" that was available in all rooms. The author's aunt and uncle operated the Evening Star Motel for many years prior to their retirement. Today the building remains in place but has been converted to condominium ownership.

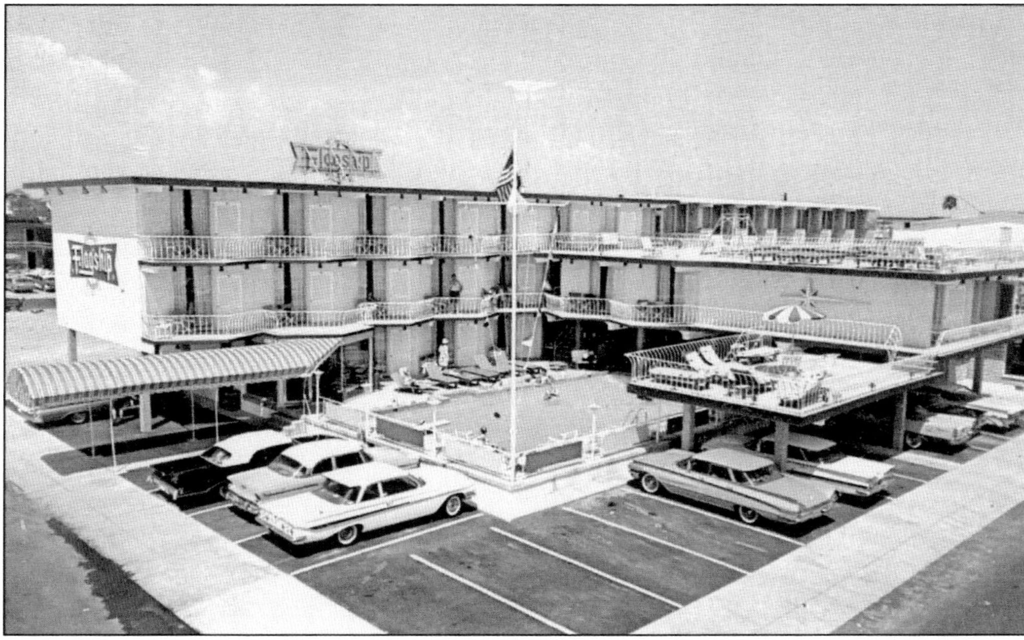

The Flagship Beach Motel was located on the oceanfront at Lavender Road and is seen in this postcard view from the 1960s. The eclectic accommodations offered by the facility included motel rooms, efficiencies, and suites. Unfortunately the Flagship Beach Motel has given way to time and progress and is now just a memory.

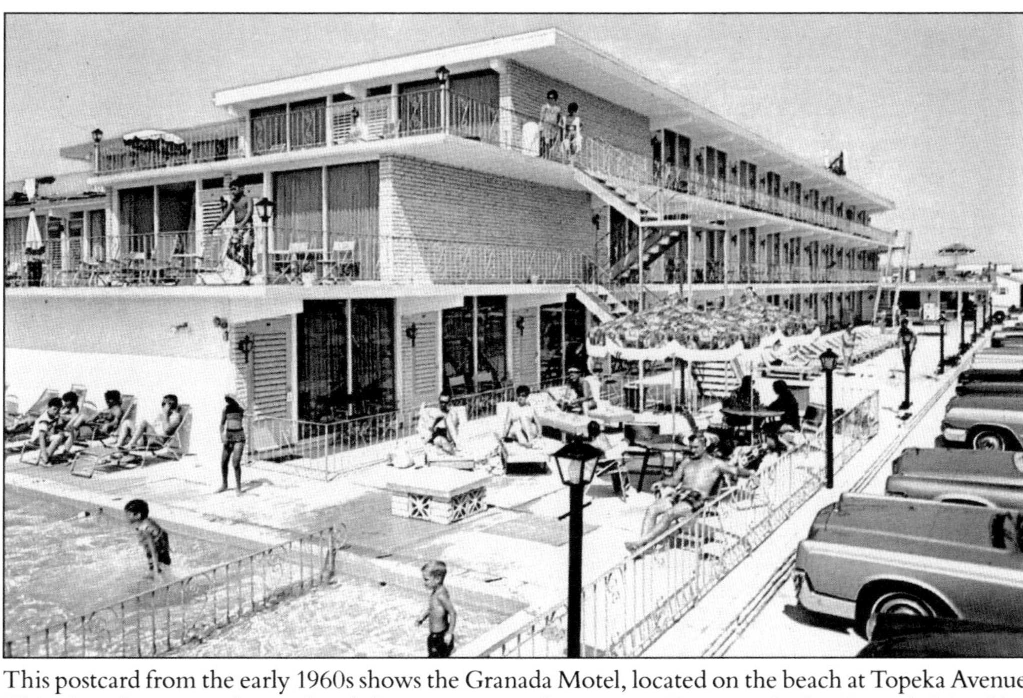

This postcard from the early 1960s shows the Granada Motel, located on the beach at Topeka Avenue. This view showcases the pool and three-story motel structure. Fortunately the Granada Motel has survived the demolition craze in Wildwood Crest and still welcomes visitors and tourists.

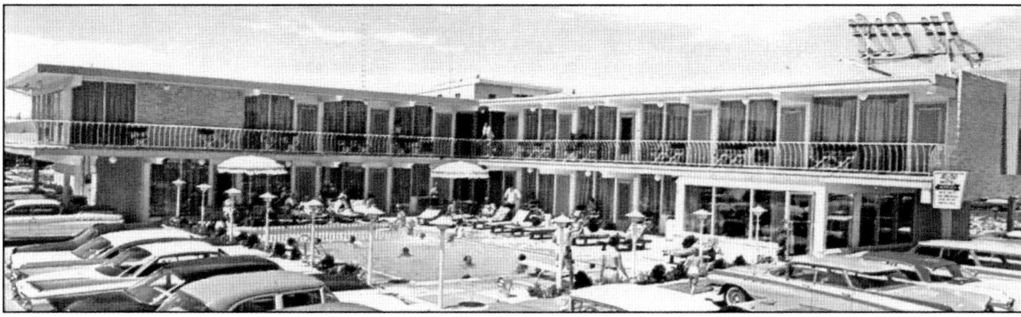

This view from the 1960s shows the Hi-Lili Motel, located on the ocean at Stockton Road. The rear of the card advertised the complimentary "ice service and daily maid service." Despite a successful business, the Hi-Lili Motel was demolished to make way for new condominiums.

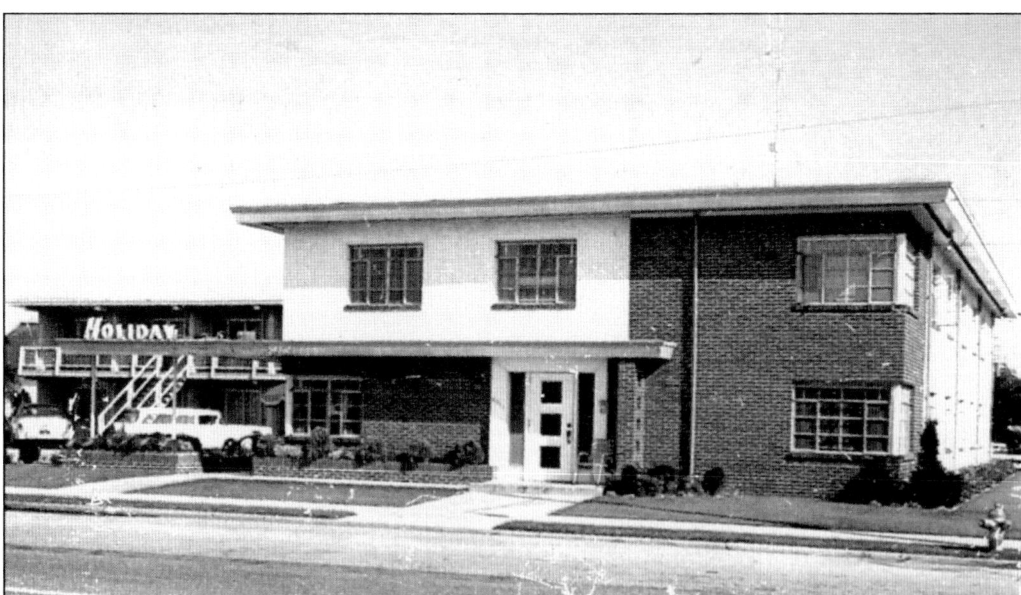

The Holiday Motel and Hotel was located at the intersection of Columbine Road and Pacific Avenue. The back of the card spoke proudly of the facility's "tile baths with neo-angle tubs." Unfortunately the modest motel was demolished. As of 2007, the former site is an empty lot awaiting redevelopment.

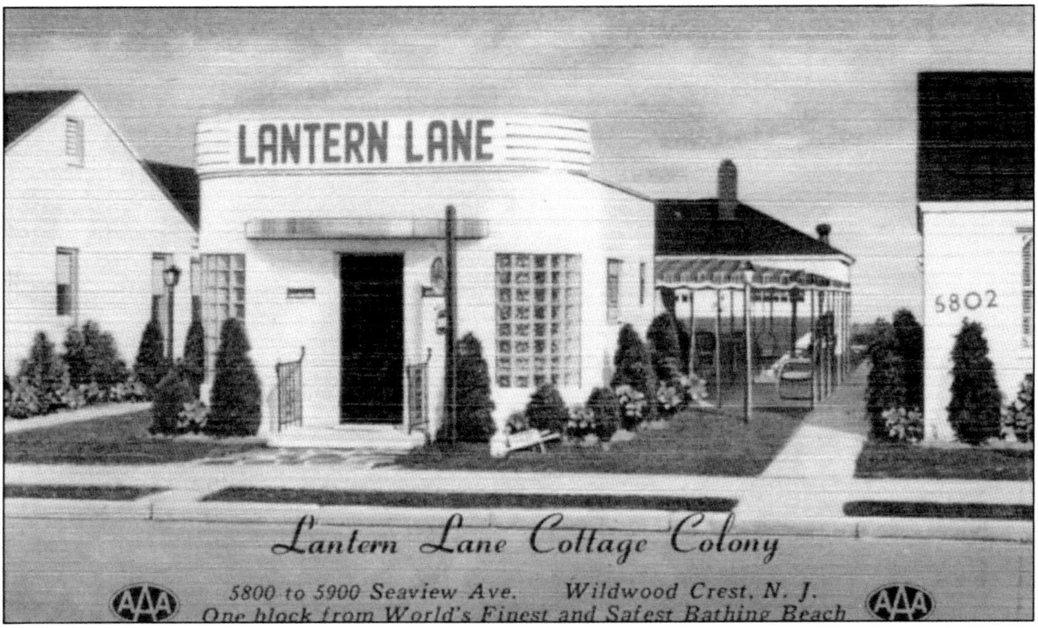

This postcard from the early 1950s shows the Lantern Lane Cottage Colony. This grouping of small cottages is located along Seaview Avenue, spanning the 5800–5900 blocks. Fortunately the cluster of buildings has survived for decades and this unique piece of Wildwood Crest's architecture remains, albeit having been converted to condominium ownership.

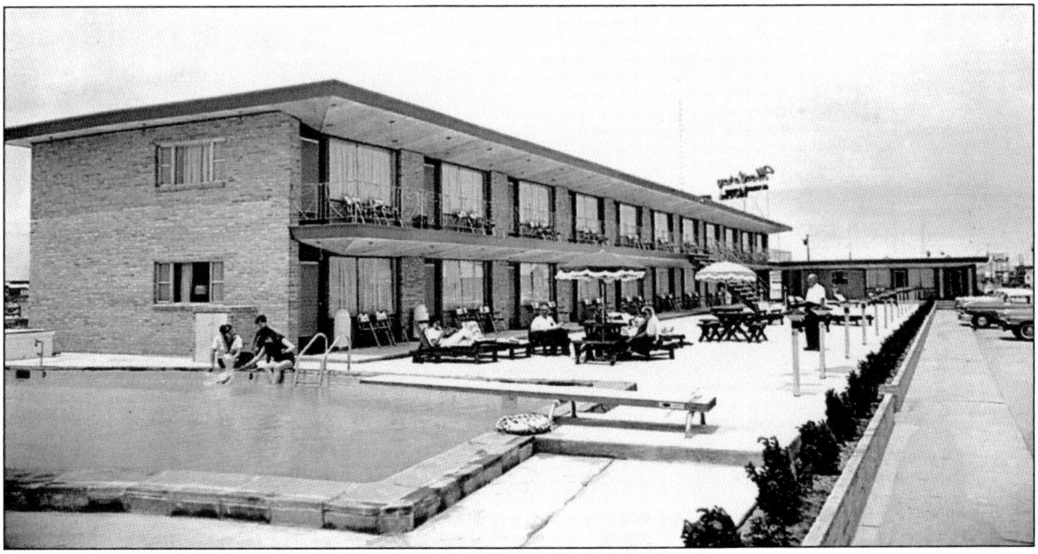

This postcard from the late 1950s shows the Monterey Motel and Apartments, aptly named for its location on Monterey Avenue at the beach. The rear of the card touts amenities such as chaise lounges, shuffleboard, and an on-site barbecue pit. Although no longer operating as a motel, the Monterey Motel and Apartments survives under an arrangement of condominium ownership.

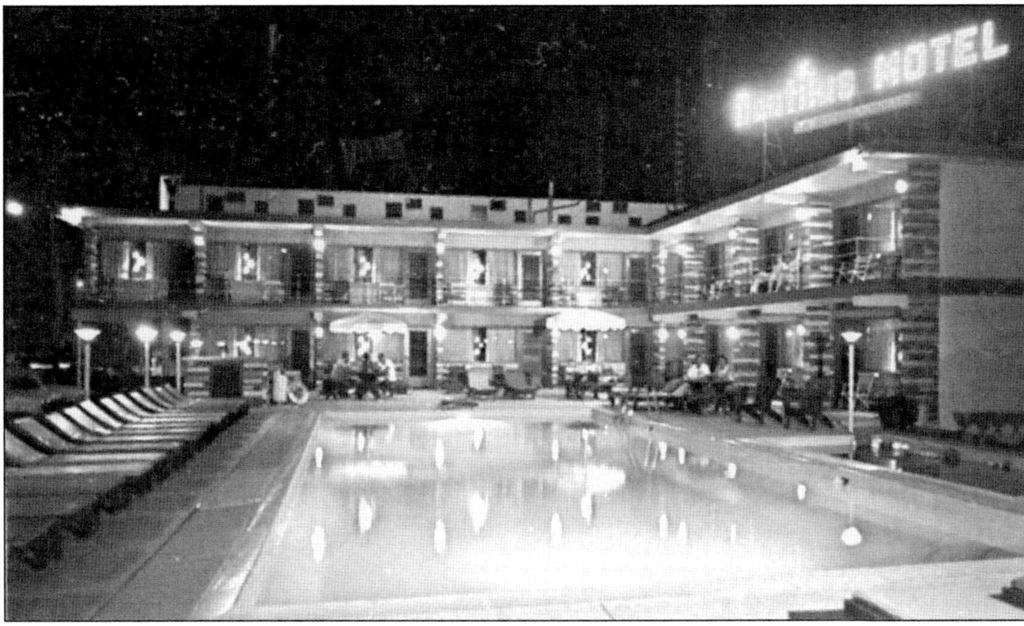

The Nautilus Motel is seen in this view from the early 1960s. The motel was located at 6401 Atlantic Avenue, at Columbine Road. Among the amenities listed on the card are a heated swimming pool and sun patio. Unfortunately the Nautilus Motel was lost to progress, and the site is now home to condominiums.

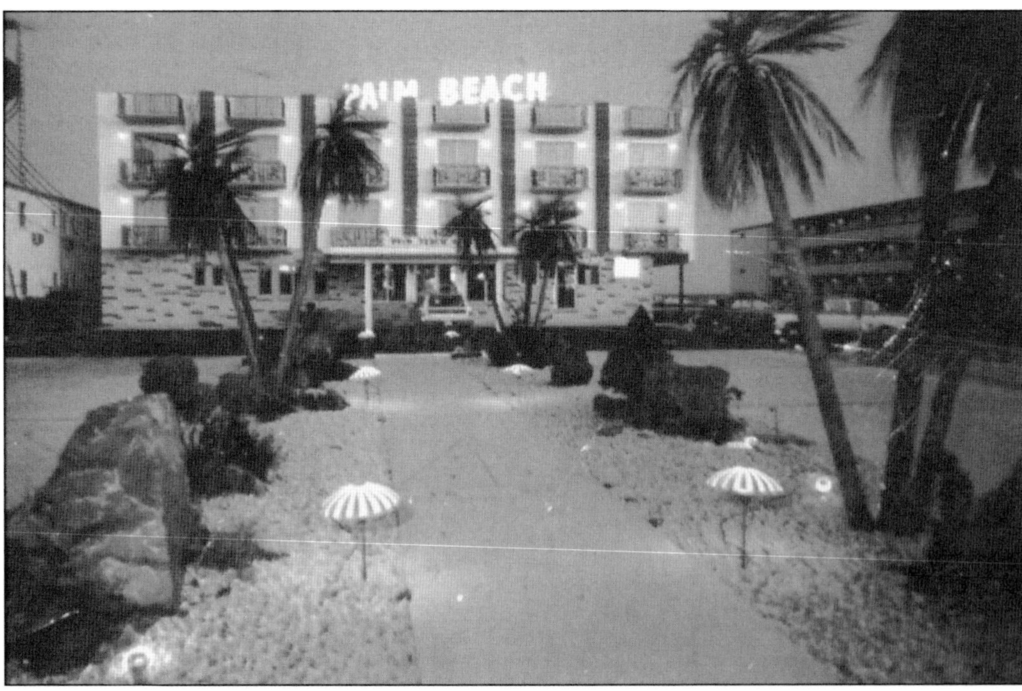

This postcard from the 1960s lauds the Palm Beach Motel as "the newest and finest ocean front motel" in Wildwood Crest. Note the palm trees that lined the walkway leading up to the motel in this view. The Palm Beach Motel was located at the corner of Atlantic Avenue and Palm Road for decades before meeting its fate.

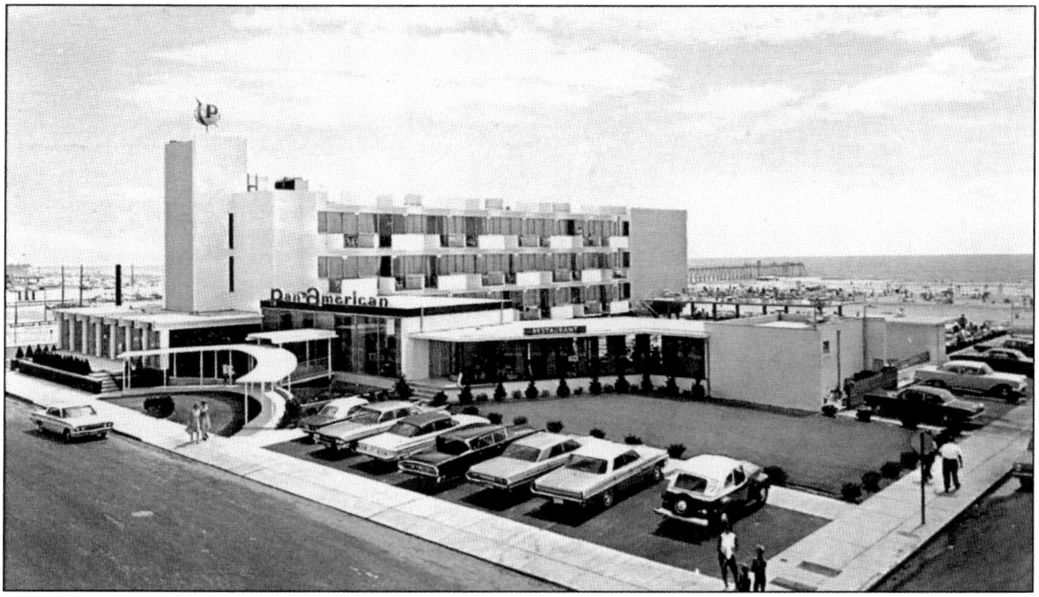

This postcard from the 1960s shows the Pan American Motor Inn as it was known then. The extensive room categories proffered on the rear of this card include standard motel rooms, efficiencies, apartments, as well as executive and bridal suites. This facility is located on the beach at Crocus Road and operates today as the Pan American Hotel.

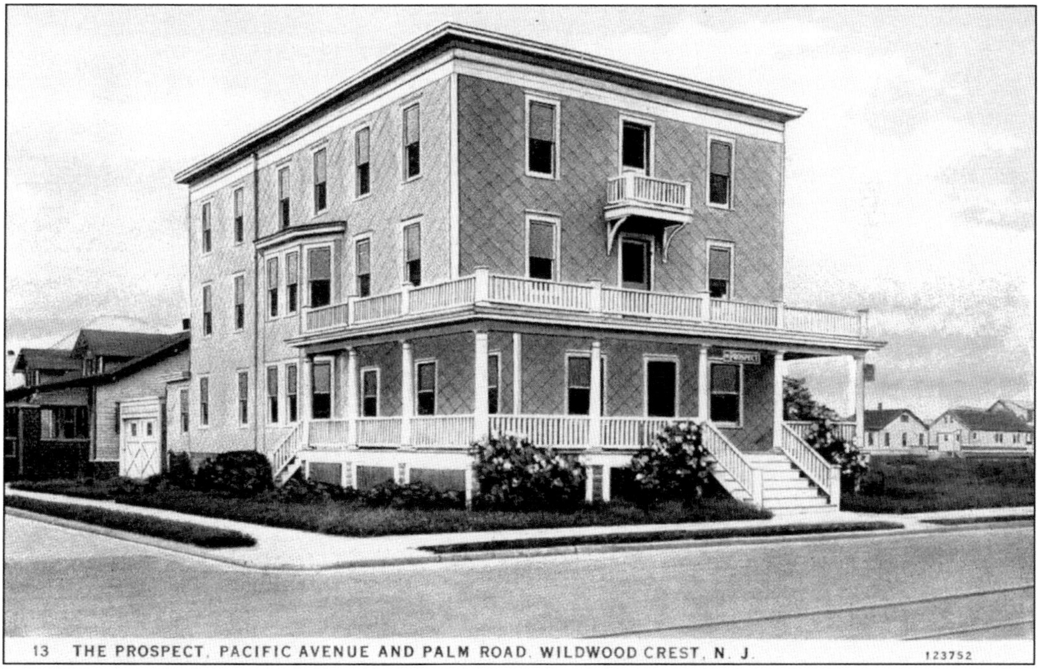

This postcard from the late 1920s shows the Prospect, located at the corner of Pacific Avenue and Palm Road. The fairly nondescript three-story building featured a two-tier porch and a serene setting. Incredibly this building is still in existence at the time of this writing. This structure has seen better days and no longer operates as a hotel, its future is uncertain.

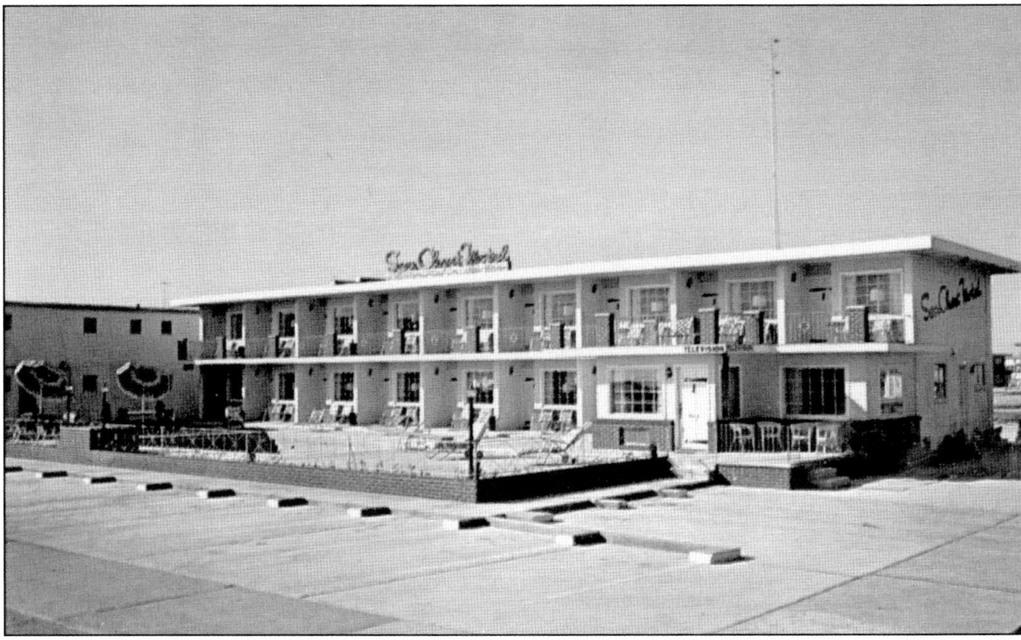

This postcard from the early 1960s shows the Sea Chest Motel, located at the corner of Stockton Road and Atlantic Avenue. In addition to the free beach umbrellas advertised on the rear of the card, it also states that the motel is close to several churches and restaurants. As of 2007, the Sea Chest Motel has been partially boarded up and is currently for sale.

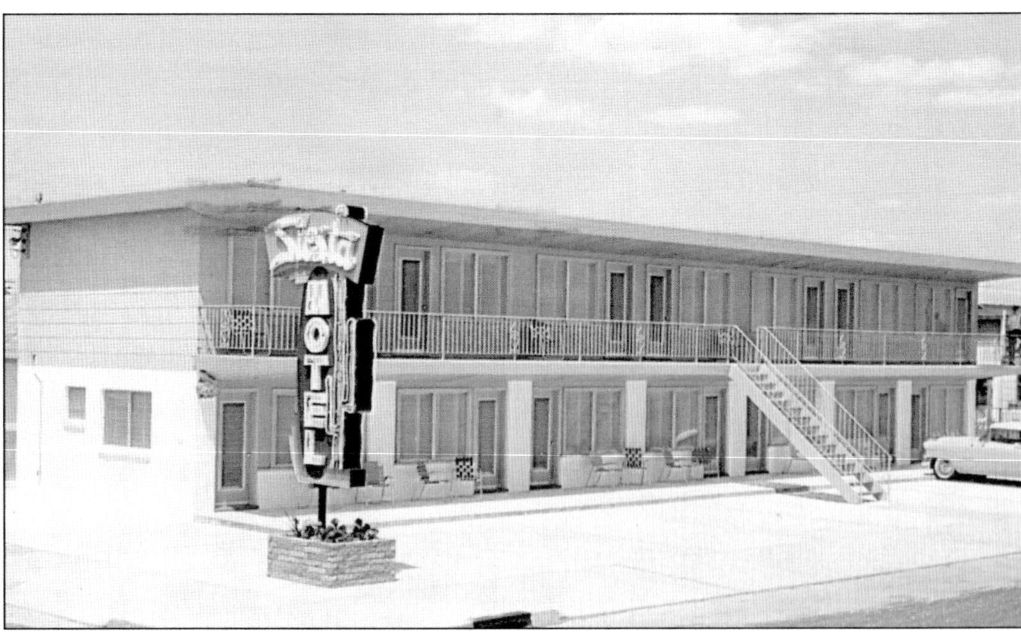

The Siesta Motel is seen in this postcard from the late 1950s. The motel was located at the corner of Morning Glory Road and Ocean Avenue and offered motel rooms as well as efficiency units. Today the former site of the Siesta Motel is now home to condominiums.

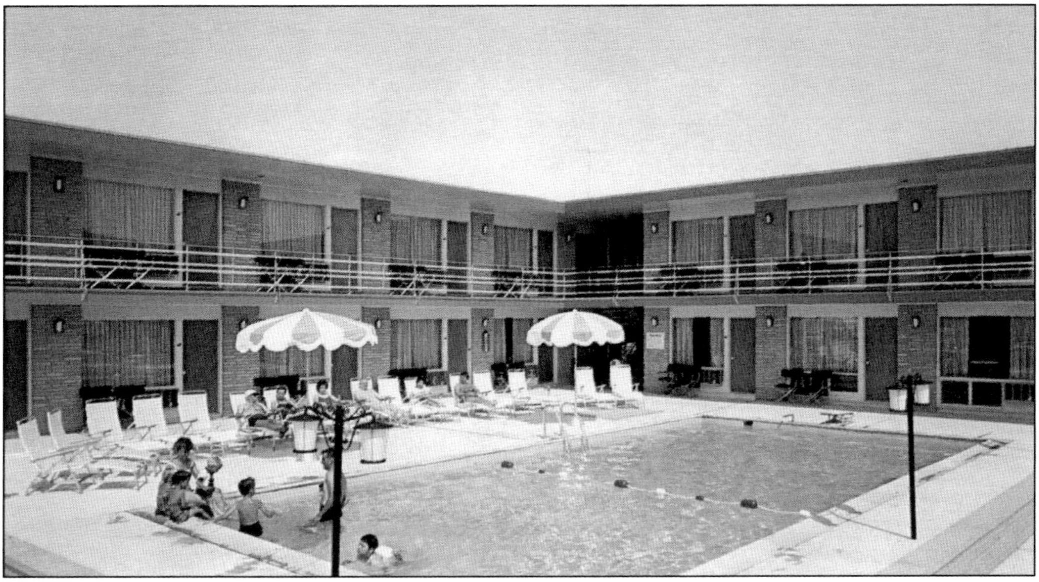

This view shows the Silver Dollar Motel, located on Ocean Avenue at Stanton Road. The back of the card mentions several amenities offered by the motel and further suggests that additional information can be obtained via "wire." Sadly the Silver Dollar Motel is yet another Wildwood Crest motel that has fallen to time and progress.

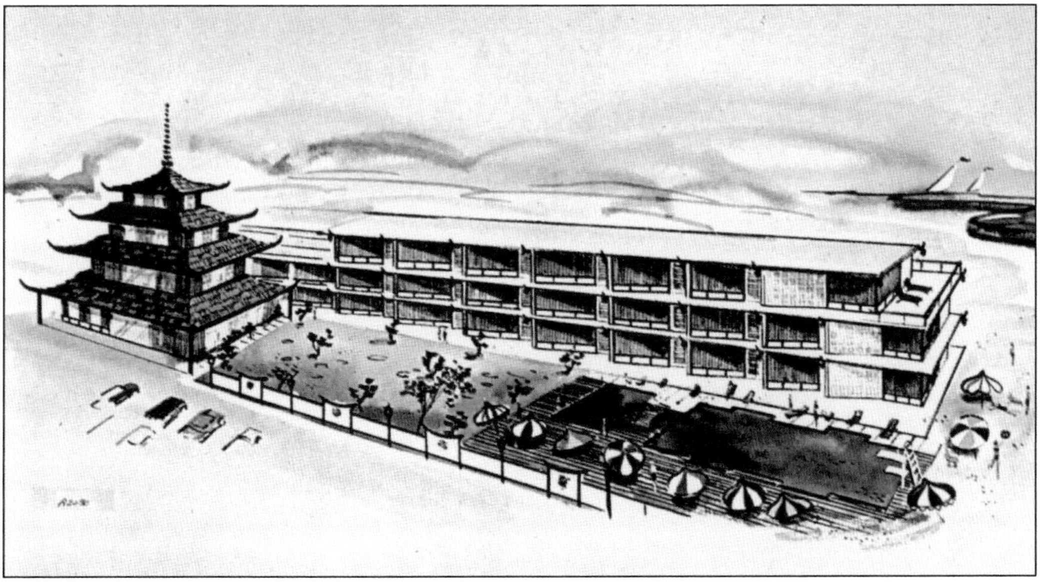

This postcard shows an artist's rendering of the Singapore Motel, located on the ocean at Orchid Road. The Asian-inspired design of the Singapore Motel makes this motel one of the true architectural standouts in all of the Wildwoods. Fortunately the motel is still operating and has managed to maintain much of its original and unique design.

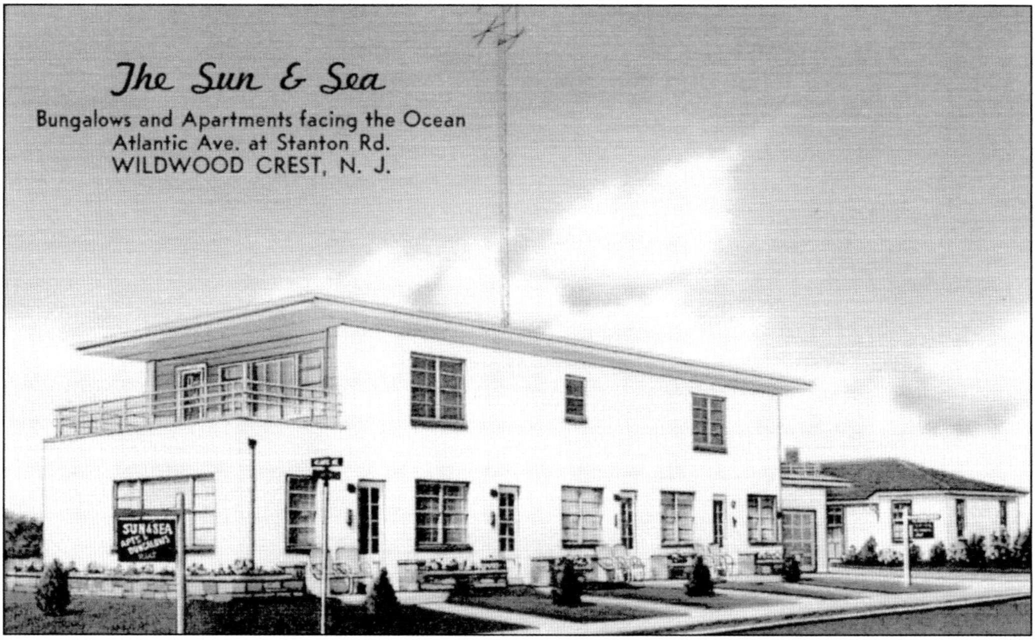

The Sun and Sea Bungalows and Apartments are seen in this postcard from the early 1950s. These units were located on Atlantic Avenue at Stanton Road and offered modest accommodations at reasonable rates. Today the former site of the Sun and Sea Bungalows and Apartments is now home to private residences.

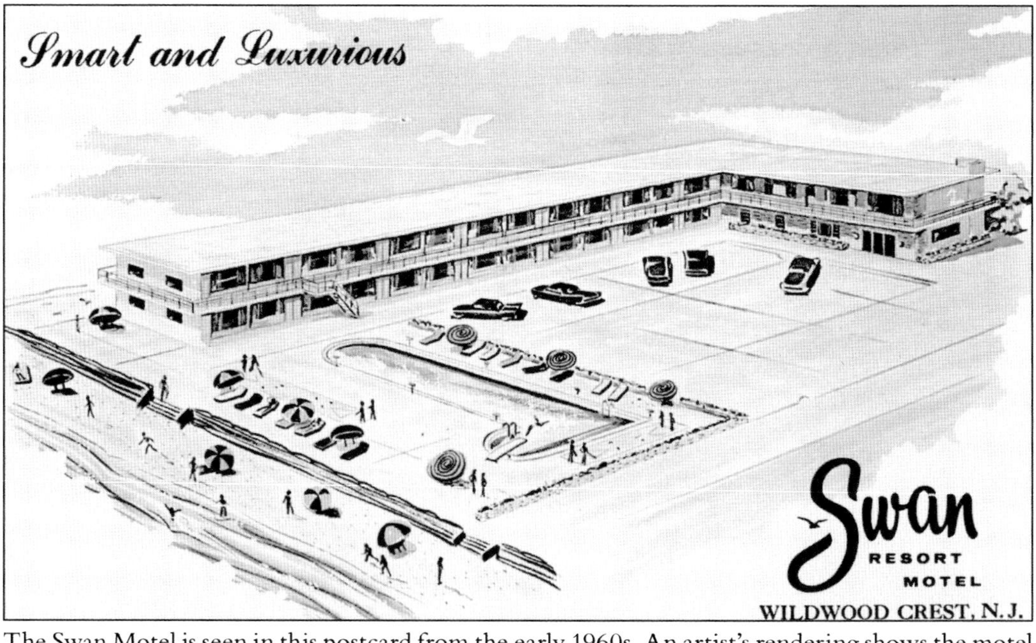

The Swan Motel is seen in this postcard from the early 1960s. An artist's rendering shows the motel from an aerial perspective, as the text on the card refers to the motel as "smart and luxurious." The motel offered efficiencies, standard rooms, as well as a variety of suites. Today the motel is gone, and its former site on the ocean at Stockton Road is now home to condominiums.

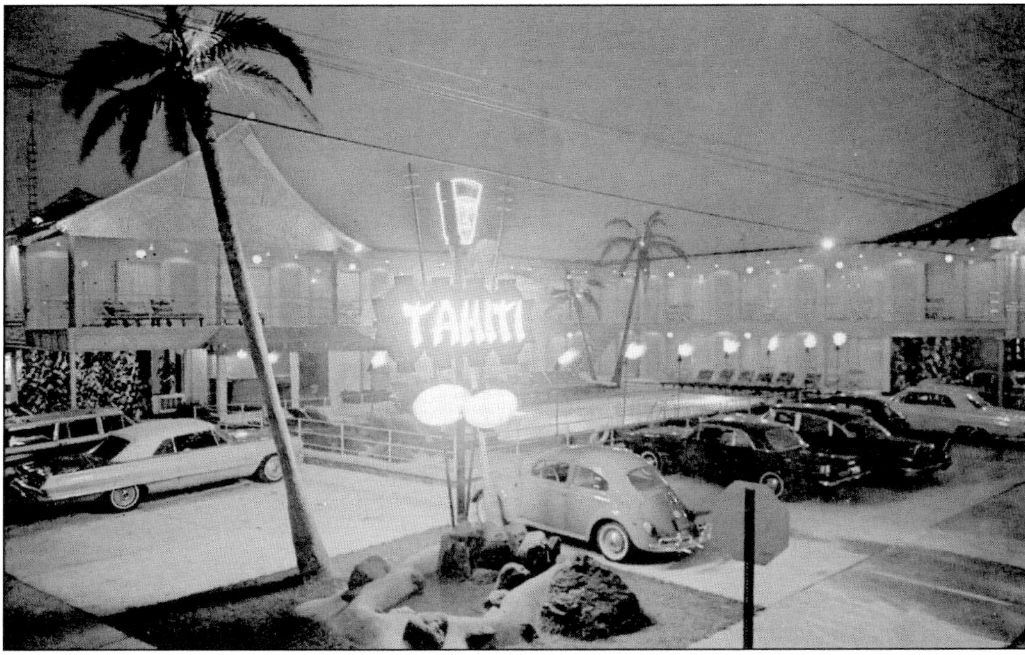

This postcard from the early 1960s shows the Tahiti Resort Motel, formerly located at the corner of Stanton Road and Atlantic Avenue. The Tahiti Resort Motel was a Polynesian-inspired motel complete with palm trees, bamboo, and lava rock. Sadly this unique and irreplaceable structure was demolished. Today condominiums stand on the former site of the Tahiti Resort Motel.

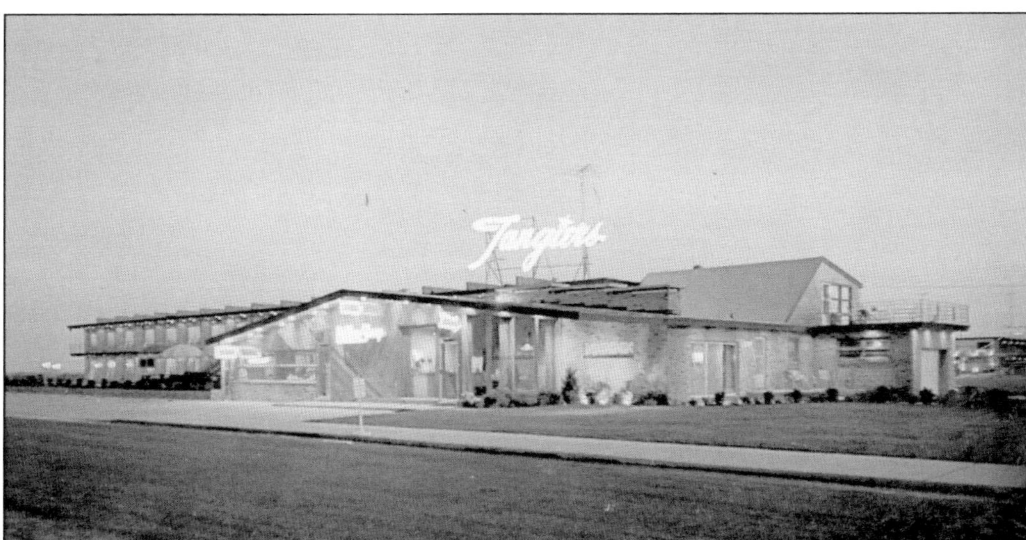

This view from 1960 shows the Tangiers Resort Motel, located at 6201 Atlantic Avenue. The rear of the card refers to the facility as "the Motel with a New Concept of Vacation Pleasure." The card's text also points out that there are televisions in every room. Fortunately the Tangiers Resort Motel survives today and is still operating as a motel.

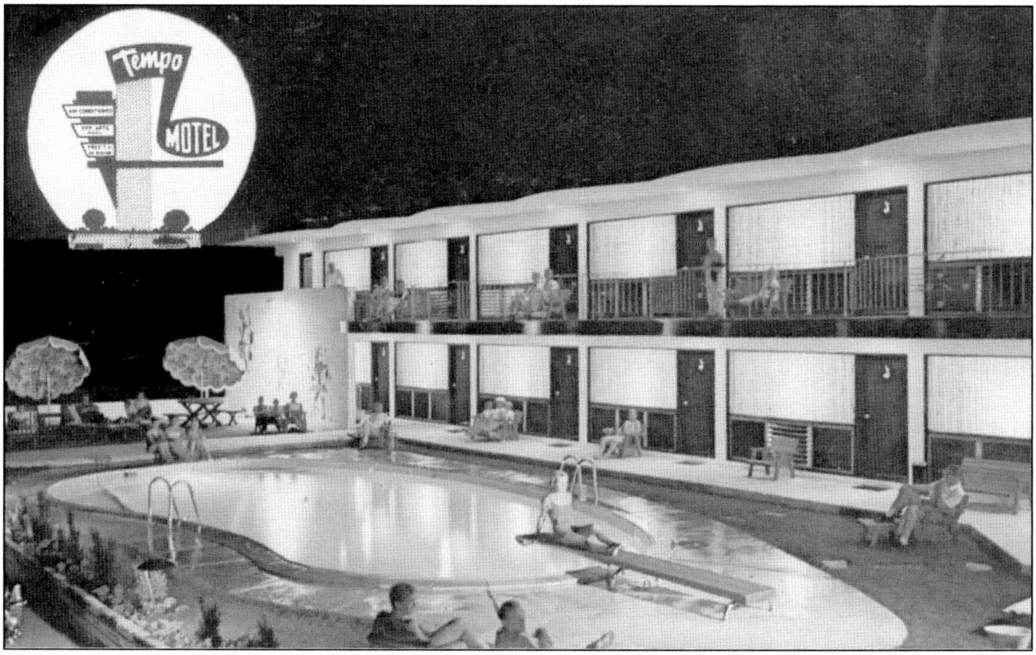

The Tempo Motel is seen in this view from the early 1960s. The Tempo Motel featured a swimming pool in addition to a lounging area and sun patio. The motel was located at 7801 Atlantic Avenue and has been replaced with condominiums.

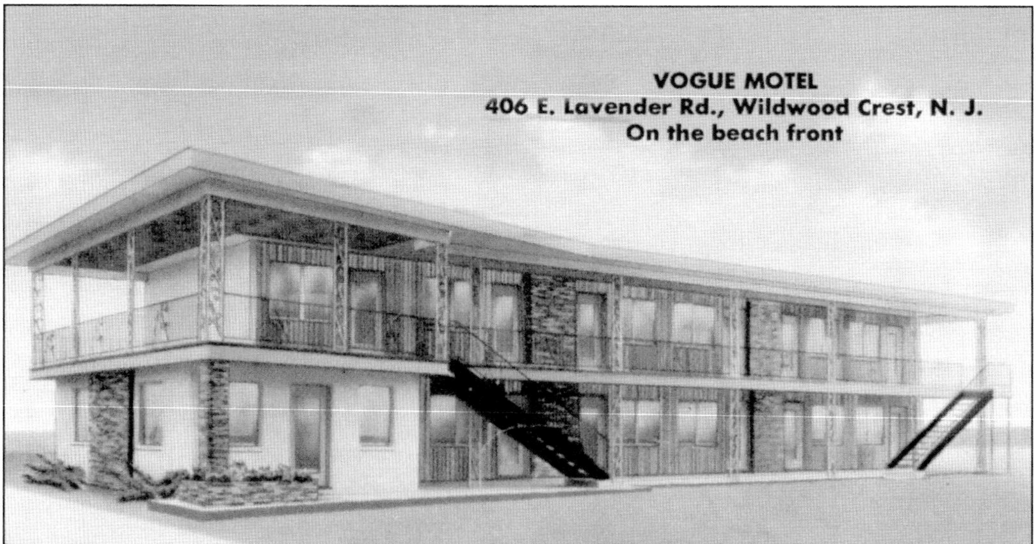

The Vogue Motel is seen in this stylized view from 1958. This two-story structure sat on the Wildwood Crest beachfront and offered kitchens and private baths for all rooms. Formerly located at 406 East Lavender Road, the site of the Vogue Motel is now home to condominiums.

Three

Accommodations in North Wildwood

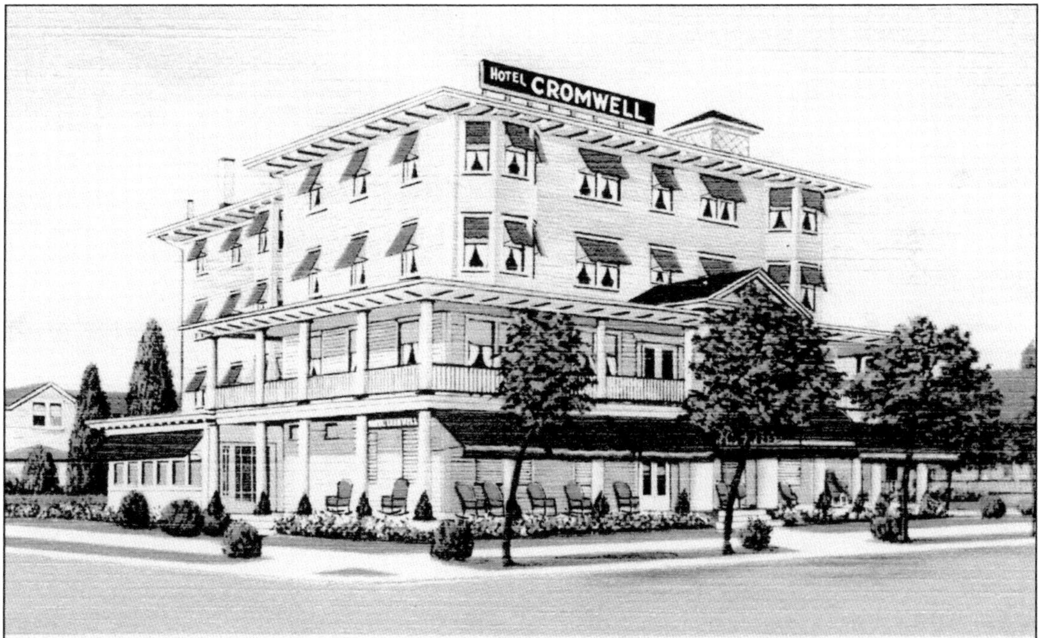

The Hotel Cromwell was located at the corner of Atlantic Avenue and Twenty-sixth Street and is seen in this view from the 1940s. The attractive four-story hotel featured rooms with "outside" views, as well as "elevator service." The Hotel Cromwell's motto was "exclusive, but not expensive." Today the Hotel Cromwell is but a memory of the past, lost to time and progress in burgeoning North Wildwood.

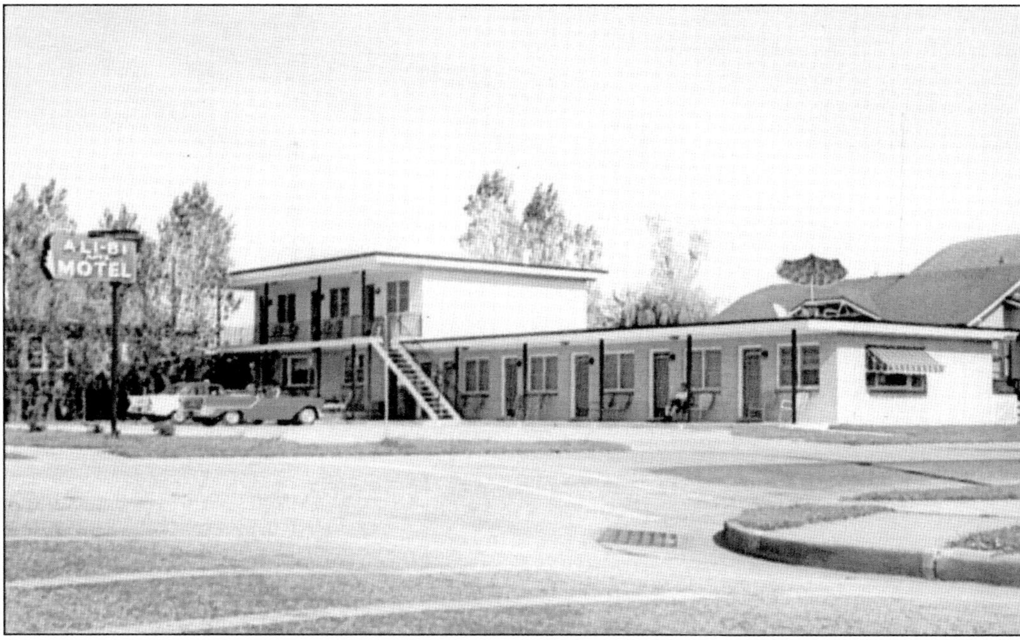

This postcard from the 1950s shows the Ali-Bi Motel, located from 1505–1509 Central Avenue. The Ali-Bi Motel featured one-, two-, and three-bedroom apartments for guests to choose from and also offered "ample" off-street parking. Today the structure that was the Ali-Bi Motel survives, although it is now operated as the Central Square Condominiums.

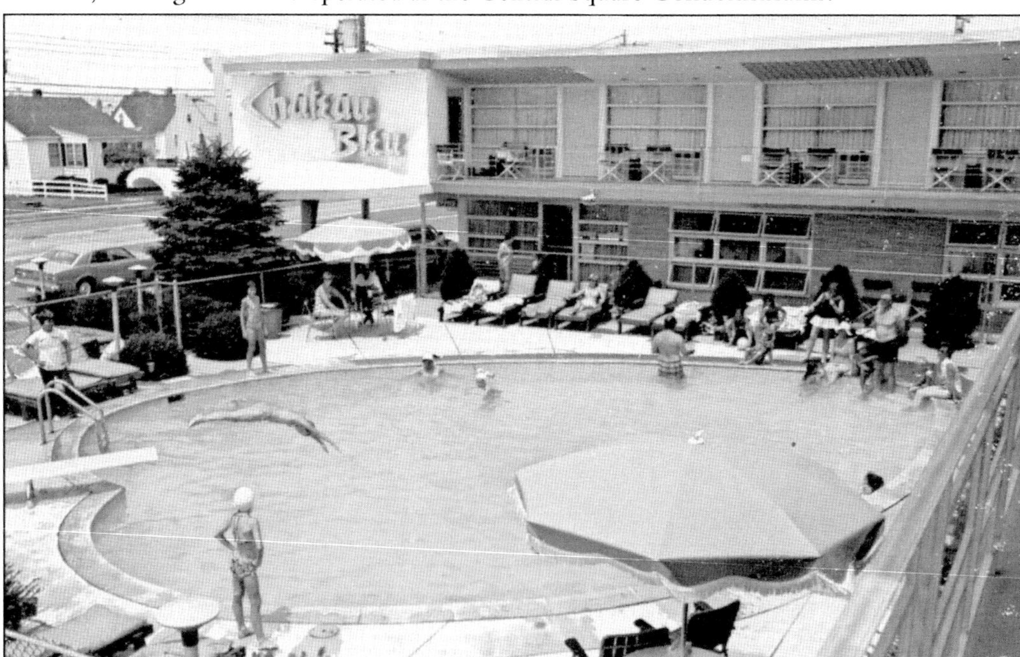

This view from the 1960s shows the Chateau Bleu Luxury Resort Motel, located at Tenth and Surf Avenues. The motel featured efficiencies in addition to standard rooms. Outside guests could luxuriate poolside or in one of the lounge areas. Today the Chateau Bleu Luxury Resort Motel is still operating as a motel.

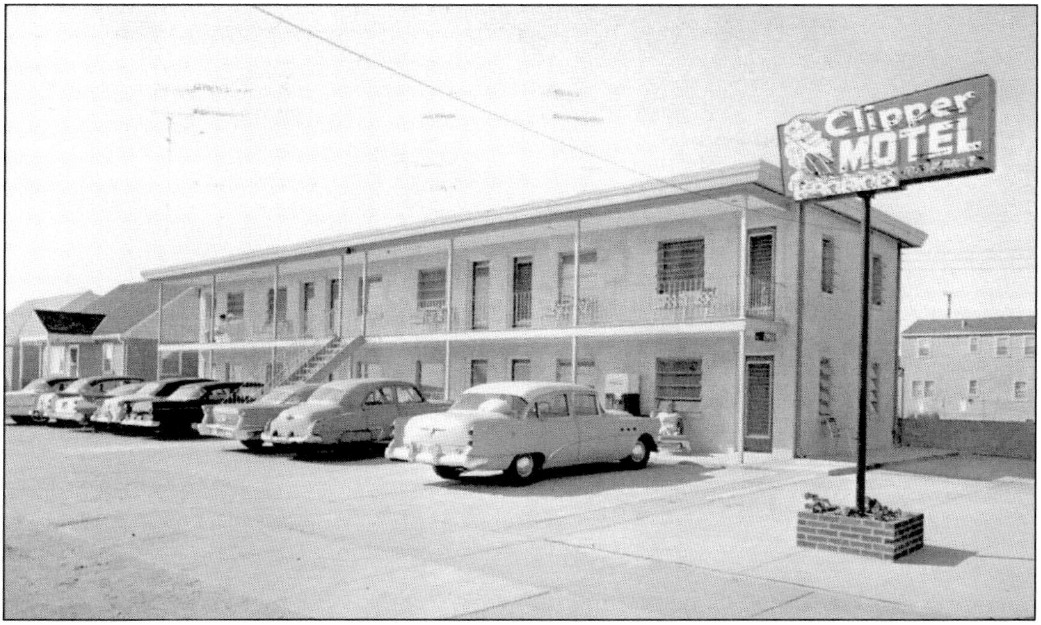

This postcard from the early 1950s shows the Clipper Motel and Efficiencies, located at 500 East Thirteenth Avenue. The facility featured "modern" bathrooms in all units, in addition to complimentary off-street parking. Today the Clipper Motel and Efficiencies' building remains, although all units have been converted to condominium ownership.

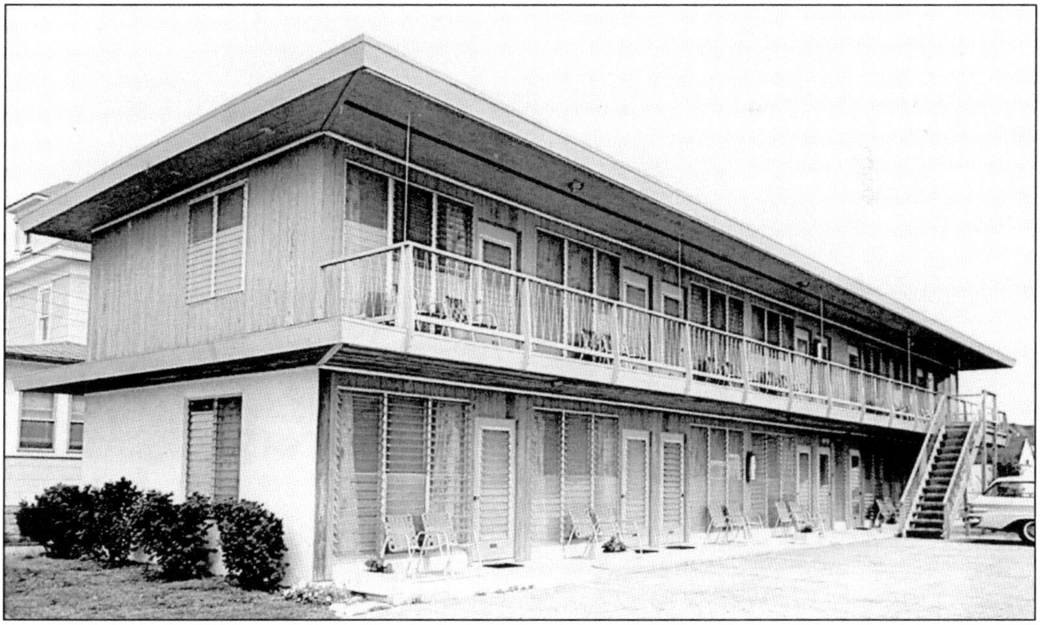

The Driftwood Motel is seen in this postcard from the late 1950s. The motel offered rooms with "modern décor" and prided itself on being in close proximity to a variety of restaurants, churches, and activities. Today the Driftwood Motel's building lives on in the form of condominium ownership at the corner of Sixteenth and Atlantic Avenues.

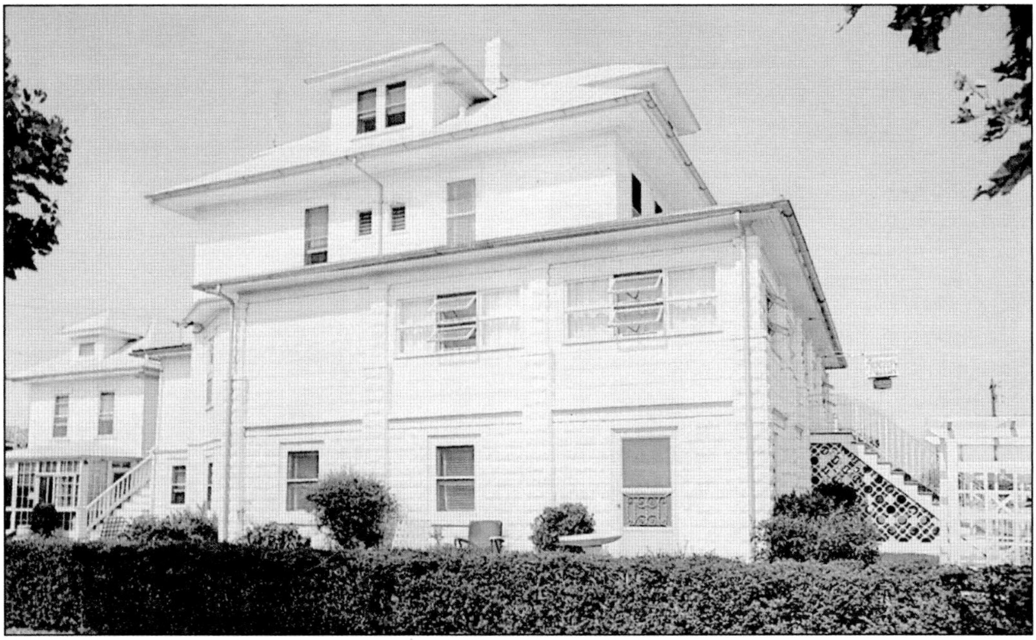

The Evergreens is seen in this view from the 1950s. Located at 2110 Atlantic Avenue, the hotel offered furnished rooms, apartments, and cottages. Today the former Evergreens has been remade as the Summer Nites Bed and Breakfast and looks remarkably similar on the outside as it did 50 years ago.

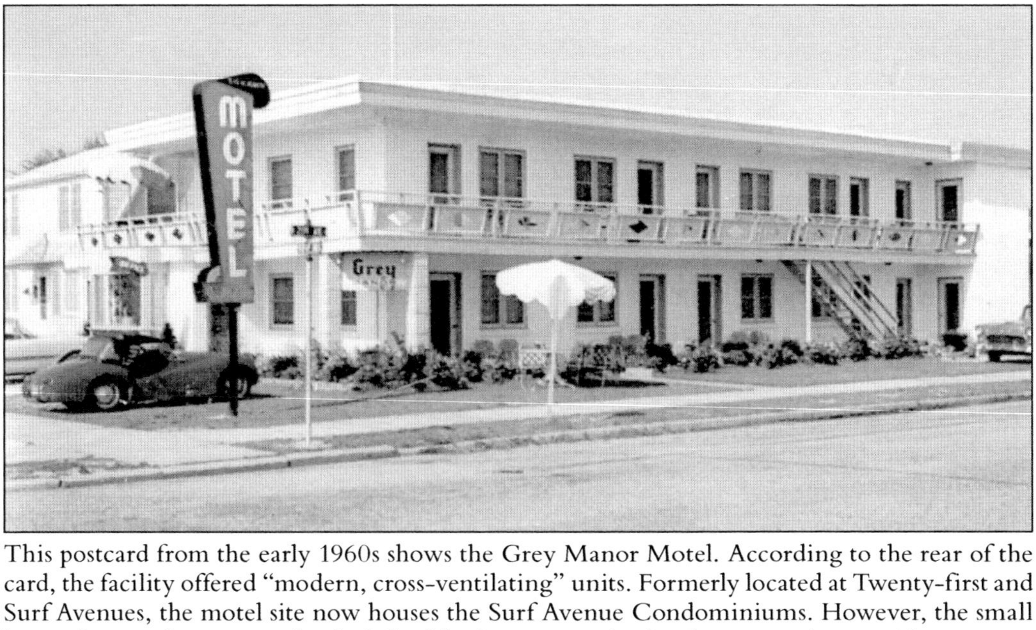

This postcard from the early 1960s shows the Grey Manor Motel. According to the rear of the card, the facility offered "modern, cross-ventilating" units. Formerly located at Twenty-first and Surf Avenues, the motel site now houses the Surf Avenue Condominiums. However, the small house that can be seen on the far left of the image remains in place as a private residence.

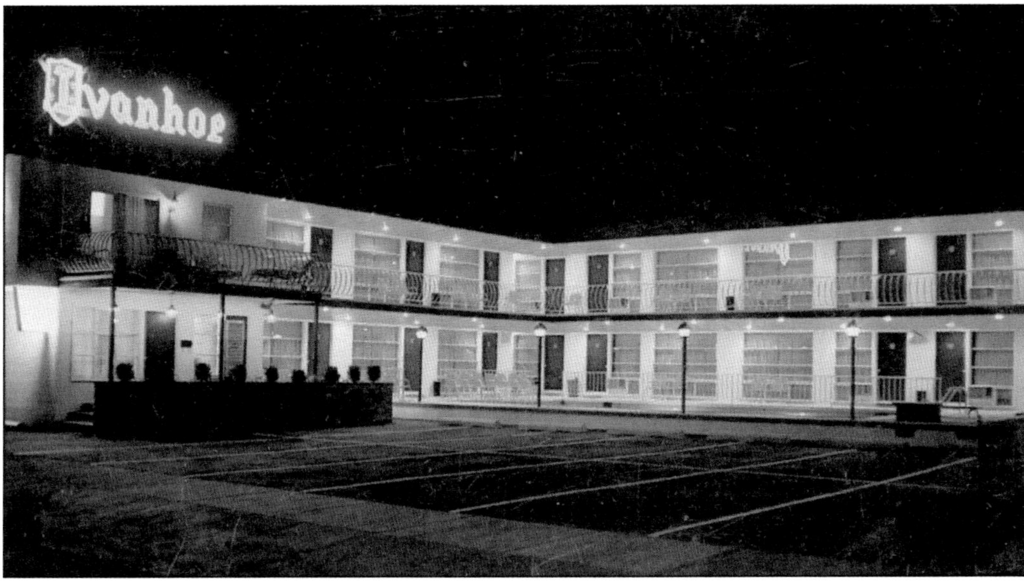

The Ivanhoe Motel is seen in this postcard from the 1960s. The motel is located at Twenty-first Avenue and the beach. The facility offered one- and two-bedroom units, in addition to efficiencies. Although the familiar Ivanhoe Motel sign was not standing atop the building at the time of this writing, the motel continues to operate in its original intended capacity.

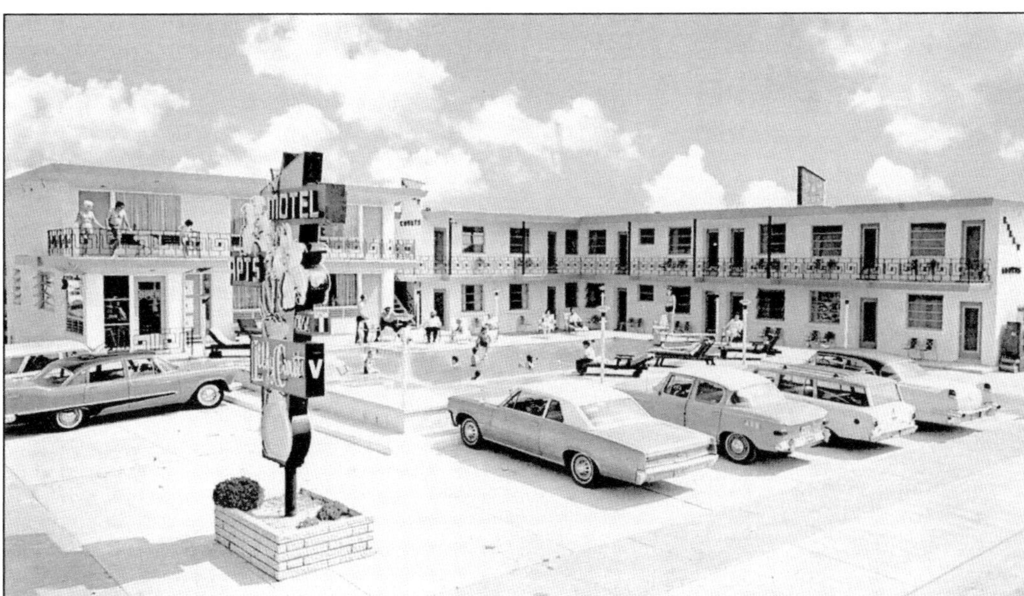

This postcard from the 1960s shows the Lilly Courts Motel. The motel offered "unsurpassed accommodations" that included standard rooms and apartments. The Lilly Courts Motel was located at Seventh and Surf Avenues for a period of many years, before being demolished to make way for condominiums.

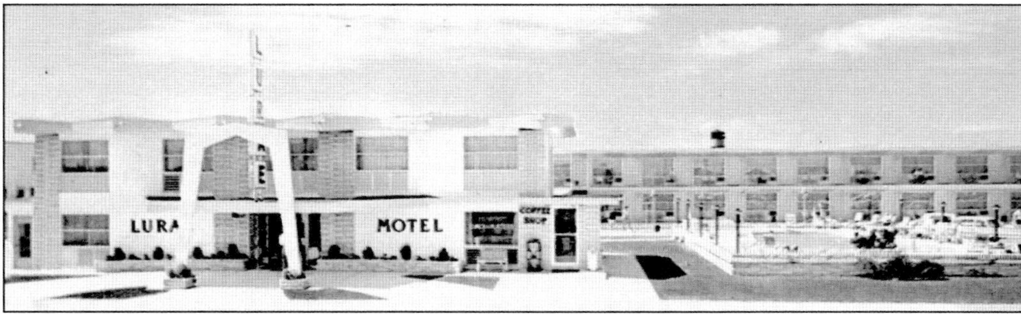

This view of the Lurae Motel from the 1960s shows the distinctive arch entrance that welcomed visitors along Surf Avenue between Sixth and Seventh Avenues. The motel offered an on-site coffee shop in addition to air-conditioned rooms and a heated pool. Today the sprawling former site of the Lurae Motel is home to a new condominium development.

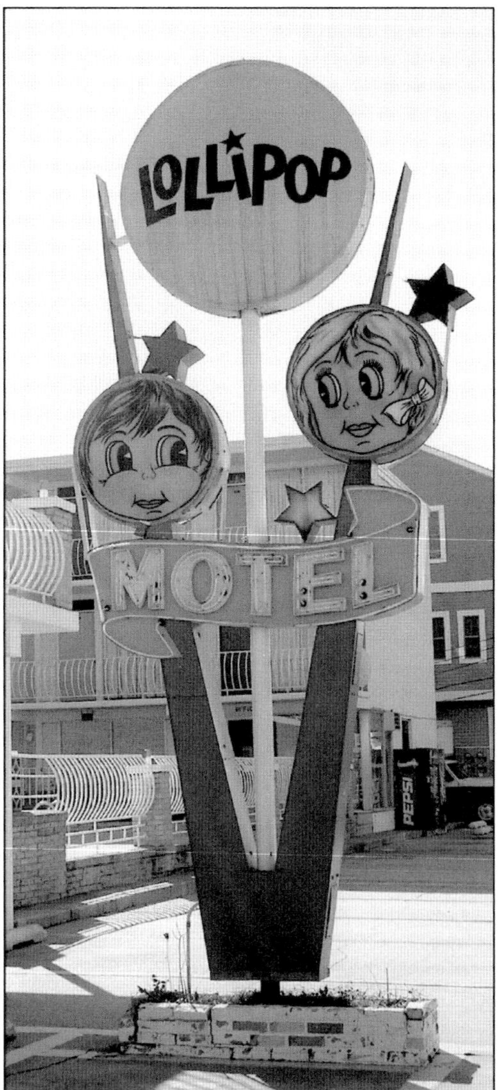

This view shows the iconic sign of the Lollipop Motel, located at Twenty-third and Atlantic Avenues. The Lollipop Motel was built in the late 1950s and has been carefully preserved so as to maintain much of its original charm and character. The motel still operates as a condominium/motel and entices visitors with brightly colored doors and one of the most recognizable signs in the Wildwoods.

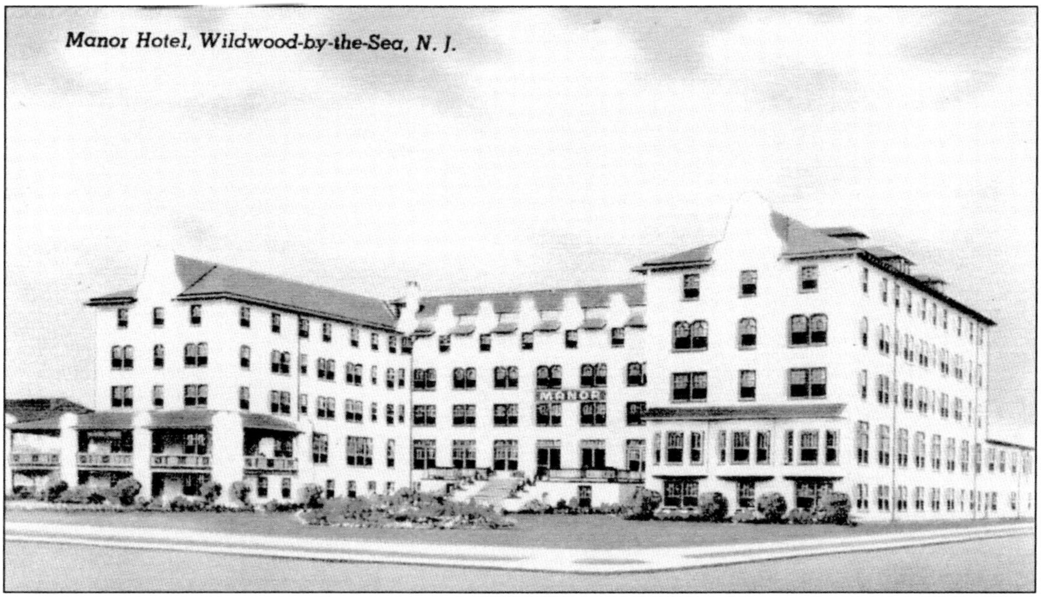

These postcards show the Manor Hotel, located at Twenty-fourth and Surf Avenues. This facility was one of the larger hotels in the Wildwoods and was easily recognizable among smaller hotels and motels in the locale of North Wildwood. The view at the top of the page shows the Manor Hotel as it appeared in the early 1940s, while the postcard at the bottom of the page shows the hotel as it looked in the late 1950s. In the later view, one can see that the hotel has been given an addition near the front-center entrance, and a sign beckons residents and vacationers to visit the Manor Hotel Supper Club, a lively entertainment venue in its day. Sadly the Manor Hotel succumbed to a devastating fire in the late 1960s. Today nothing remains of this once imposing facade.

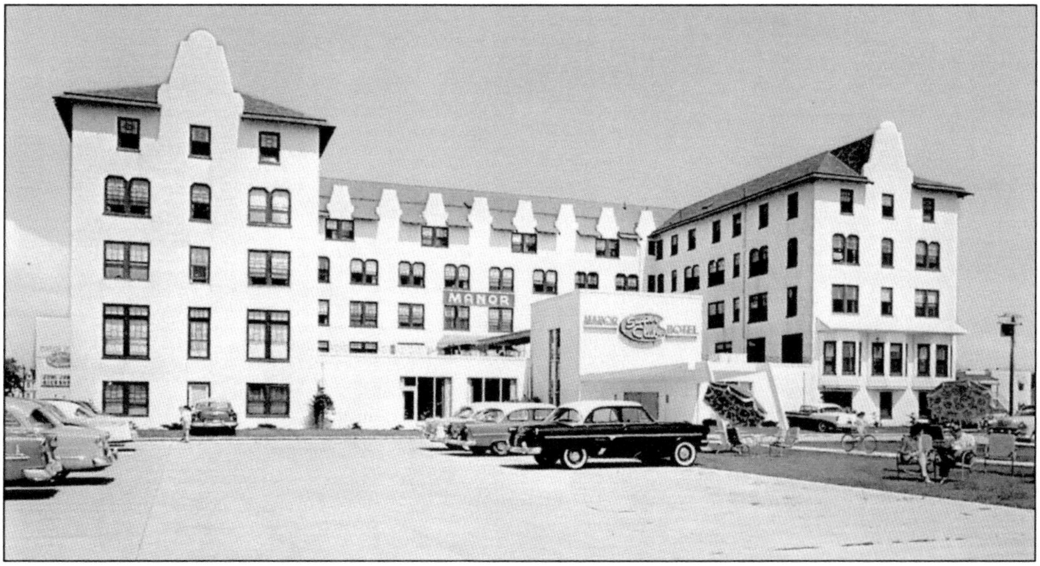

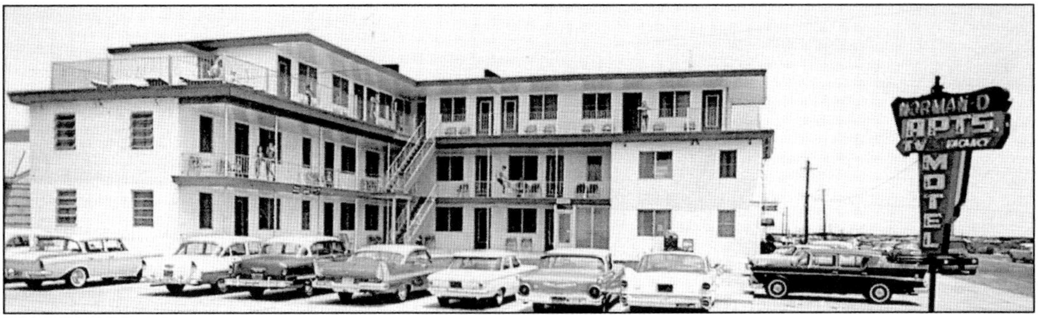

The Norman-D Apartments and Motel is seen in this postcard from the late 1950s. The facility offered one- and two-bedroom units in addition to efficiencies. Although the Norman-D complex no longer operates as a motel, the building has been preserved under condominium ownership. The unique three-story design is still evident at the corner of Seventh and Ocean Avenues, although the Norman-D is now wrapped in a neutral-colored siding.

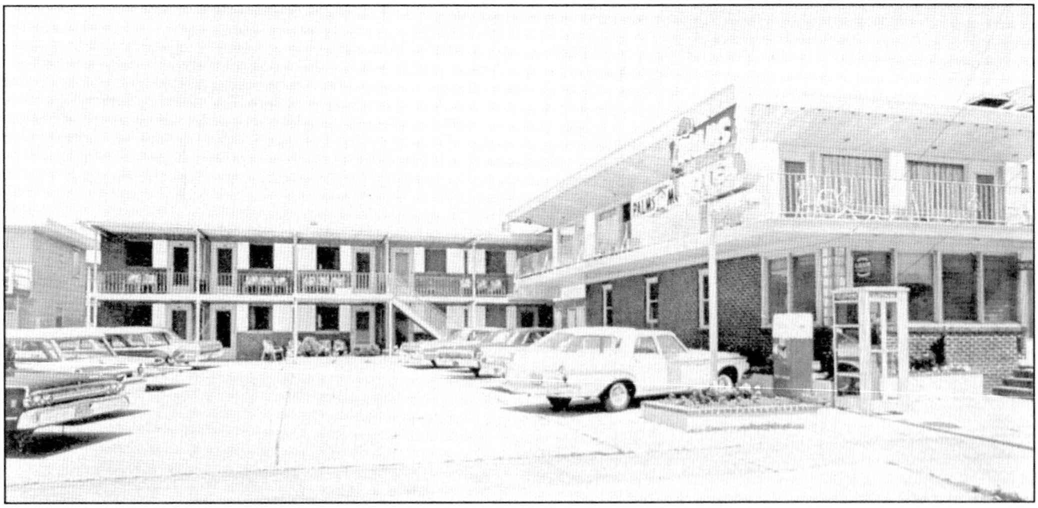

This view from the 1960s shows the Palms Motel, formerly located at 317 East Twenty-fifth Street. The rear of the card touts the motel's location as being close to "theaters, stores, and night clubs." In this view, a vintage Coca-Cola vending machine can be seen standing next to an old phone booth. Today the Palms Motel is but a memory of the past.

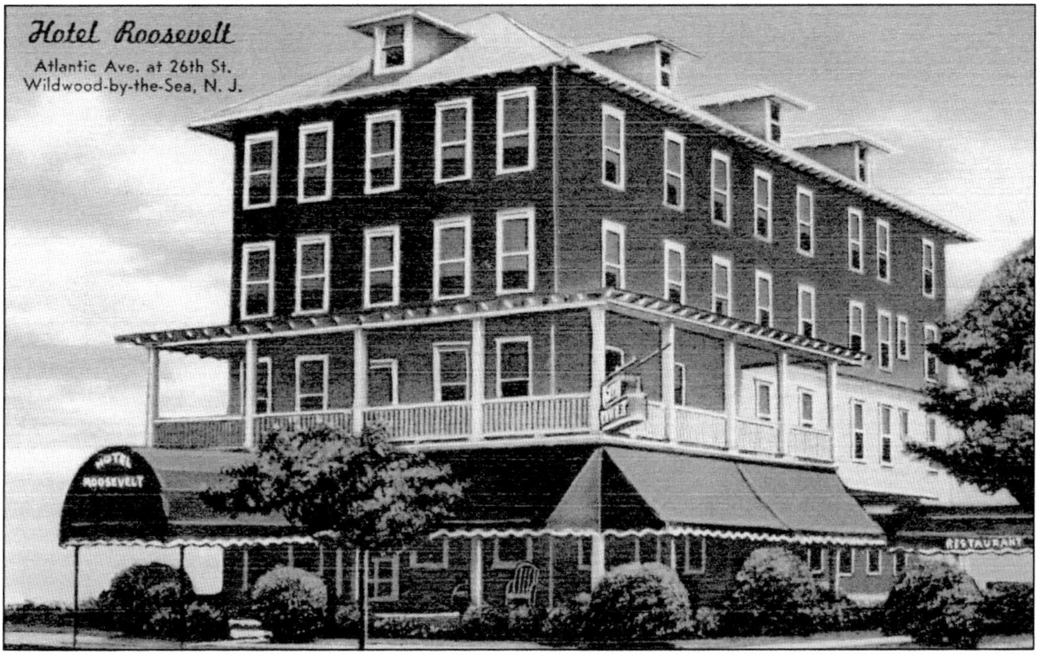

The Roosevelt Hotel is seen in this postcard from the 1940s. The hotel was located at Twenty-sixth and Atlantic Avenues and featured a restaurant in addition to year-round accommodations. Today the Roosevelt Hotel has joined the many others that have vanished and exist now only in our memories.

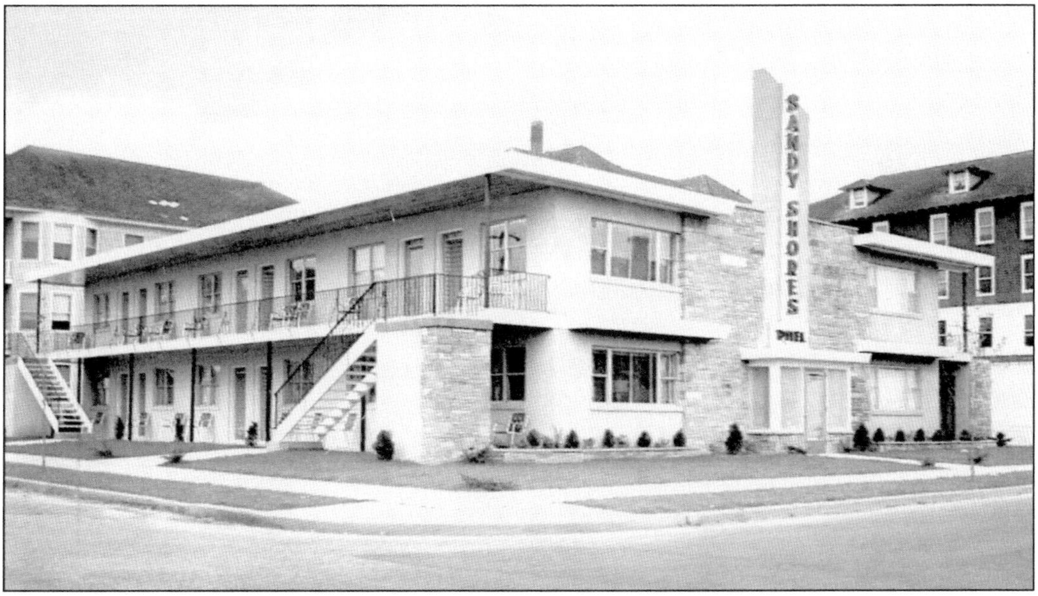

This postcard from the 1950s shows the Sandy Shores Motel, located along Atlantic Avenue between Twenty-fifth and Twenty-sixth Avenues. The rear of the card advertised the option of an "American" or "European" rate plan in addition to full baths in every room. Today the Sandy Shores still operates as a motel in North Wildwood and is recognizable despite the addition of a third story.

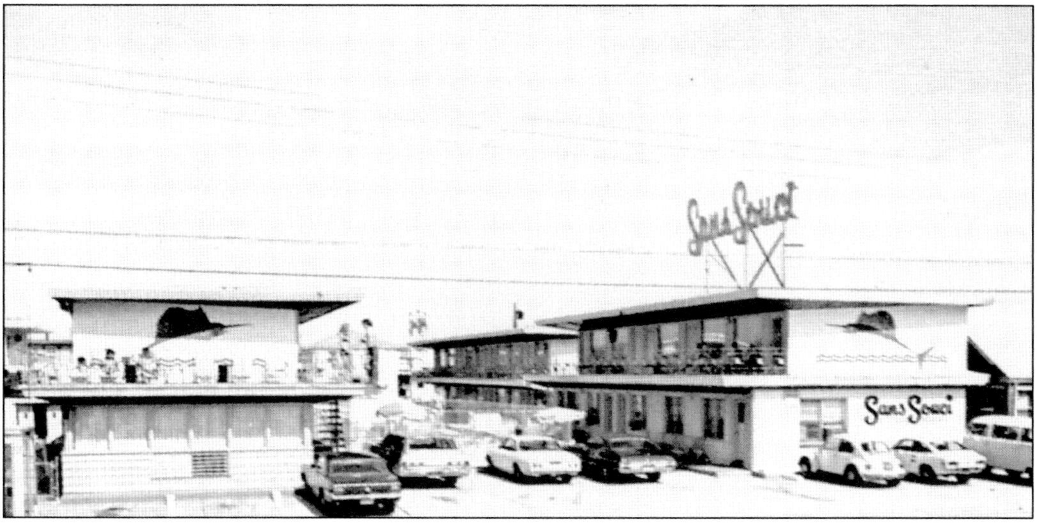

The Sans Souci Motel is seen in this postcard view from the 1960s. The motel was formerly located at Twenty-first Avenue and the beach and advertised itself as the "Ultimate in Vacation Living." All rooms featured wall-to-wall carpeting and refrigerators. Unfortunately the Sans Souci Motel has not survived the rapid pace of redevelopment underway in the Wildwoods.

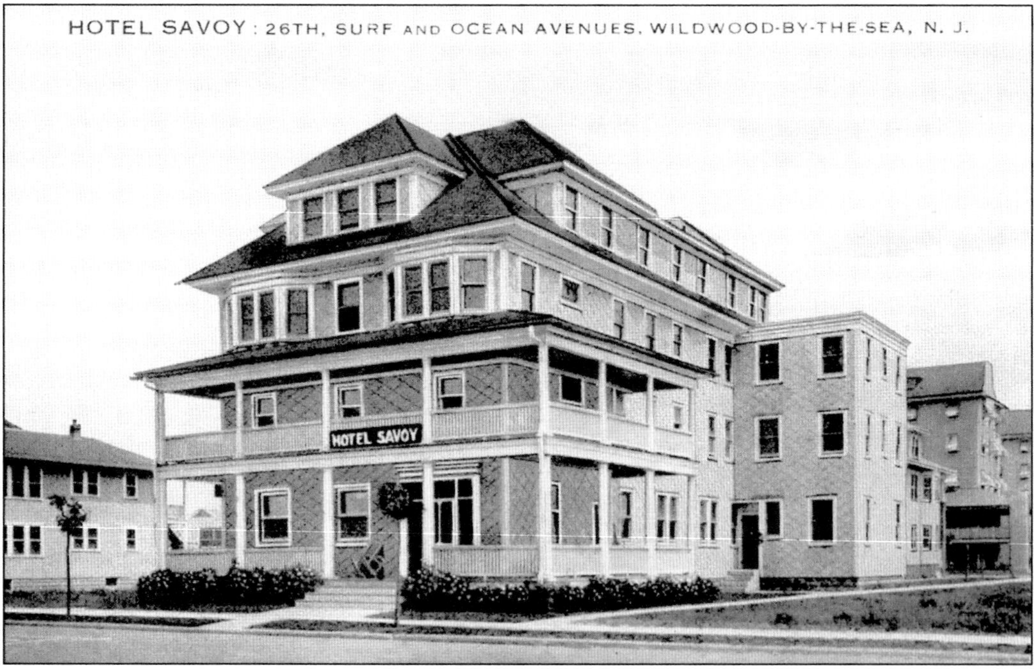

This postcard from the 1920s shows the Hotel Savoy, located on Twenty-sixth Avenue, between Surf and Ocean Avenues. The four-story hotel featured accommodations that were typical for its day, along with first- and second-story porches. Today the Hotel Savoy is yet another example of the Wildwoods' history having been lost to time and progress.

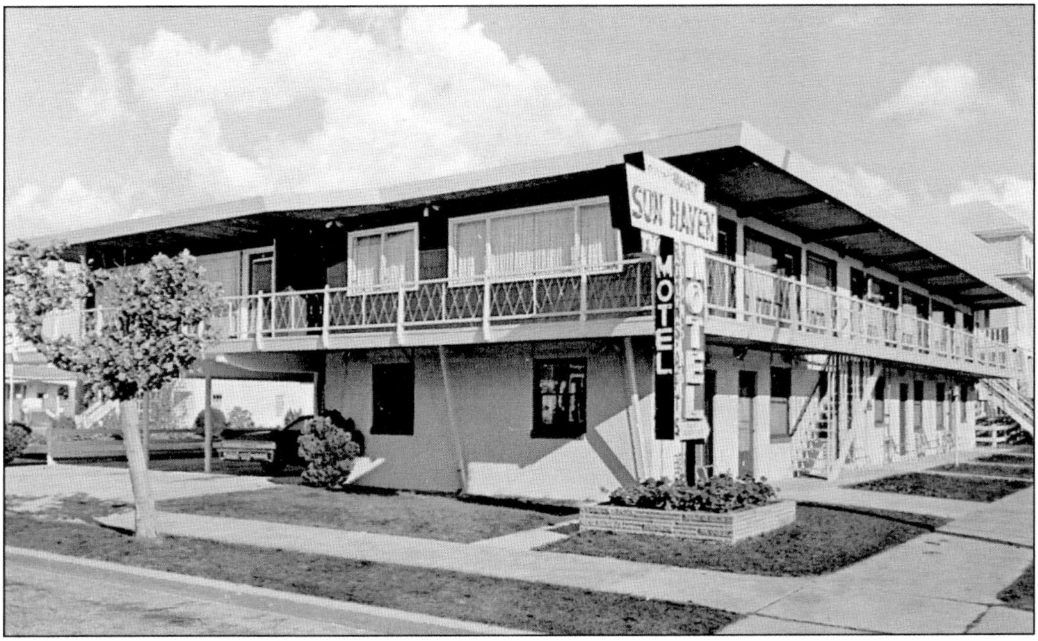

The Sun Haven Motel is seen in this postcard from the 1950s. All rooms were equipped with "tub and shower" and featured television and daily maid service. The Sun Haven Motel was located at Twenty-fourth and Atlantic Avenues and would last for decades in this spot before being demolished to make way for new residences.

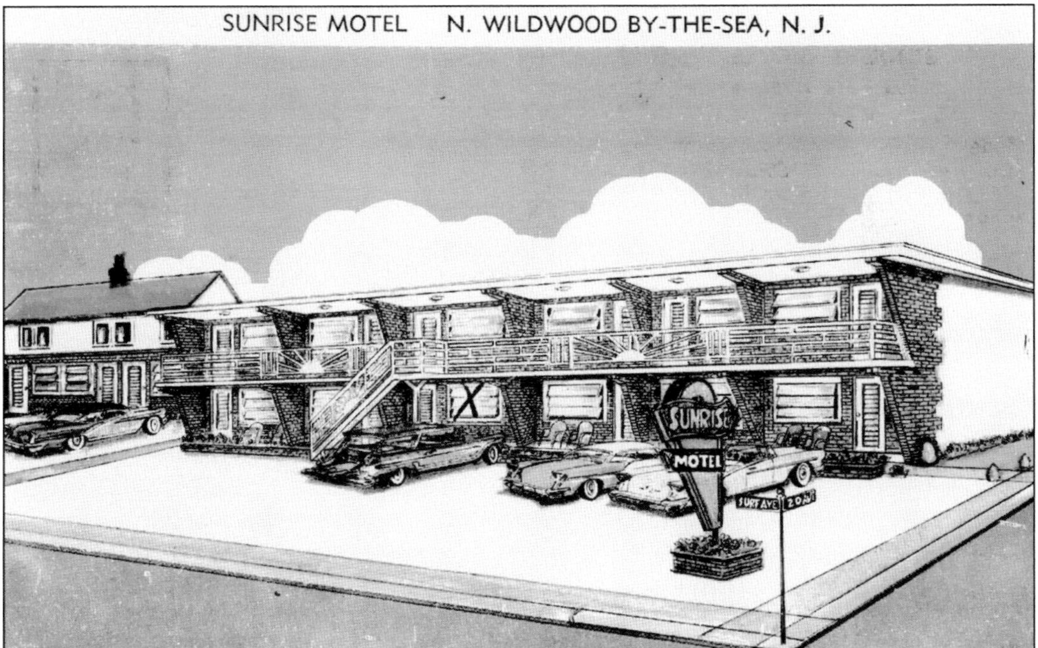

This postcard shows an artist's rendering of the Sunrise Motel as it appeared in the 1950s. The facility featured standard motel units, efficiencies, and suites. There was also an elevator for the convenience of its guests. Formerly located at 1901 Surf Avenue, the site of the Sunrise Motel now houses residential offerings.

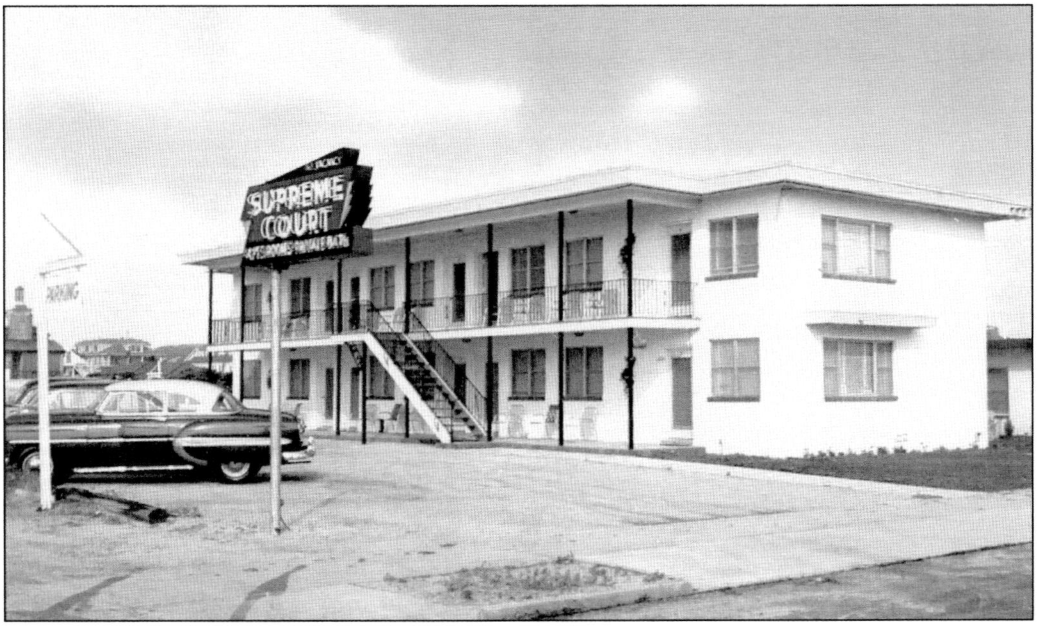

The Supreme Court is seen in this postcard from the 1950s. The motel was located just a short distance from the boardwalk and offered private bathrooms for each unit. Although the structure survives at Twenty-second Avenue and the boardwalk, the Supreme Court would eventually have its sign removed and become part of the King's Inn Motel, based one block over on Twenty-third Avenue.

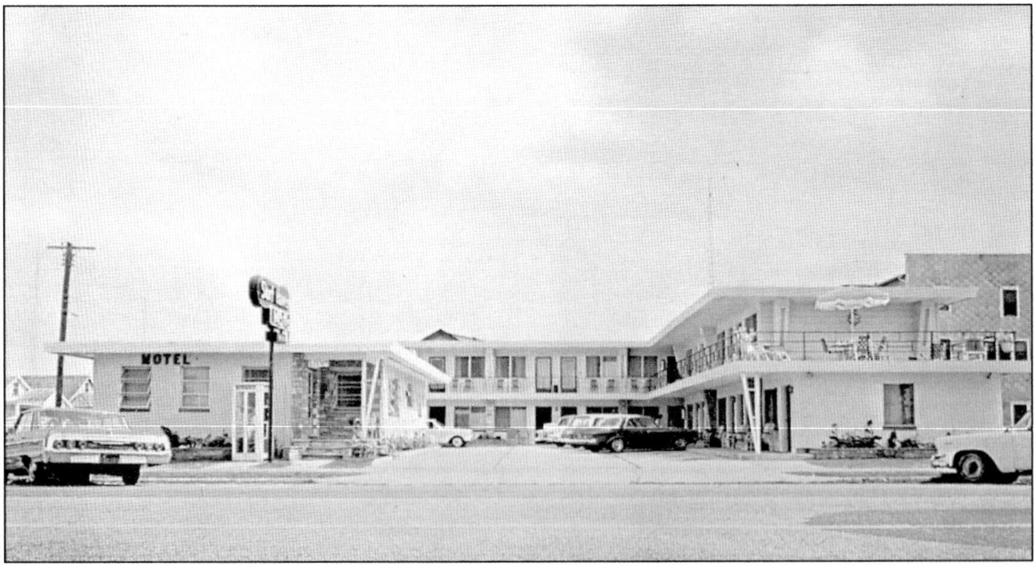

This postcard from the 1960s shows the Surf Haven Motel, located at 1601 Surf Avenue. When built, the motel offered 23 units, each with private bath. Despite the fact that almost 50 years have elapsed since this postcard was produced, the Surf Haven Motel is still operating and has managed to retain much of its original design.

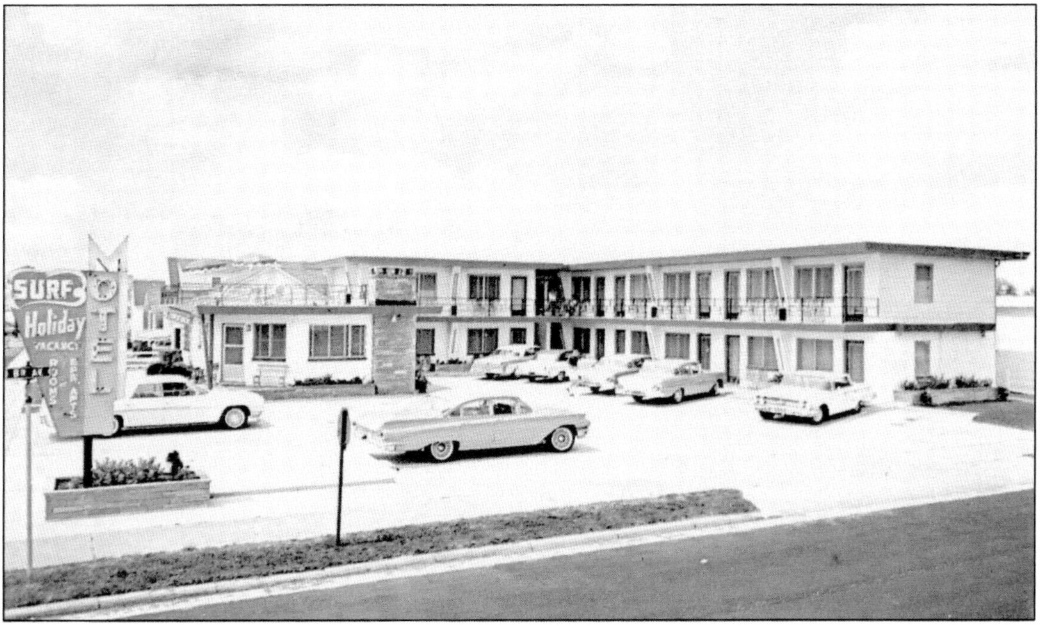

The Surf Holiday Motel is seen in this postcard from the early 1960s. The rear of the card touts the motel's location in a "quiet atmosphere," yet states that it is located near all types of activities. Sadly the two-story motel building no longer graces the corner of Eighth and Surf Avenues; instead a condominium has risen in its place.

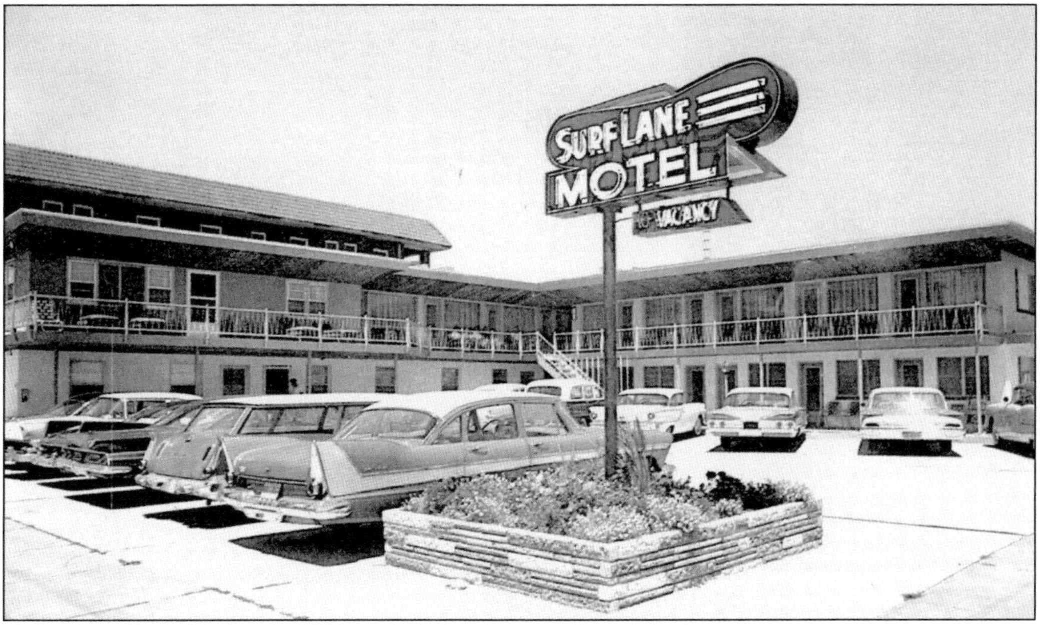

This postcard from the early 1960s shows the Surf Lane Motel and Apartments, formerly located at 349 East Twenty-fourth Avenue at Surf Avenue. The motel offered one- and two-bedroom units, complete with private bath. Sadly the two-story Surf Lane Motel and Apartments has been demolished and new residences stand on its former site.

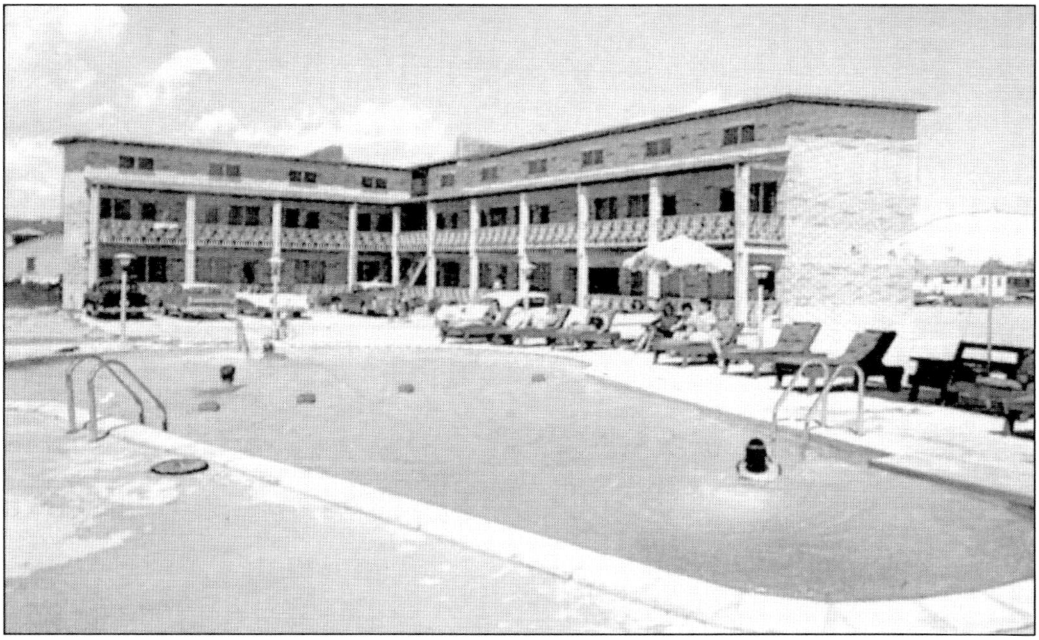

The Trylon Motel is seen in this postcard from the late 1950s. The motel is located along the beachfront, between Twelfth and Thirteenth Avenues. The Trylon Motel offered fully equipped kitchens in addition to two swimming pools. Today the Trylon Motel continues to operate but has seen some expansion since this postcard was produced.

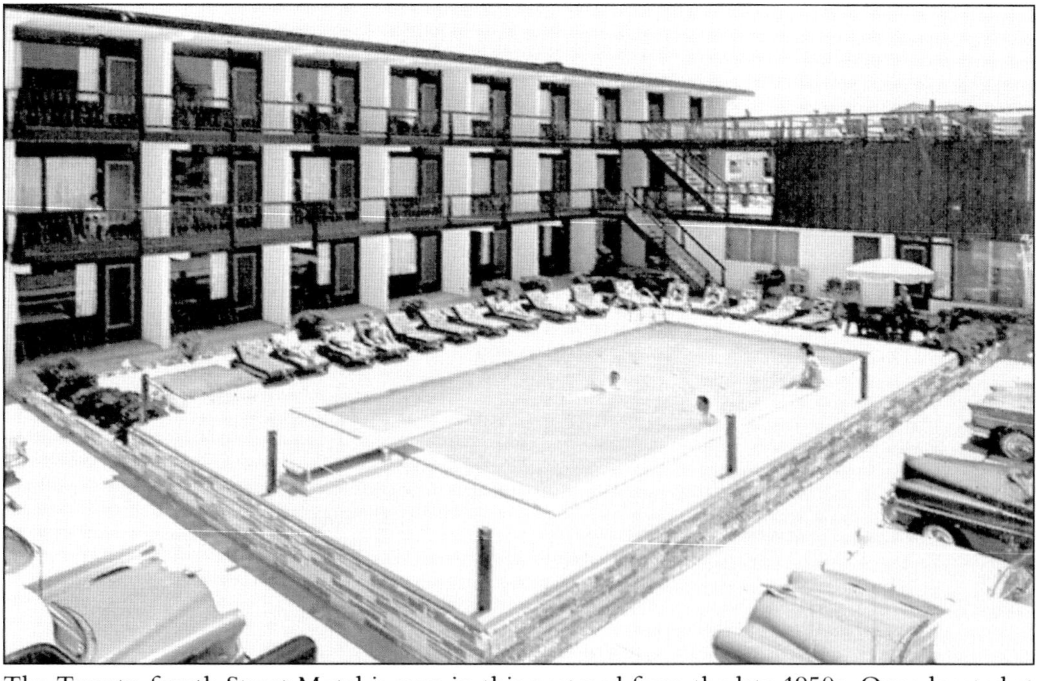

The Twenty-fourth Street Motel is seen in this postcard from the late 1950s. Once located at the corner of Twenty-fourth and Surf Avenues, the Twenty-fourth Street Motel featured a sun patio, swimming pool, and television in every unit. Unfortunately the motel has succumbed to the residential development that is gripping several areas of North Wildwood these days.

Four

Businesses, Bars, and Restaurants

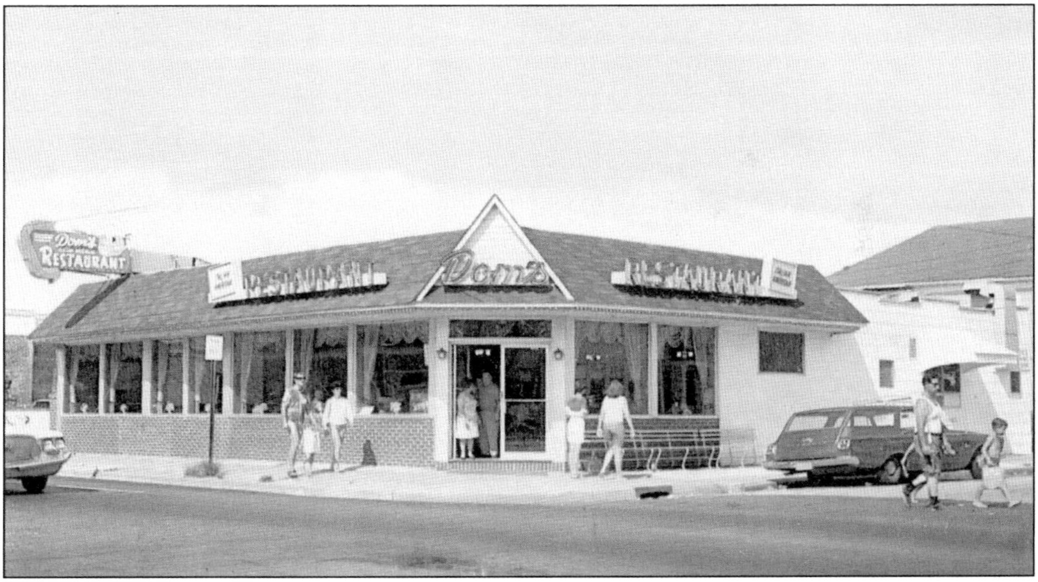

This postcard from the early 1960s shows Dom's Italian-American Restaurant in its location at Burk and Pacific Avenues in downtown Wildwood. The author's extended family operated this popular eatery for decades prior to selling the business in the 1980s. Dom's Italian-American Restaurant offered breakfast, lunch, and dinner between the hours of 8:00 a.m. and 9:00 p.m., welcoming hungry vacationers and residents alike. The building seen in this image once had multiple stories, but was cut down to one floor for various practical reasons. Today the space is occupied by another restaurant, La Piazza Cucina.

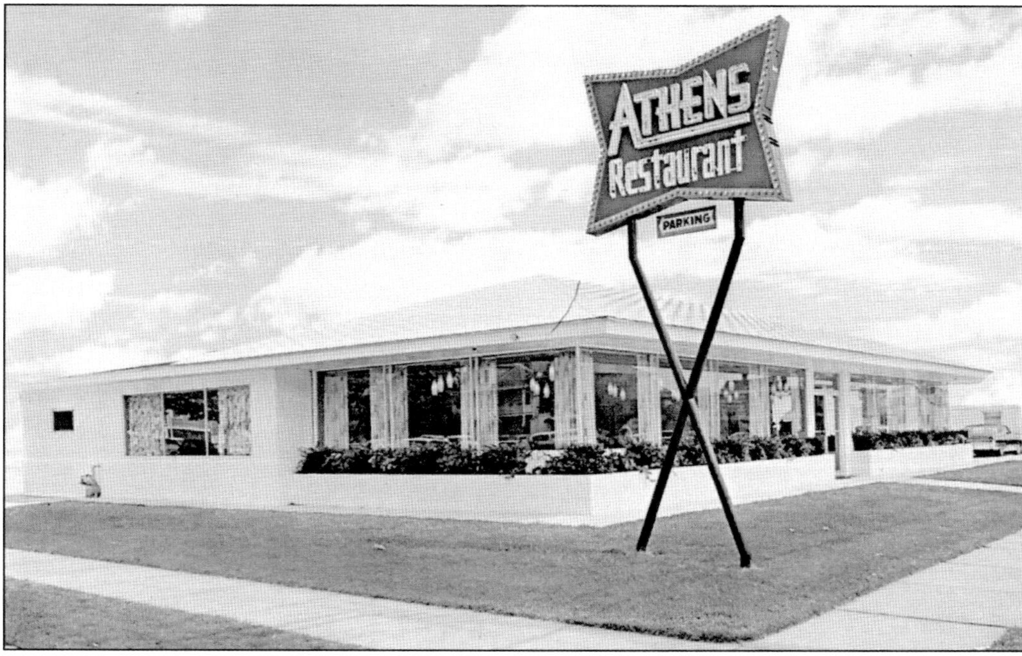

The Athens Restaurant is seen in this postcard from the early 1960s. The building seen here is located at the corner of Atlantic and Twenty-fifth Avenues in North Wildwood. The rear of the card touts air-conditioned dining and free parking for its patrons. Although the sign has been changed since this postcard was produced, the building remains as of 2007 and is currently for sale.

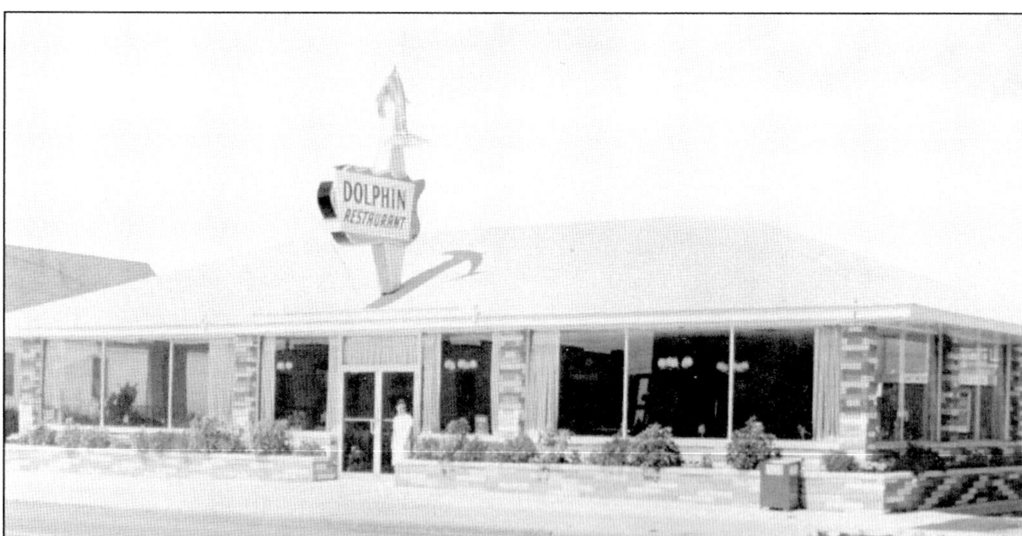

The rear of this postcard proclaims the Dolphin Restaurant as being "Brand New in 1965" and is seen in its former North Wildwood location. The Dolphin Restaurant featured steaks, chops, and seafood in pleasant air-conditioned comfort. The large dining room could seat 160 people, and the restaurant was located at 1002 Ocean Avenue, just one block from the beach. Unfortunately the Dolphin Restaurant is but a memory today.

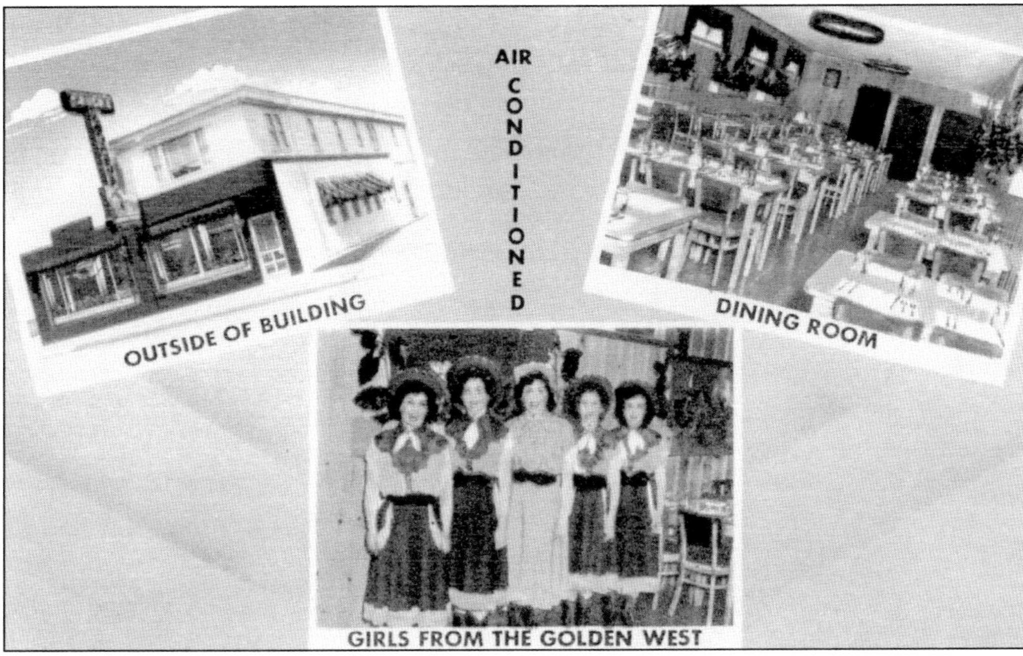

This postcard from the early 1960s shows Chuck's Round Up, formerly located at 245 East Cedar Avenue in Wildwood. The restaurant's motto was "food at its best, served by the girls from the golden west." The multi-view postcard shows the building's exterior, the waitresses, and the dining room. Today the restaurant is but a distant memory.

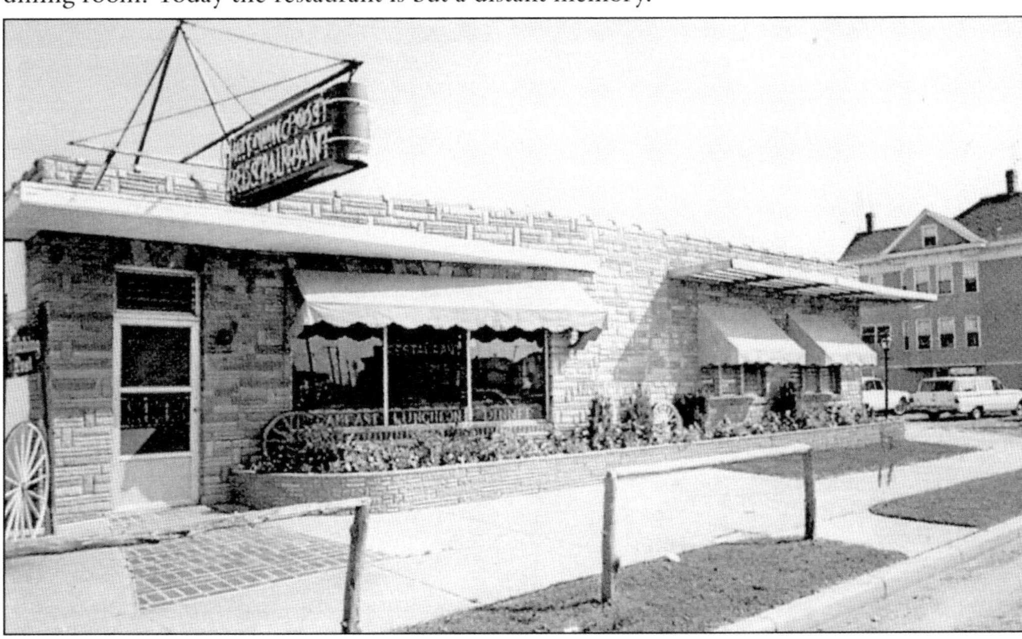

The Hitching Post Restaurant is seen in this view from the early 1960s. Formerly located at the corner of Seventeenth and Atlantic Avenues in North Wildwood, the Hitching Post Restaurant was a popular eatery for decades. The building seen here was given a face lift several years after this postcard was produced, but alas, the Hitching Post Restaurant is gone today. The former site is part of an area dominated by residential offerings.

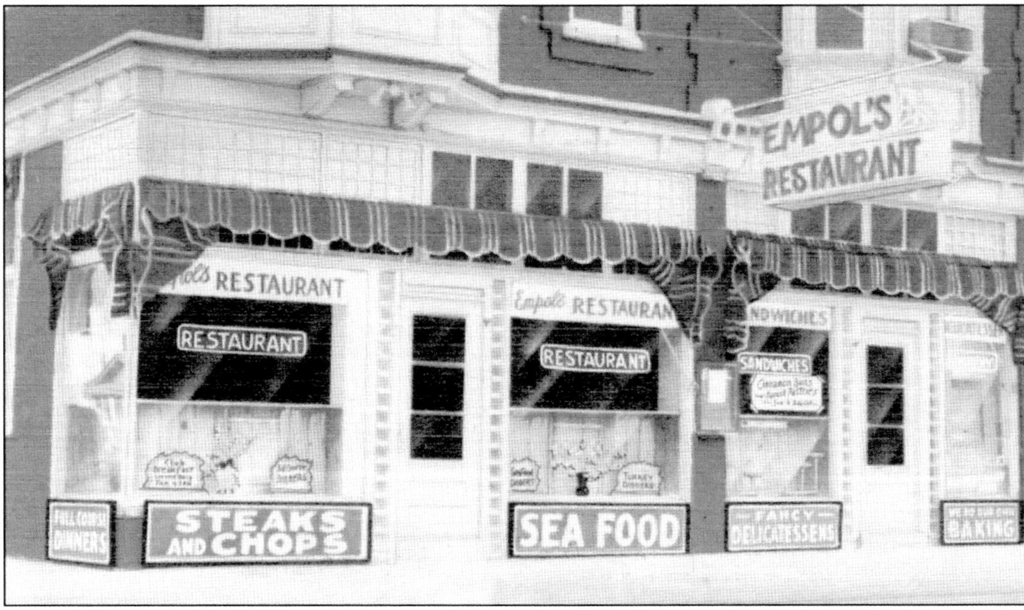

Empol's Restaurant and Pastry Shop is seen in this postcard from the 1950s. This facility was located at the corner of Pacific and Garfield Avenues in downtown Wildwood. Empol's Restaurant and Pastry Shop was famous for its "quality food, whipped cream pies, and cheese cakes." Today the space is occupied by Juan Pablo's Margarita Bar. Despite significant changes to the interior, the building's exterior is still easily recognizable today.

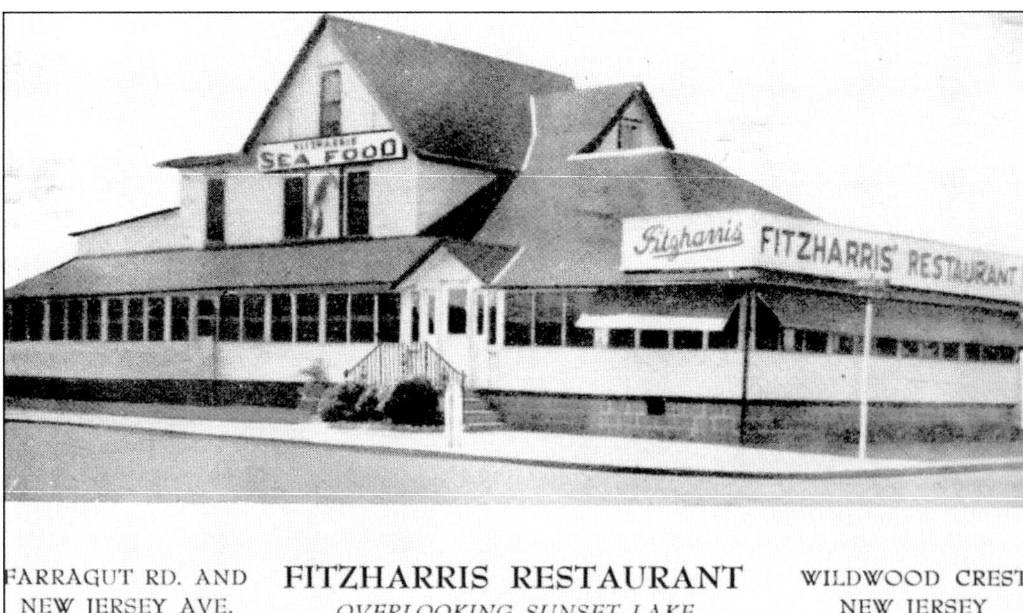

This postcard from the 1950s shows the Fitzharris Restaurant, located in Wildwood Crest at the corner of Farragut Road and New Jersey Avenue. The restaurant overlooked Sunset Lake and served "portions of superior sea food and meats." Today most people familiar with the area will recognize this building as Duffy's on the Lake, the popular eatery that replaced the Fitzharris Restaurant.

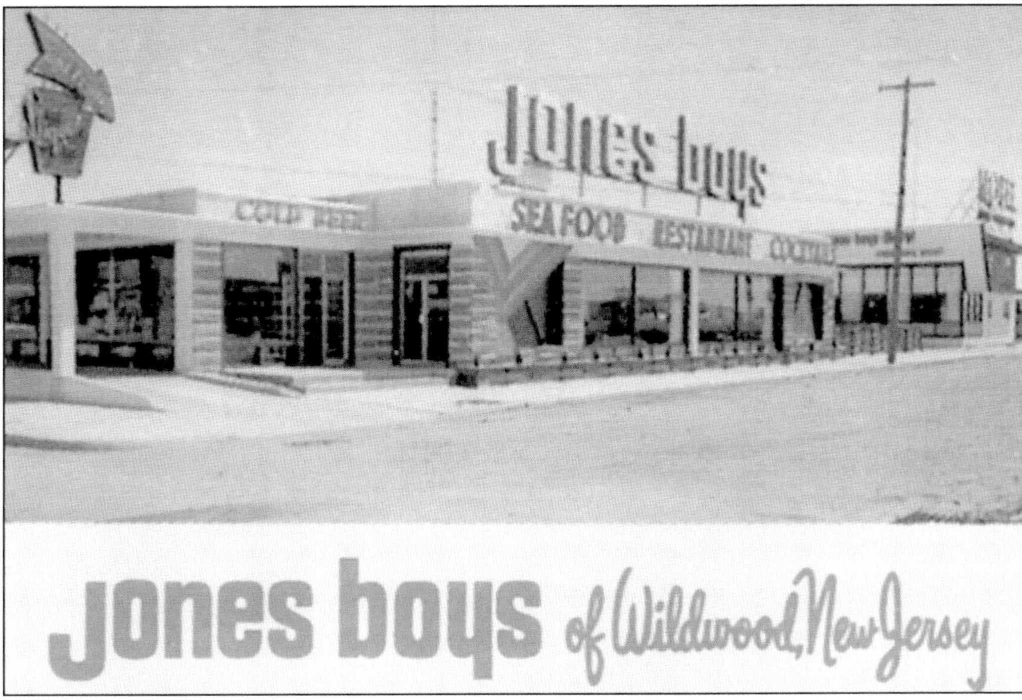

This view from the early 1960s shows the Jones Boys restaurant, located at 448 West Rio Grande Avenue in Wildwood. The Jones boys operated this location, which featured a restaurant, bar, take-out beer, and an on-site motel. Although the Jones Boys name is but a memory of the past, other restaurants have subsequently occupied this space.

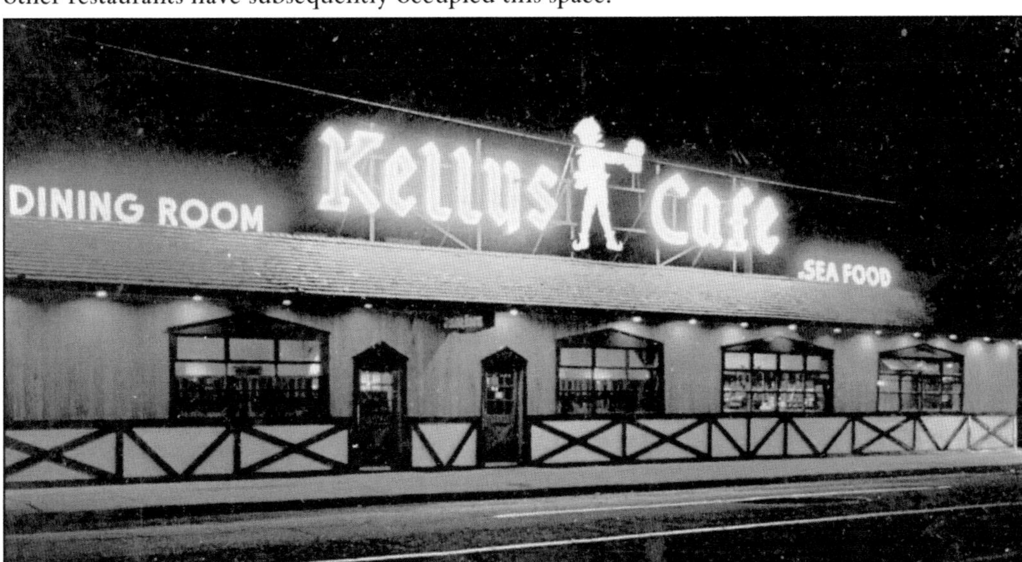

The iconic Kelly's Cafe is seen in this postcard from the 1960s. The bar and restaurant is located at 4400 Atlantic Avenue in Wildwood and is still in operation today. The rear of this postcard advertises Kelly's Cafe's seafood dinners, prime rib, and filet mignon. Today the familiar illuminated sign still beckons patrons to Kelly's Cafe on Atlantic Avenue, and the building looks much the same today as it did then.

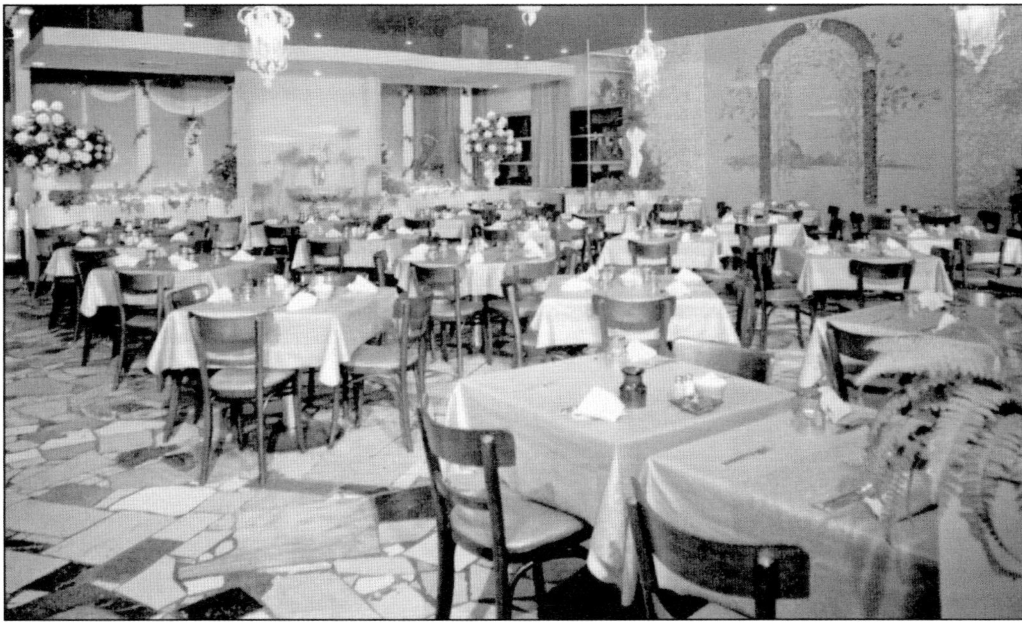

This 1950s-era interior view shows Dino's Restaurant located at 5401 Atlantic Avenue, once located at the northern end of Wildwood Crest. The decorating scheme shown in the dining room was quite typical for many restaurants of its day. As of 2007, the former Dino's Restaurant site is now home to Little Italy Restaurant.

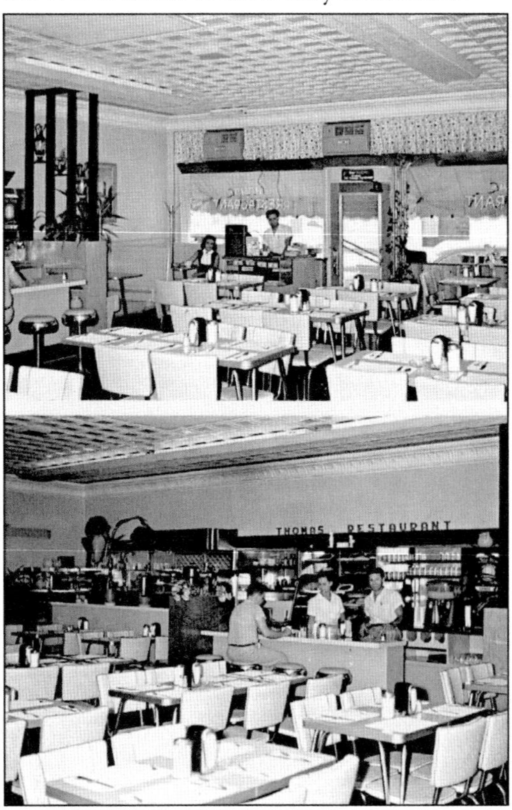

This double-view postcard shows Thomas' Restaurant, as it appeared in 1961. Formerly located at 3813 Pacific Avenue in downtown Wildwood, this small eatery featured "delightful meals at modest prices." Today the former restaurant site is now an empty storefront.

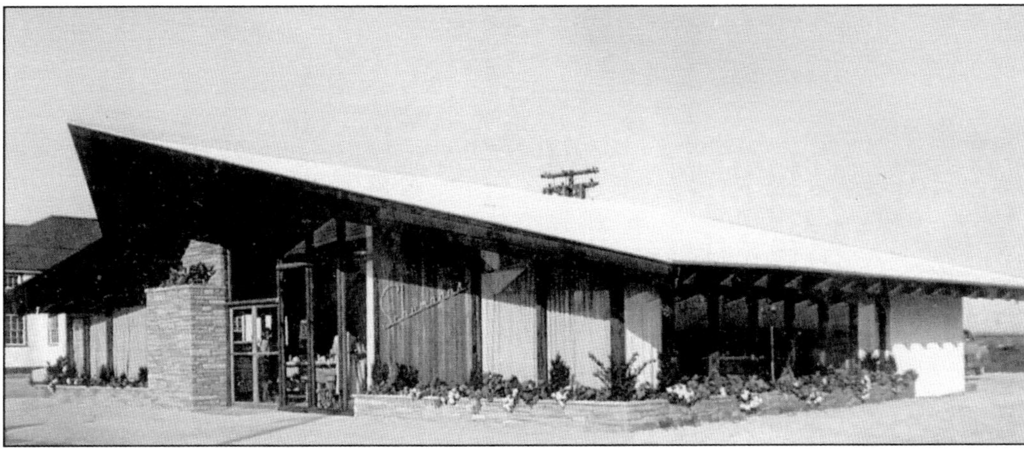

Schumann's Restaurant is seen in this postcard from the 1960s. The restaurant was located near Crest Pier at the corner of Crocus Road and Atlantic Avenue in Wildwood Crest. The uniquely designed Schumann's Restaurant was famous for "fountain service," in addition to its breakfast, lunch, and dinner offerings. Unfortunately Schumann's Restaurant has been lost to progress. The former site is home to a condominium development.

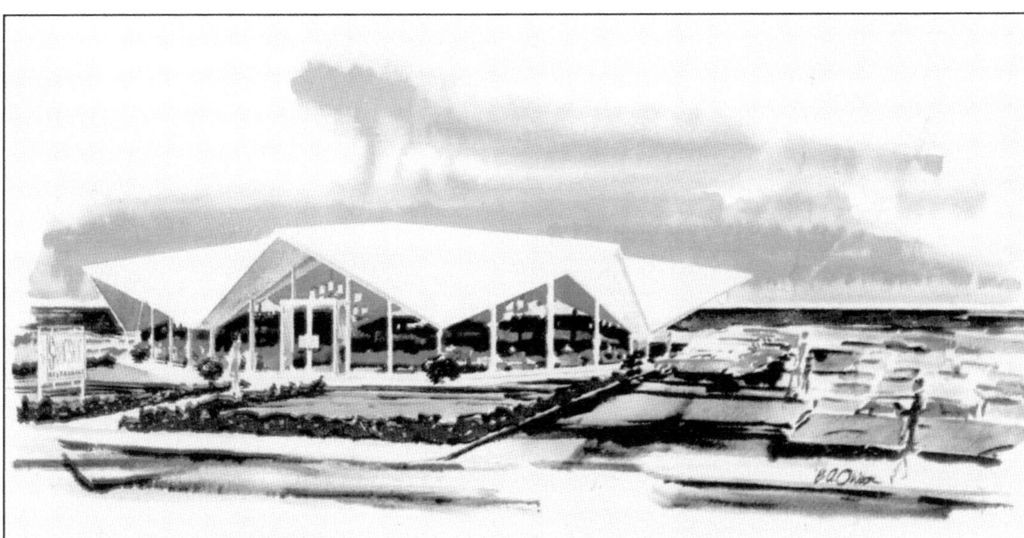

This postcard from the 1960s shows an artist's rendering of the Surf Side Restaurant, formerly located at Ocean Avenue and Lavender Road in Wildwood Crest. The Surf Side Restaurant featured breakfast, lunch, and dinner in an air-conditioned atmosphere. Although the business is gone, the Surf Side Restaurant's building was moved, and many original elements are being reassembled across from the new convention center and will eventually open as a doo-wop museum.

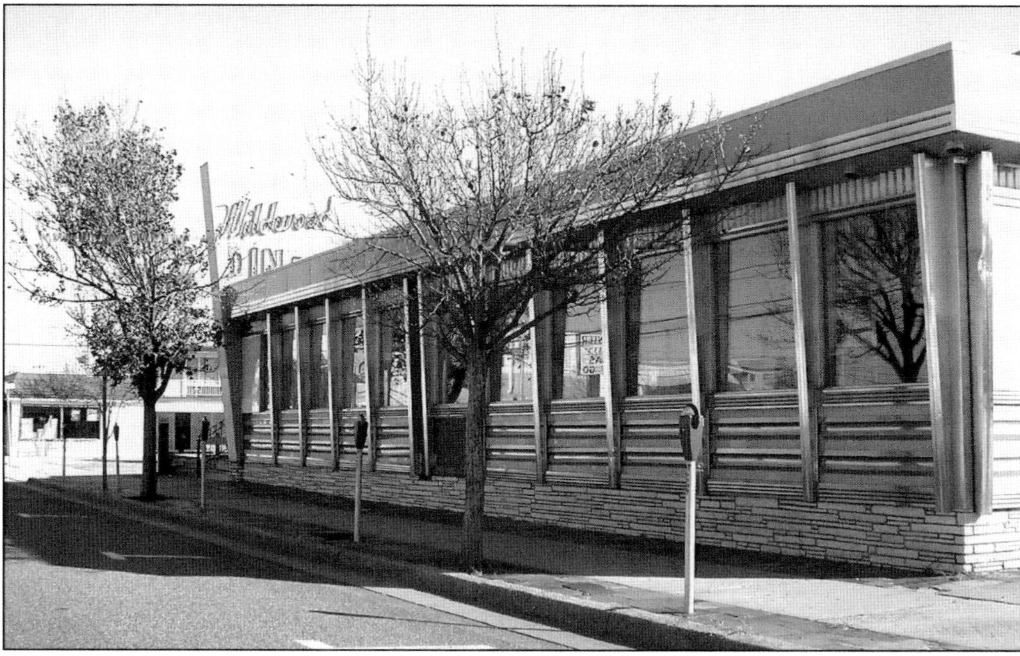

This view from late 2005 shows the Wildwood Diner near the end of its days. This iconic Wildwoods institution was located for decades along Atlantic Avenue at Spencer Avenue. The uniquely designed diner featured an aqua blue and stainless steel facade that represented a timeless late-1950s and early-1960s trend in the construction of such businesses. Sadly the Wildwood Diner was demolished during the summer of 2006. As of 2007, an empty lot sits in its place.

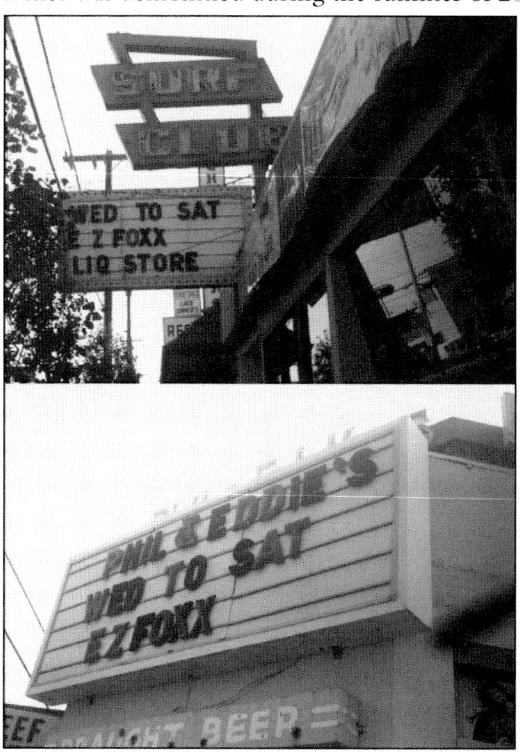

This double-view from 1992 shows Phil and Eddie's Surf Club, located along Atlantic Avenue at Cedar Avenue in Wildwood. This bar and club was one of the more popular venues in the Wildwood of the 1960s, and featured an enormous wrap-around bar. Today the classic signage has been removed and Phil and Eddie's Surf Club has been rebranded under another name but still operates as a bar and restaurant.

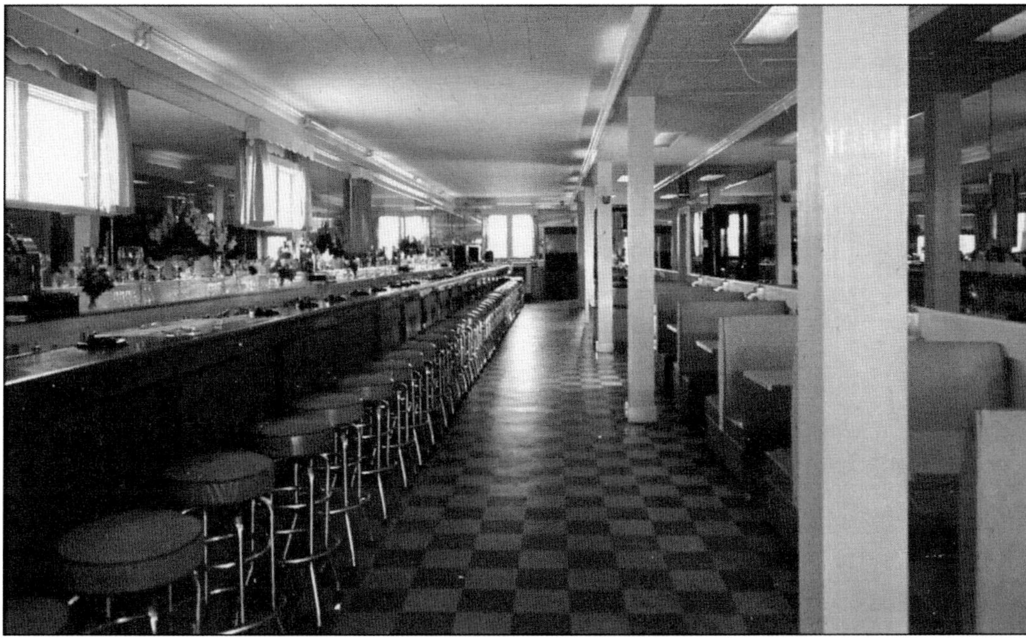

This interior-view postcard from the 1950s shows the Mirror Room, located within the Hotel Lincoln. The hotel was located at the corner of Lincoln and Ocean Avenues in Wildwood. The bar's name is derived through the fact that mirrors adorned opposite-facing walls in the narrow space. Today the Mirror Room is just a memory, as the Hotel Lincoln has long ago disappeared from the Wildwood landscape.

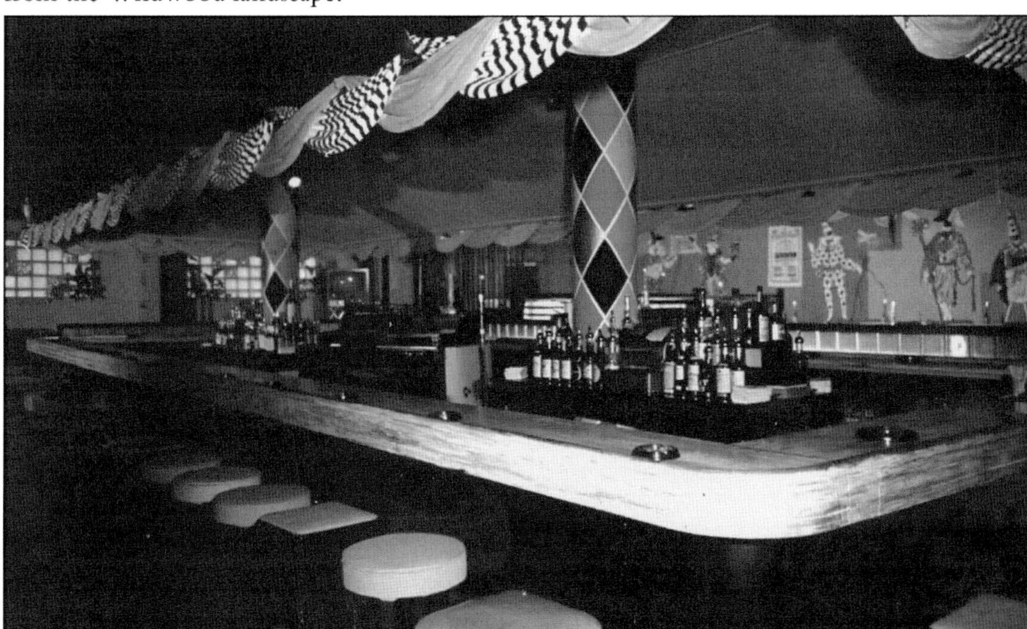

The ornate bar and lounge seen in this 1950s-era interior-view postcard was known as Ricci's Capri and was located at New Jersey and Oak Avenues in Wildwood. In addition to cocktails, Ricci's Capri was renowned for its famous steaks and salad bar. Although Ricci's Capri is no more, the former site hosts a variety of businesses.

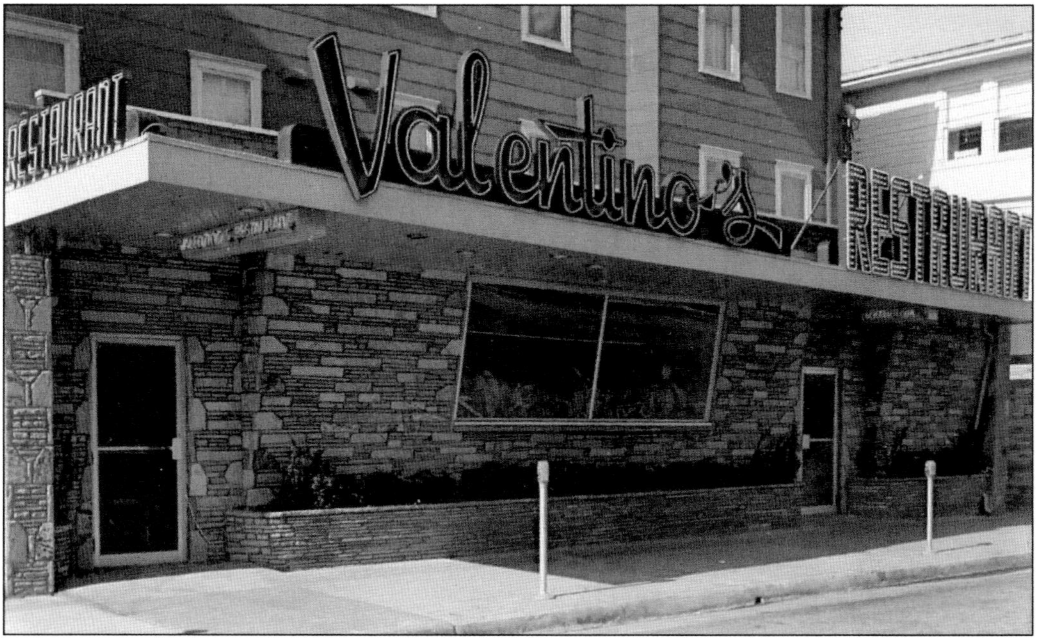

These postcards from the early 1960s show an exterior and interior view of Valentino's Restaurant. The bar and restaurant were located within the Hotel Hof Brau at the corner of Oak and Atlantic Avenues in Wildwood. The view at the top of the page shows the entrance to the restaurant that was described on the rear of the postcard as having "the most beautiful dining room in Cape May County." The interior view at the bottom of the page shows the fully stocked cocktail bar, clearly decorated in a classic late-1950s style. Today the Hotel Hof Brau is but a memory of the past, taking Valentino's Restaurant along with it.

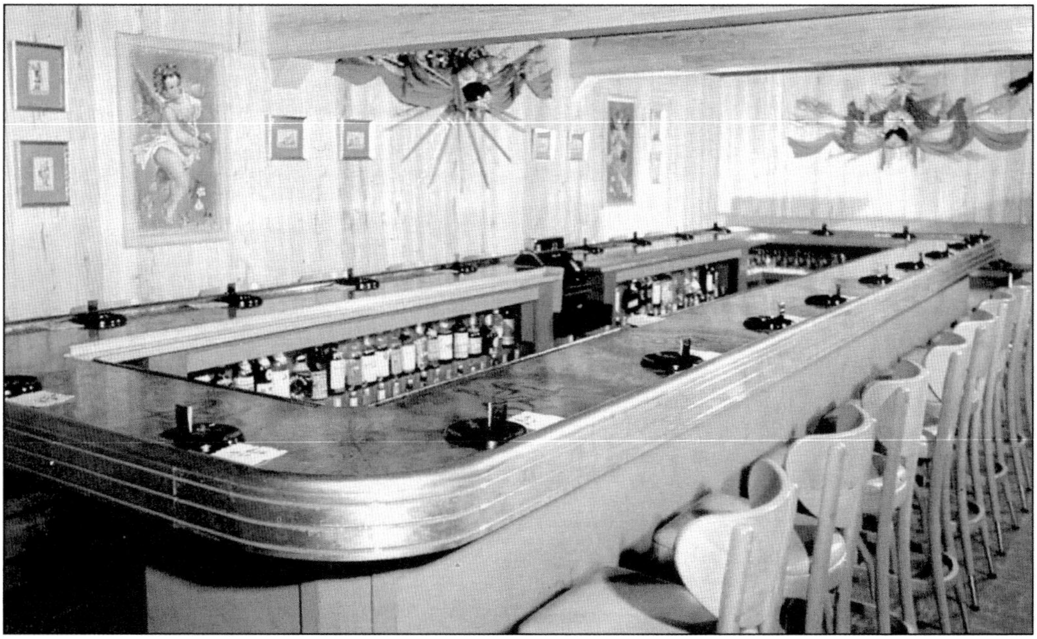

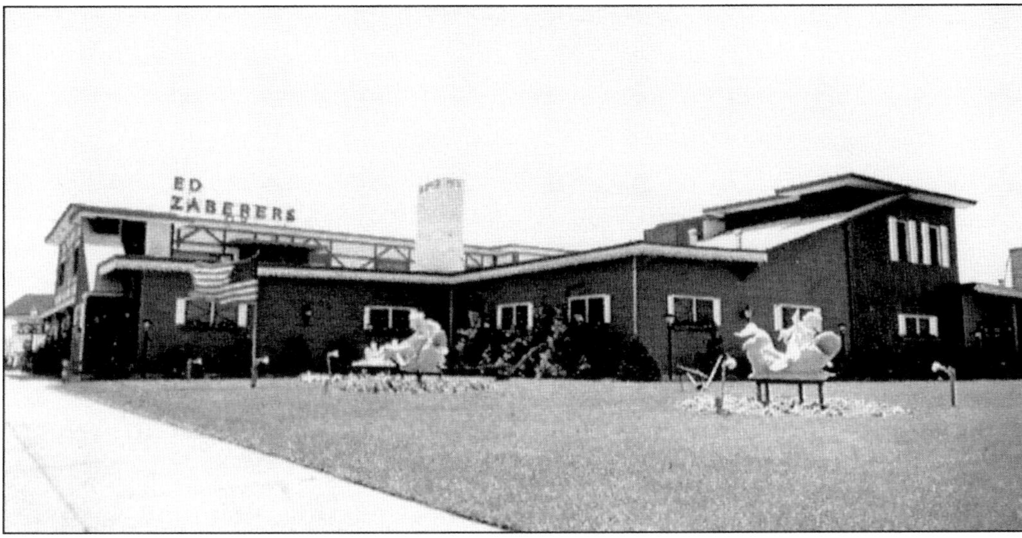

This postcard from the 1960s shows Zaberer's Restaurant. The restaurant was located in North Wildwood along Route 147 and was the largest restaurant in the Wildwoods. At the time of this postcard's printing, Zaberer's was open everyday except for Christmas and featured banquet facilities for up to 400 people. Eventually the facility would accommodate well over 1,000 patrons at any given time. The restaurant was sold in the late 1980s and given a new theme. Just a few years later, the building was destroyed by fire.

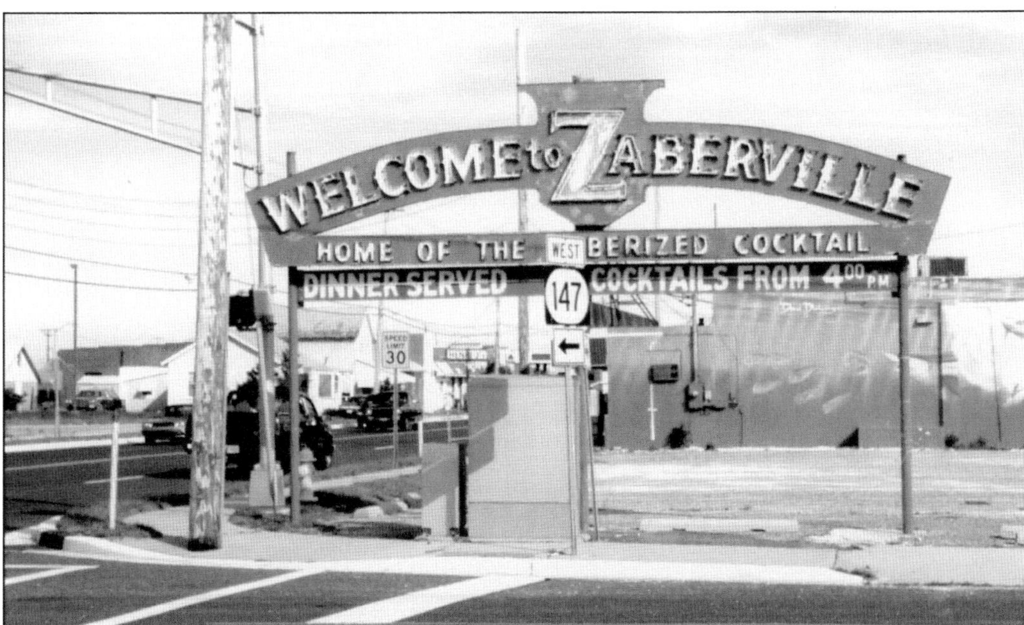

This view from the late 1990s shows the last surviving remnant of Zaberer's. This sign was placed strategically along the entrance to North Wildwood at the corner of Spruce and Maryland Avenues. The large metal sign beckoned all who gazed upon it to eat at Zaberer's, a veritable institution in the Wildwoods' heyday. Today the sign has been removed, thus bringing to an end the physical memory of what was once one of the Wildwoods' most renowned attractions.

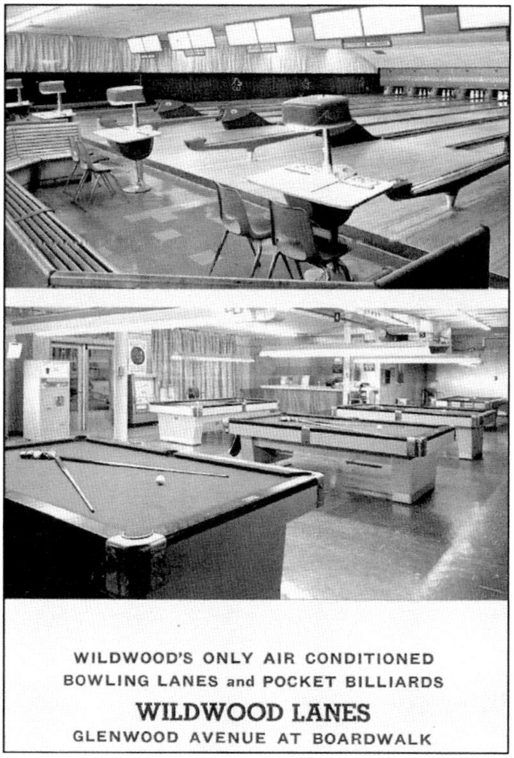

This double-view postcard from the 1960s shows Wildwood Lanes, located on the boardwalk at Glenwood Avenue. At the time, this facility was known as the Wildwoods' only air-conditioned bowling alley and pocket billiards hall. It featured 20 lanes in addition to an on-site pro-shop. Today the boardwalk bowling alley is just a memory of the past.

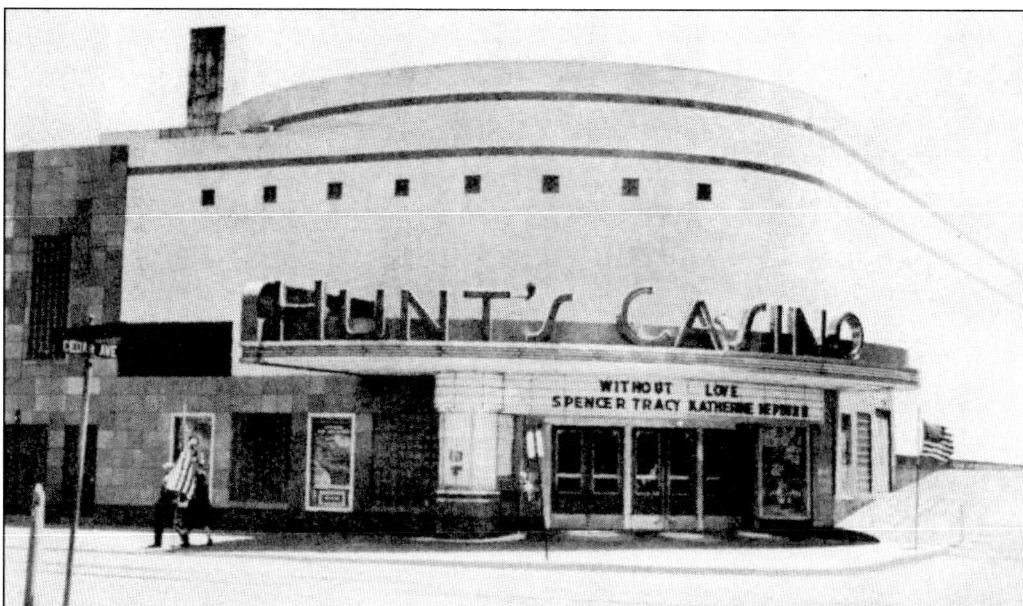

This view from 1945 shows Hunt's Casino movie theater located along Atlantic Avenue at Cedar Avenue. The theater opened in 1940 and featured first-run movies for decades before closing as a movie house in the 1980s. Various businesses would occupy the theater space in the coming years before the building began to fall into disrepair. It was demolished in the late 1990s and remains an empty lot as of 2007.

The view at the top of the page is from 1939 and shows the Shore Theater at the corner of Atlantic and Schellenger Avenues. This picture was taken shortly after the theater opened and shows the great art deco facade and signage. This theater was open year-round and would show first-run movies for decades before closing finally in the late 1990s. The image at the bottom of the page was taken in December 2005, just weeks before the theater would be irrevocably demolished. As of 2007, an empty lot remains on the former site of the Shore Theater.

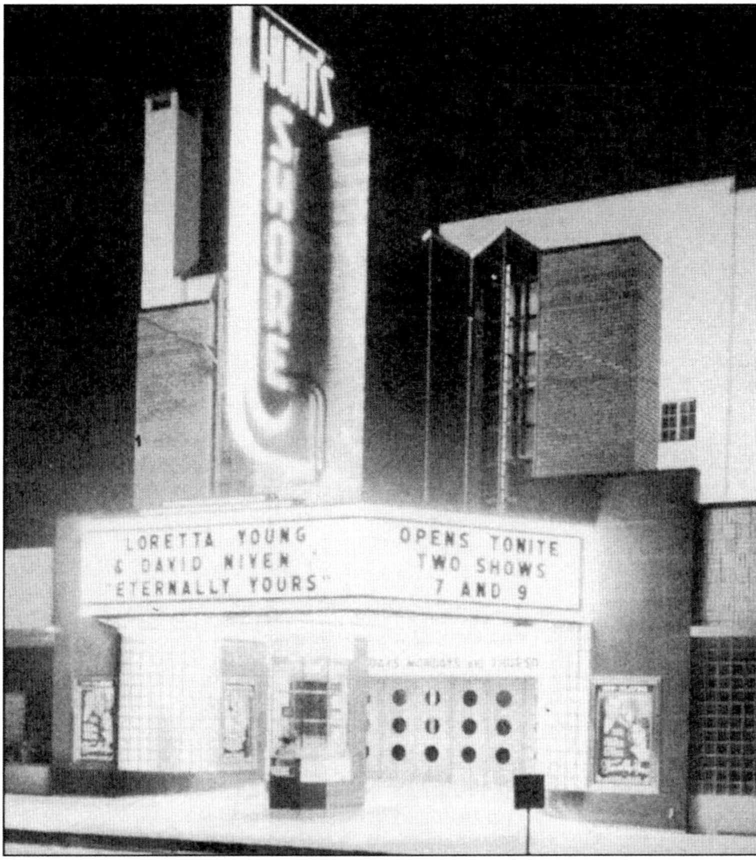

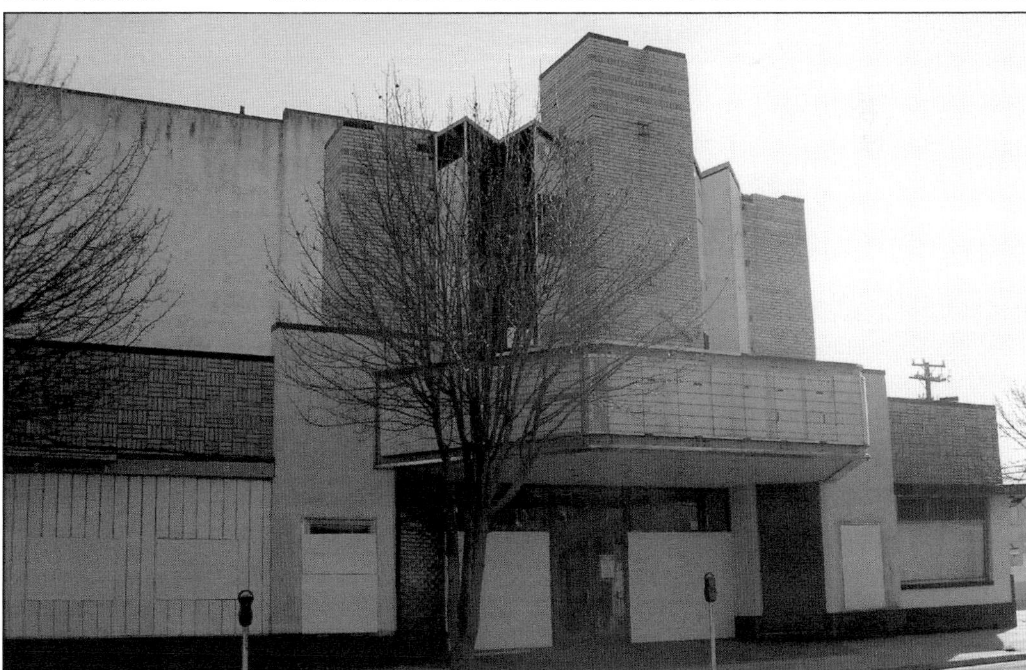

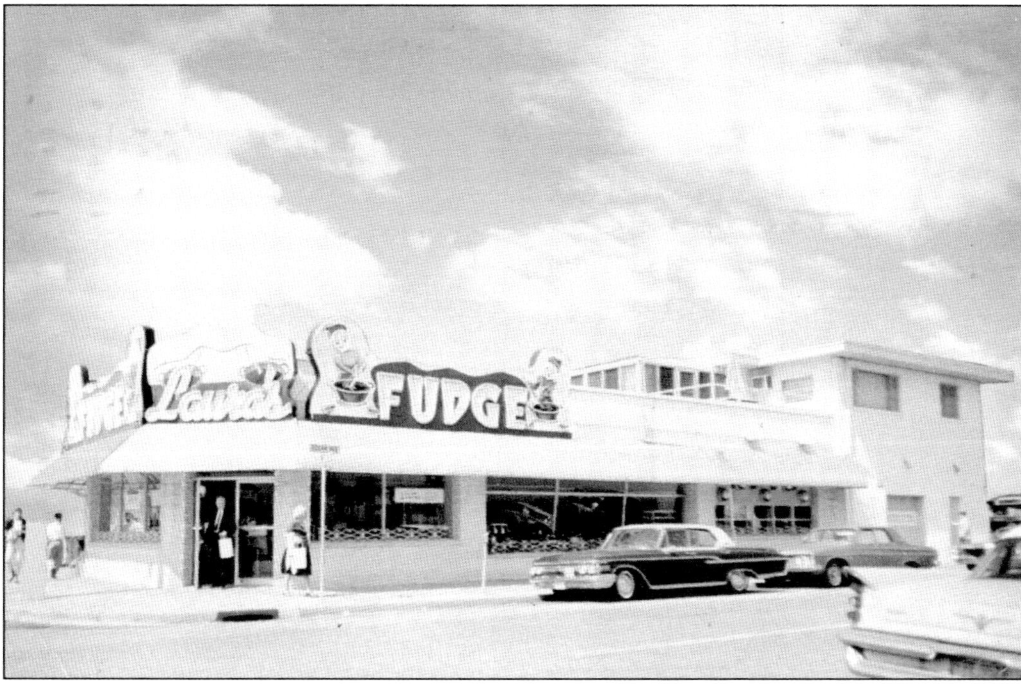

The postcard seen at the top of the page shows Laura's Fudge shop, located at the corner of Wildwood and Ocean Avenues as it appeared almost 50 years ago. The rear of the card indicates that the business was established in 1926, and that Laura's Fudge is "the Cadillac of all Fudge." At the bottom of the page, one can see a view of Laura's Fudge Shop as it looks today. Although the cars in the views might have changed over the decades, Laura's Fudge shop remains almost frozen in time. With the exception of some additional signage and a row of new townhouses having risen beyond the shop, the scene is remarkably unchanged.

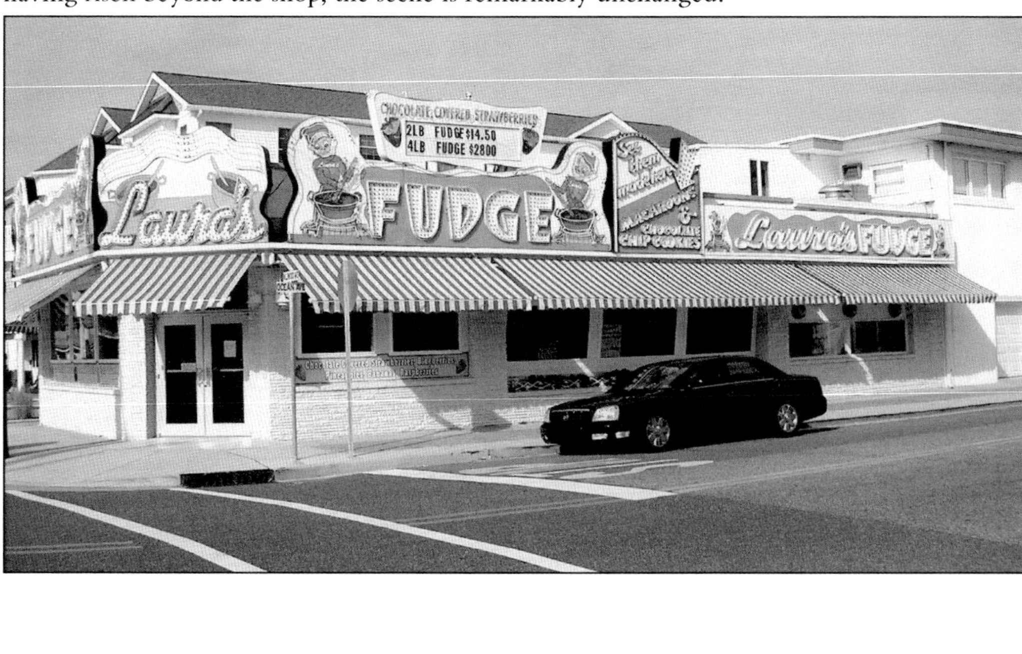

Five

The Boardwalk

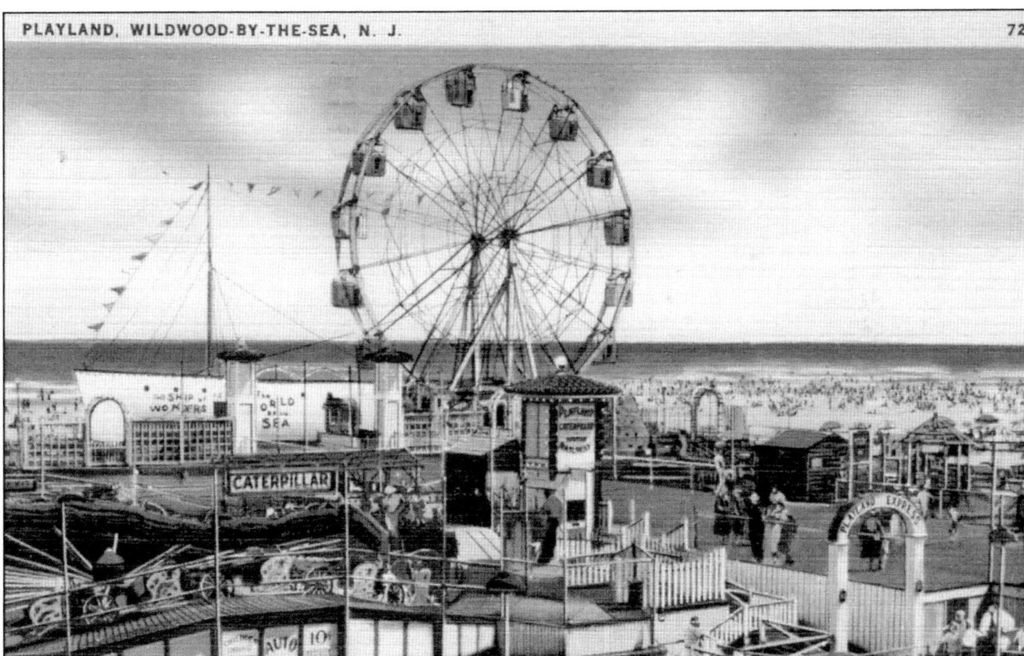

This postcard from the 1940s shows Playland Amusement Pier, located on the boardwalk between Cedar and Schellenger Avenues. Playland Amusement Pier anchored the boardwalk in an area where the boards shifted course and headed in a slightly different direction. In this view, one can see the Ferris wheel, Caterpillar ride, Playland Express, as well as the Ship of Wonders. Although elements of Playland Amusement Pier date to the late 19th century, the pier would amuse visitors for decades before evolving into Marine Pier West. Today amusements still exist in this place but with an entirely different theme.

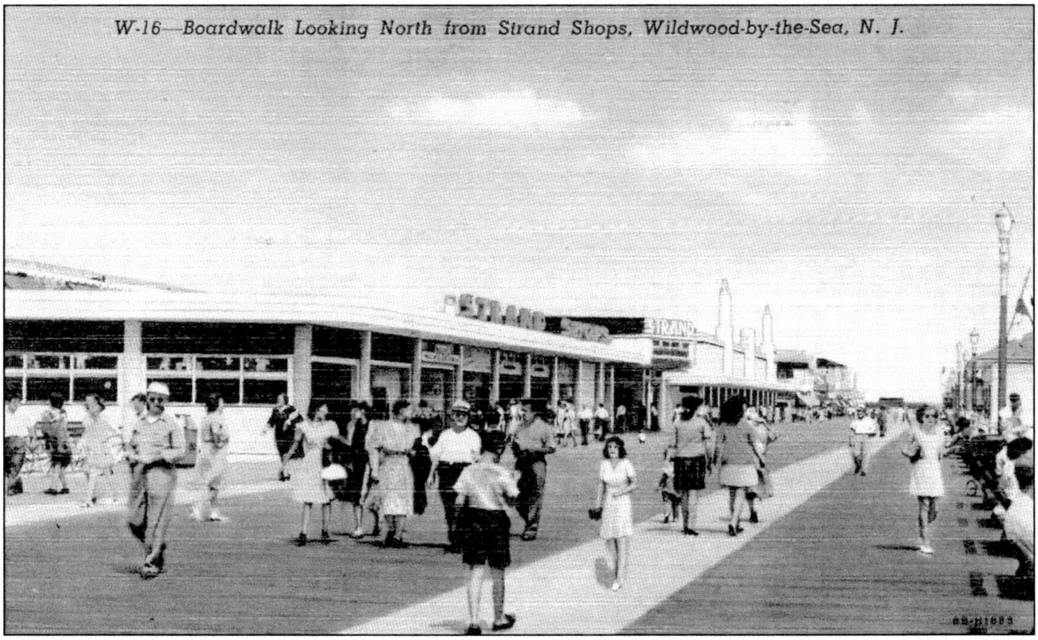

This view of the boardwalk looks north from the Strand Shops. These shops were located on the boardwalk between Maple and Pine Avenues. Although the shops have certainly changed since this postcard was produced in the 1940s, this strip of the boardwalk is still anchored by the Strand Theater as it was then.

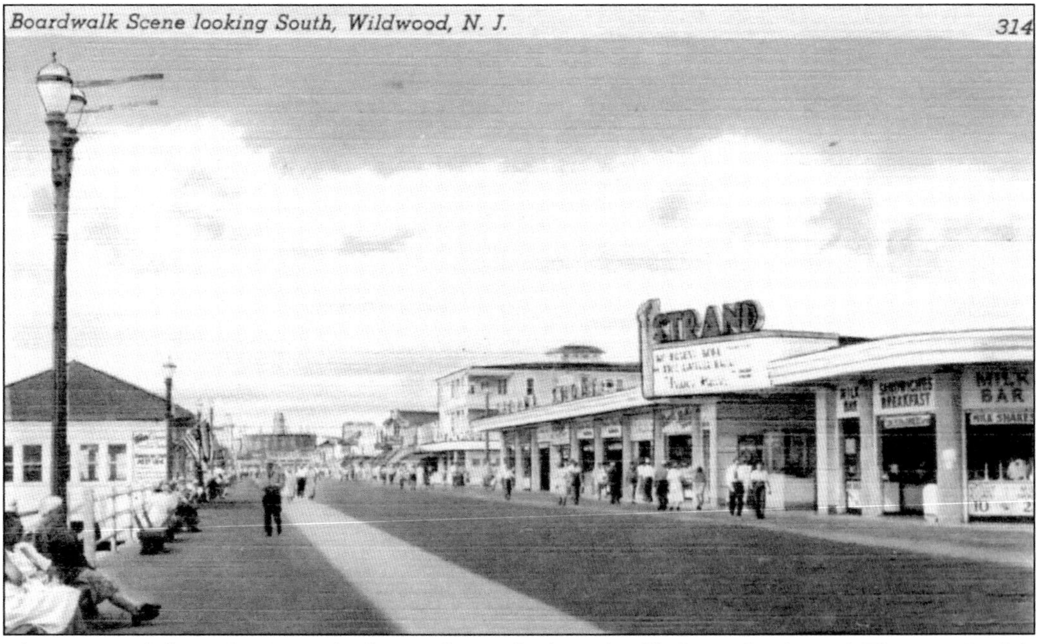

This postcard from the 1940s looks south on the boardwalk from the Strand Theater. In this view, Playland's merry-go-round can be seen off in the distance in addition to the Milk Bar in the foreground. The Milk Bar has a small sign indicating that ice-cream cones can be purchased for 10¢. Although ice cream is still enjoyed by visitors to the boardwalk, the prices have increased exponentially since then.

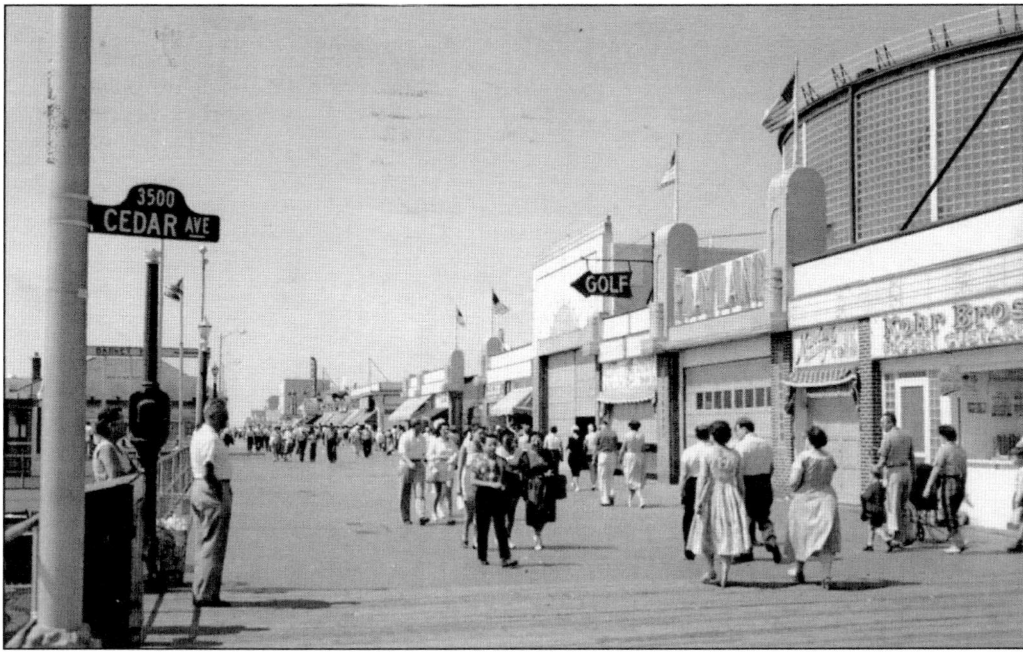

This postcard shows the boardwalk at Cedar Avenue in the 1950s. At the right side of the card, one can see the base of Playland's merry-go-round perched on top of the Kohr Brothers Frozen Custard stand. Although the merry-go-round was destroyed by fire many years ago, this area of stores has been rebuilt. Visitors can still be seen enjoying Kohr Brothers' custard on warm nights, while strolling the boards.

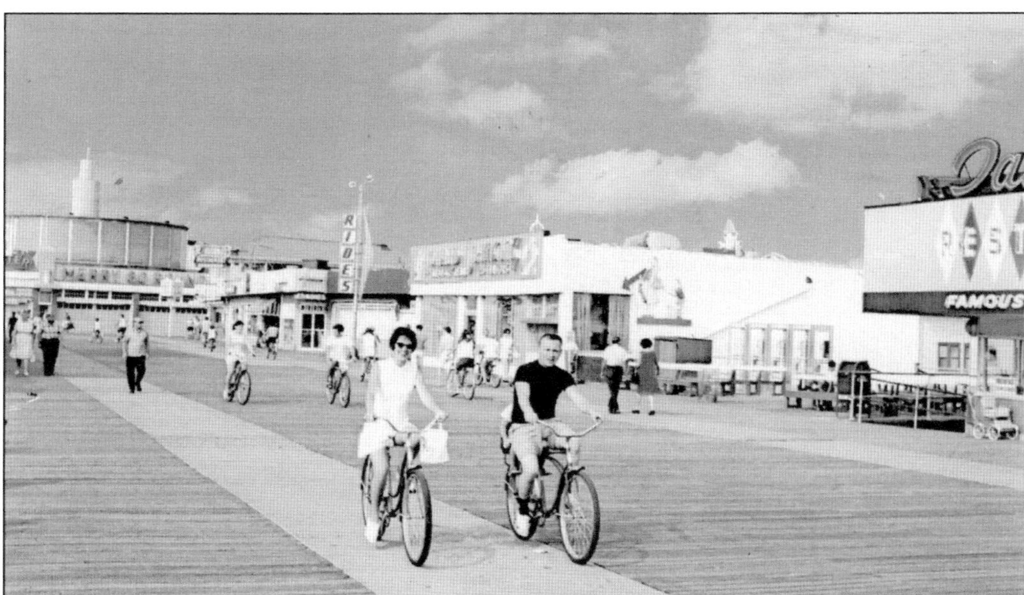

This postcard from the 1950s shows a view of the boardwalk looking toward Cedar Avenue with an almost full view of Playland's merry-go-round. Also visible in this shot are Grandma's Restaurant and Howard Johnson's Restaurant. Even today, early morning bike rides remain a popular Wildwood past time.

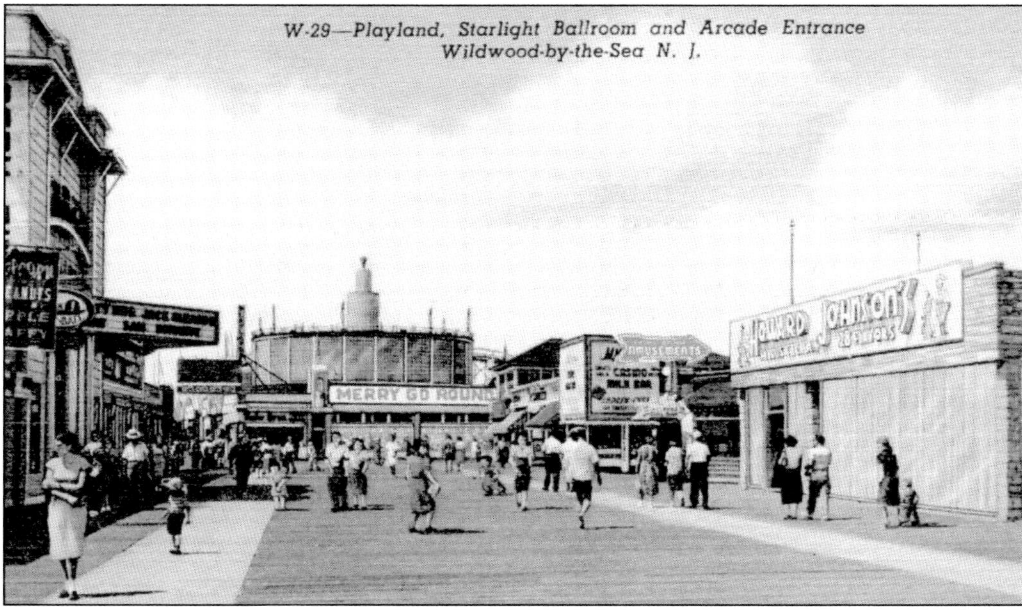

In this postcard, yet another popular view of the boardwalk is seen, looking toward the merry-go-round at Cedar Avenue. However, in addition to the familiar restaurants noted in previous views, this shot also shows the legendary Starlight Ballroom. Although this view has changed quite significantly over the last 60 years since this postcard was made, restaurants and amusements still line this block of the boardwalk.

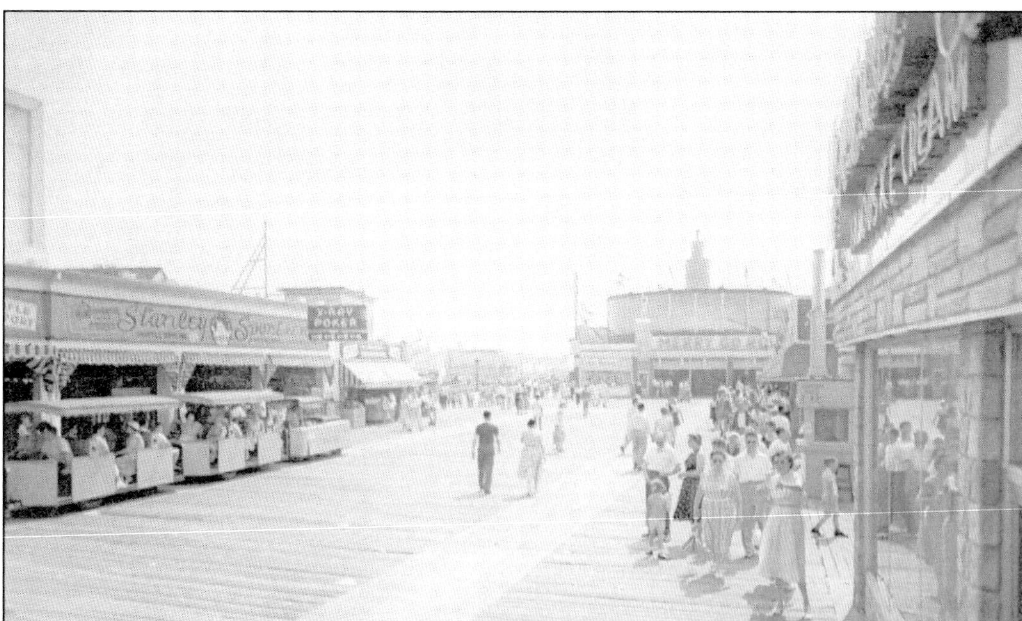

This postcard shows the boardwalk at Cedar Avenue and features the iconic Playland merry-go-round, in addition to some amusements that include X-Ray Poker in the storefronts adjacent to the Starlight Ballroom. On the right side of the image, one can see the faux stone facade of the Howard Johnson's Restaurant. Although this postcard is more than 50 years old, the familiar shift in course of the boardwalk is still evident in this spot.

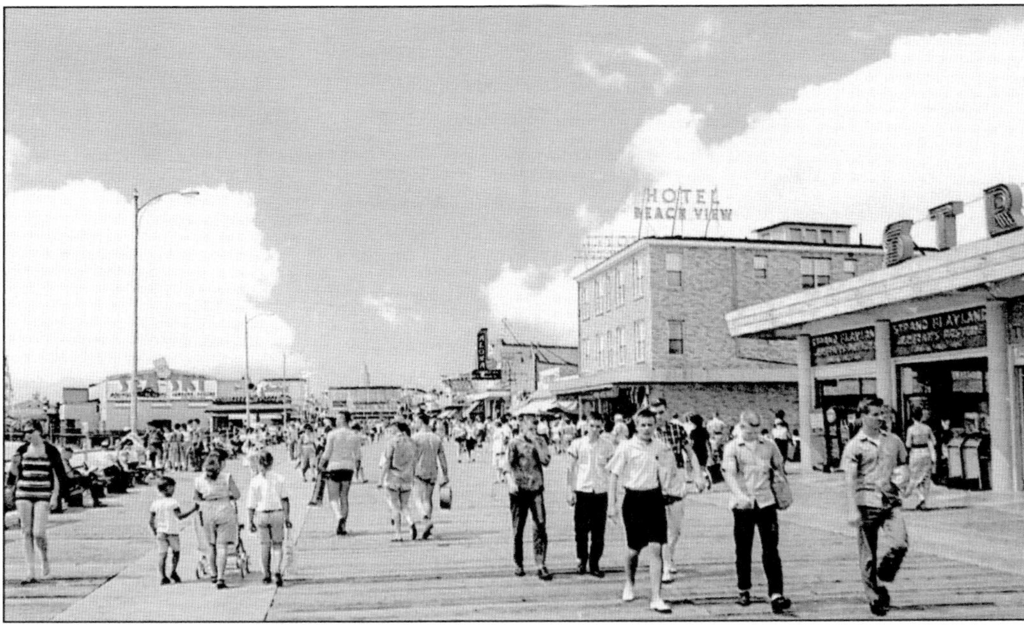

This postcard from the 1950s looks south on the boardwalk from the area around Pine Avenue. To the immediate right in the view are the Strand Shops, and just past the shops the Hotel Beach View can be seen. And once again, the Playland merry-go-round is off in the distance. Today some of these storefronts remain, while the Hotel Beach View has seen its number of stories reduced from three to one.

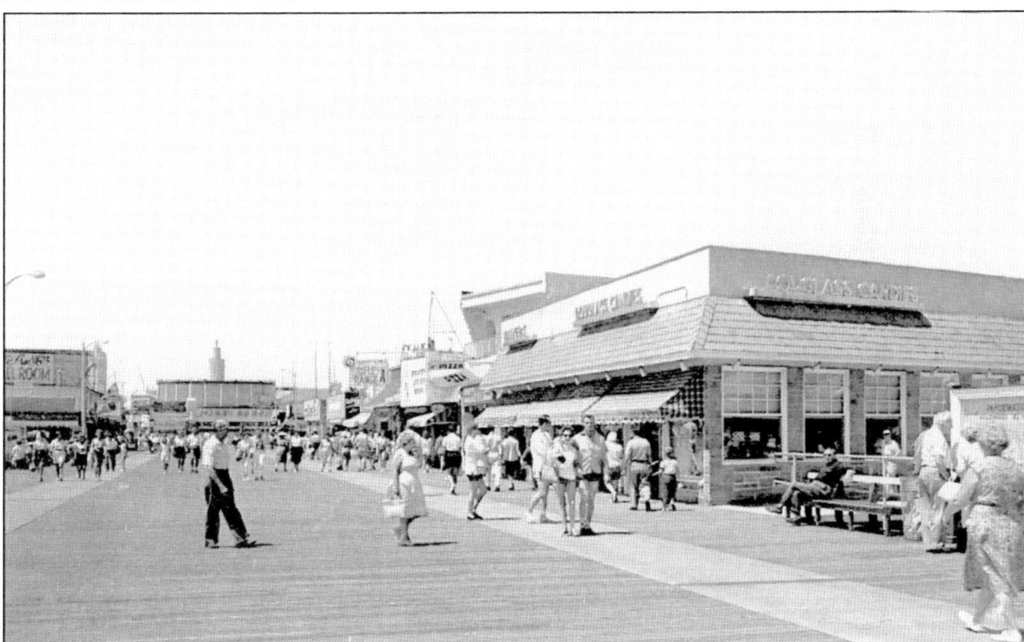

This view from the 1950s looks south on the boardwalk from Wildwood Avenue. In the foreground at the right, the still-operating Douglass Candies shop can be seen, more commonly known today as Douglass Fudge. Yet again, this vista provides another distant view of the Playland merry-go-round.

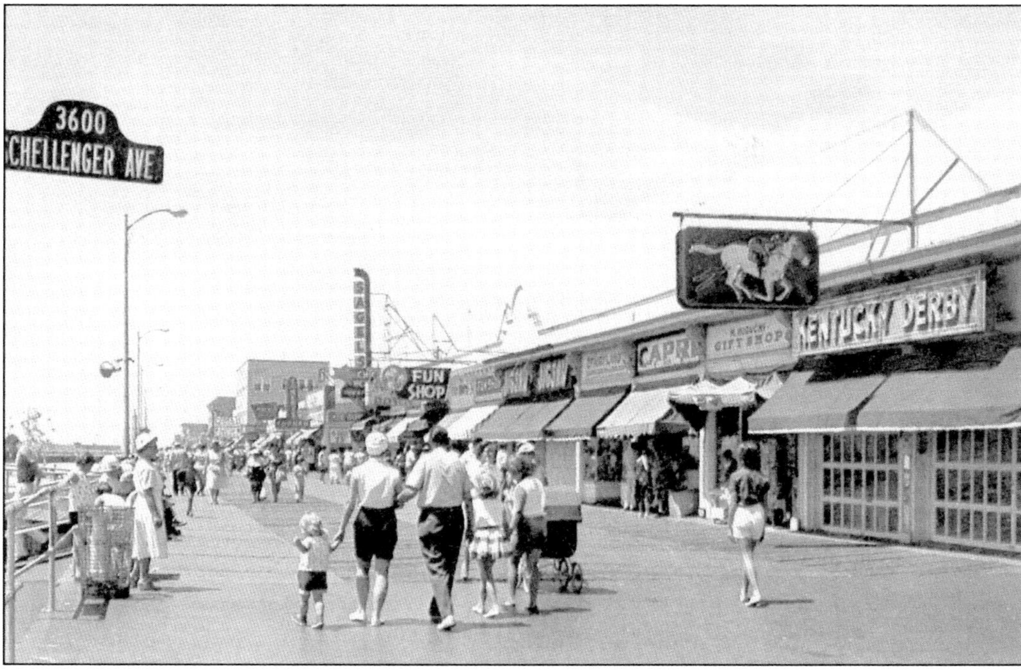

This postcard of the boardwalk shows a view looking south from Schellenger Avenue in the late 1950s. In the foreground is the popular Kentucky Derby horse racing game. Further in the distance, one can see Sagel's Candies and just a glimpse of the Regent movie theater.

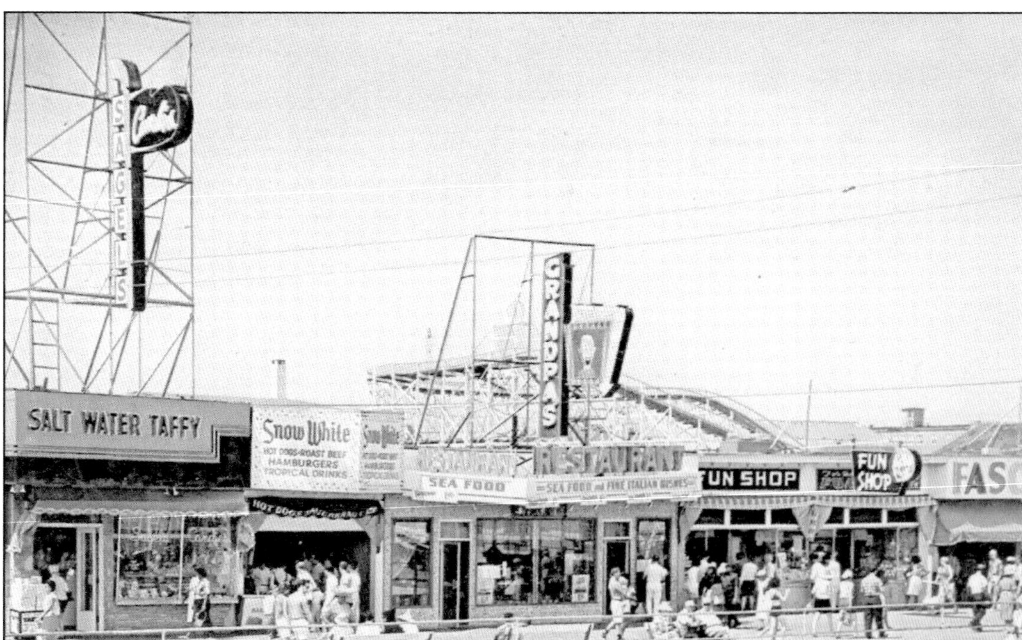

This view from the 1950s shows the boardwalk between Lincoln and Schellenger Avenues. Some of the many shops and restaurants visible in this view are Sagel's, Snow White's, Grandpa's, and the Fun Shop. These stores were destroyed by fire in the early 1980s, although the block was eventually rebuilt.

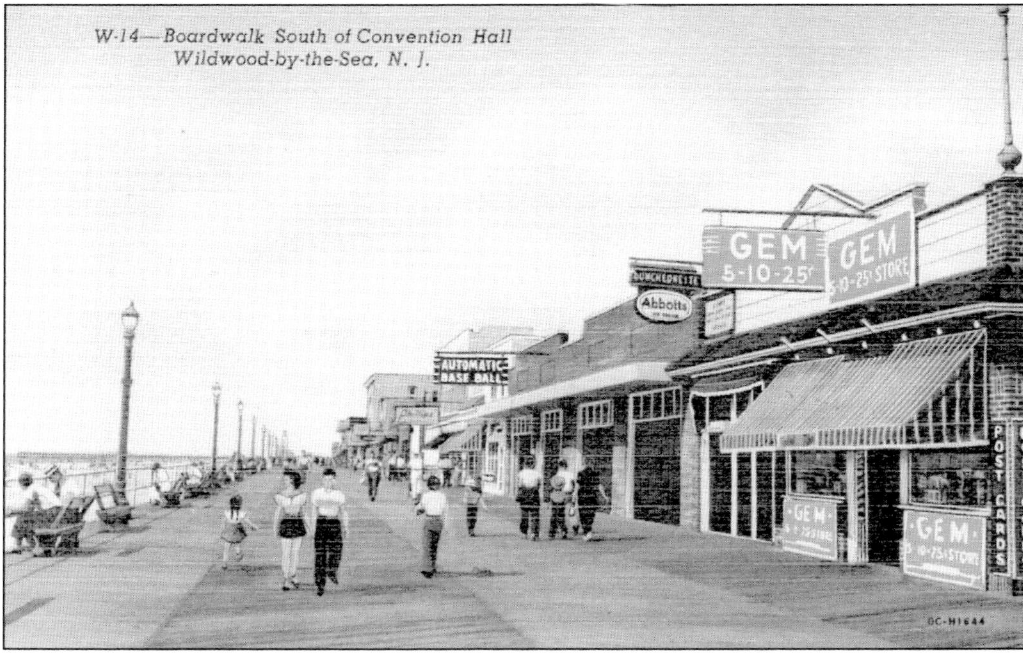

This postcard from the 1940s shows the boardwalk looking south from Baker Avenue. In this view, the Gem Store is seen, with a vertical sign at its corner advertising postcards. Further along, one can see a sign advertising Abbott's Ice Cream at a luncheonette, as well as a game called Automatic Base Ball. Today these stores and amusements are but a memory of the distant past.

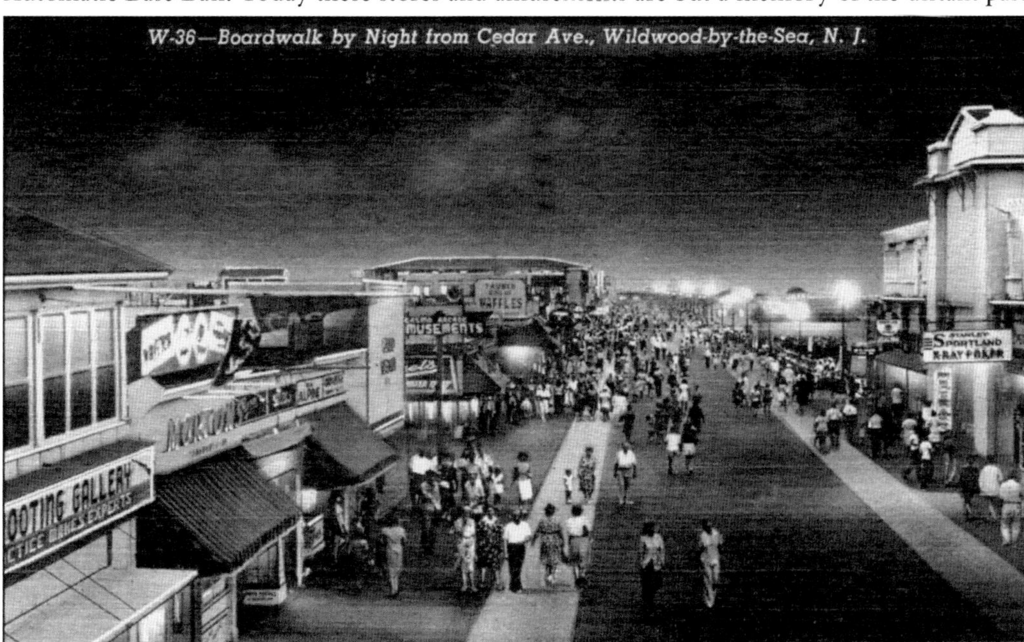

This postcard shows a night view of the boardwalk, looking north from Cedar Avenue. The Starlight Ballroom commands quite a presence along the right side of the image, while at the left a shooting gallery, arcade amusements, as well as a waffle stand are seen. More than six decades later, this view of the boardwalk looks very different.

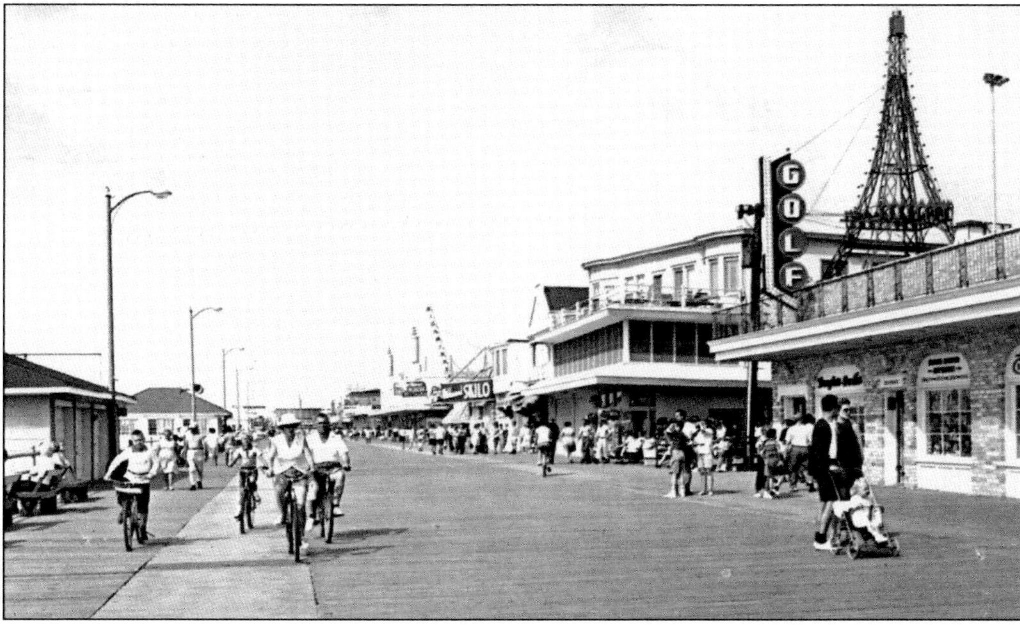

This view of the boardwalk in the 1950s looks south from Magnolia Avenue. The rooftop miniature golf no longer exists on the building to the right, and the miniature Eiffel Tower has long since been removed. In this shot, one also can see the Royal Hotel in addition to several amusements and games.

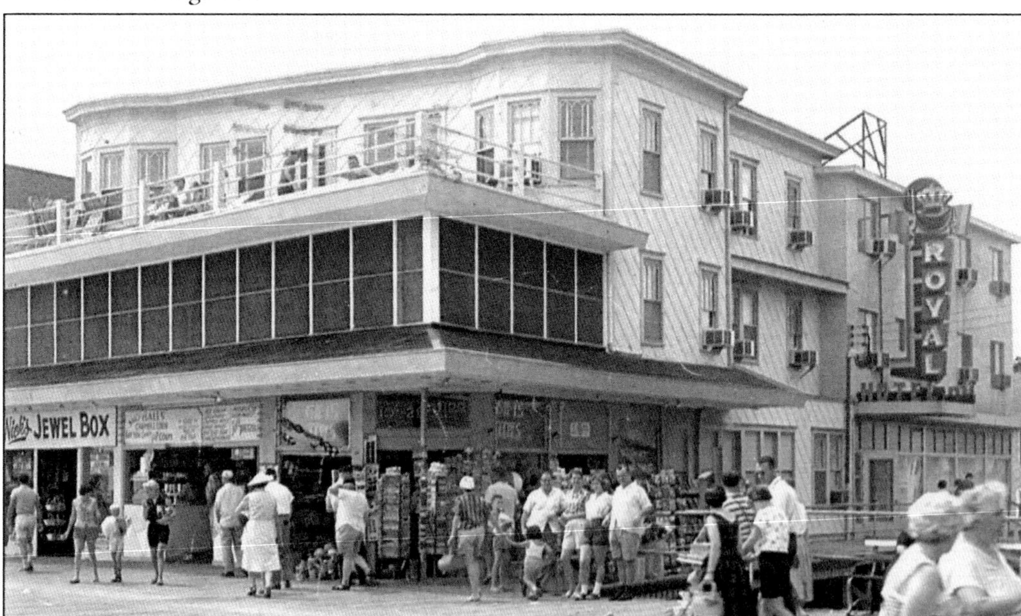

This postcard from the 1950s shows a view of the Royal Hotel, formerly located on the boardwalk at Magnolia Avenue. The Royal Hotel was one of just a few hotels that were situated directly on the boardwalk. Although the ground floor at the front of the structure was occupied by several stores, there was still plenty of room left for guests. Today the Royal Hotel is no more, but a row of stores lives on its place.

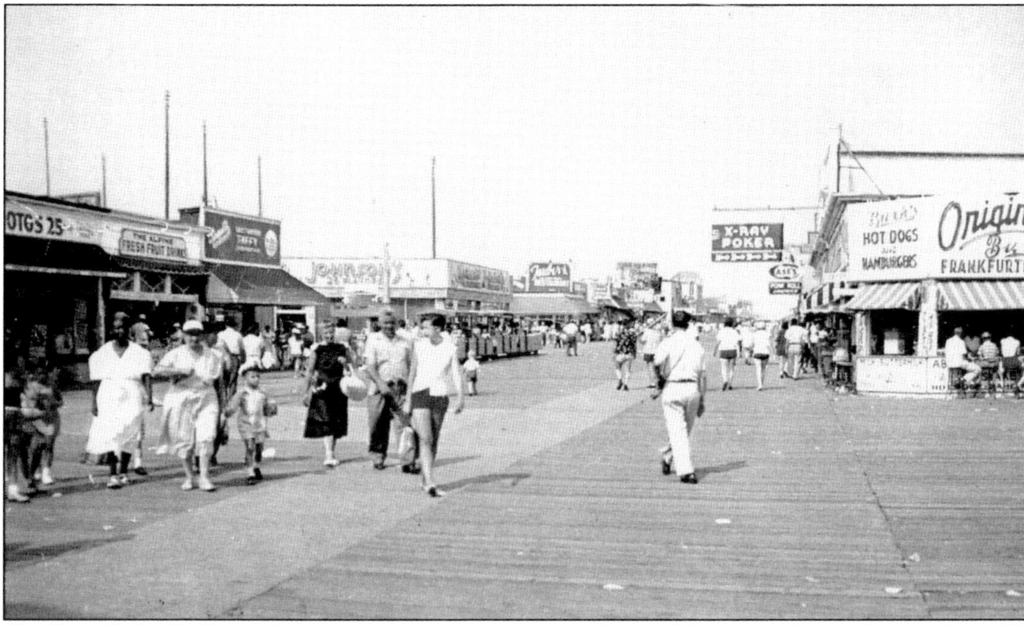

This postcard from the 1950s shows the boardwalk, looking north from Cedar Avenue. In this view, one can see signs for 25¢ photographs, fresh fruit drinks, Howard Johnson's Restaurant, X-Ray Poker, Case's Pork Rolls, as well as Burk's Hot Dogs and Hamburgers. Between the series of fires that have marred the boardwalk and the propensity for reinvention, none of these businesses survives in their place today.

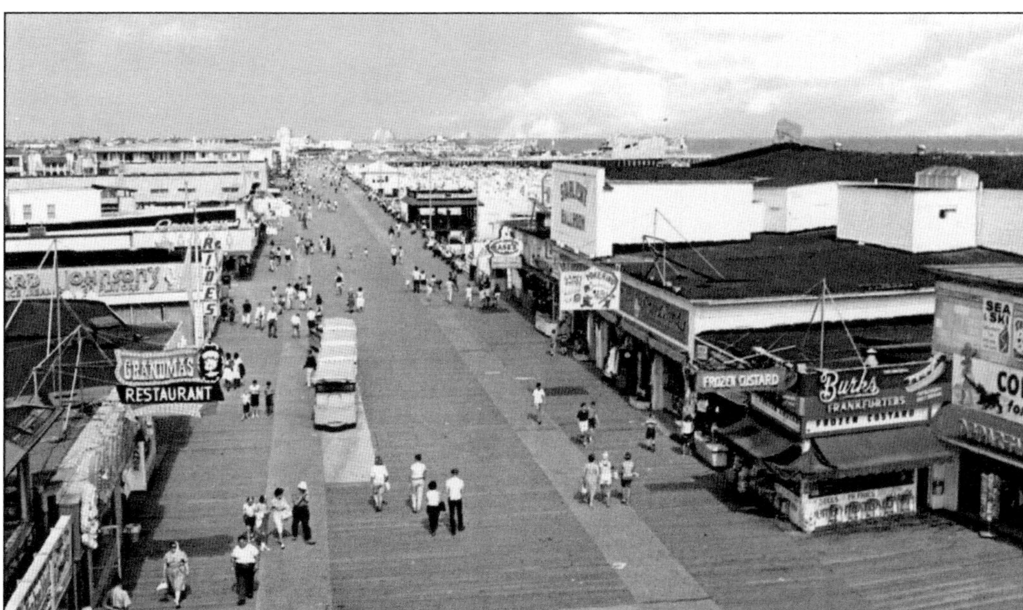

In yet another 1950s-era view looking north from Cedar Avenue, Grandma's Restaurant, Howard Johnson's Restaurant, the Starlight Ballroom, and Burk's Hot Dogs and Hamburgers can all be seen. Headed north in this view, one can see a roller coaster situated prominently on an amusement pier. Today virtually this entire scene has taken on a new look.

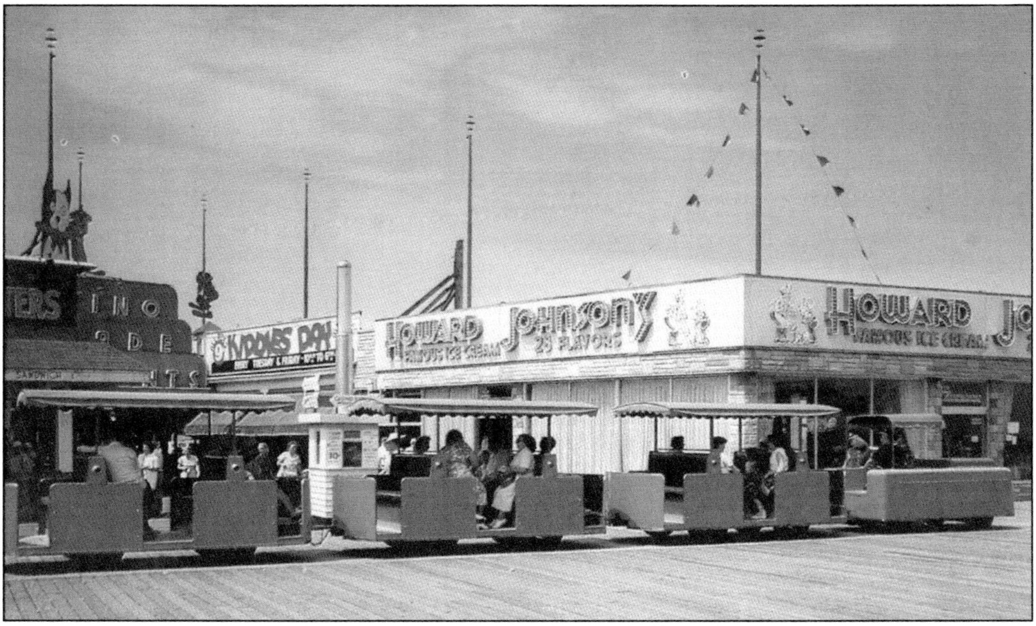

This postcard shows the boardwalk at Oak Avenue in this view from the 1950s. Clearly dominating this view is the familiar tramcar that still maintains routes up and down the boardwalk. Most who have walked the boards will recall the prerecorded and familiar taunting admonition of "watch the tramcar please." In the background of this view is the Casino Arcade and the Howard Johnson's Restaurant.

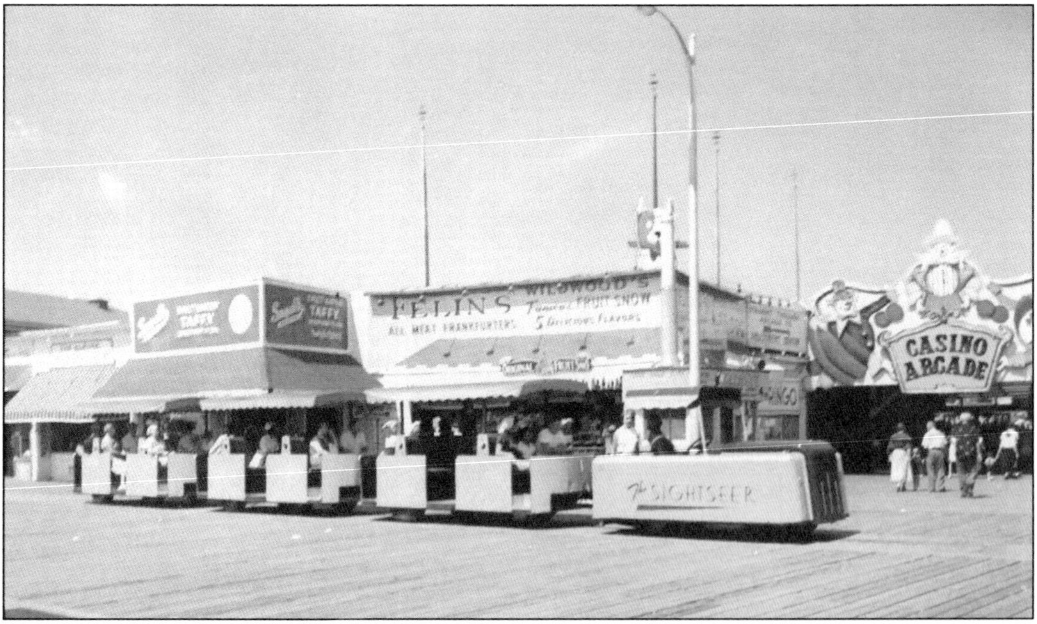

A postcard from the 1950s shows the boardwalk at Oak Avenue, with a view of the tramcar, the side of which reads, "The Sightseer." Some of the shops in the background include an outpost of Sagel's Candies, Felin's All Meat Frankfurters, and the Casino Arcade. With the exception of the tramcar, nothing in this scene would look familiar to visitors today.

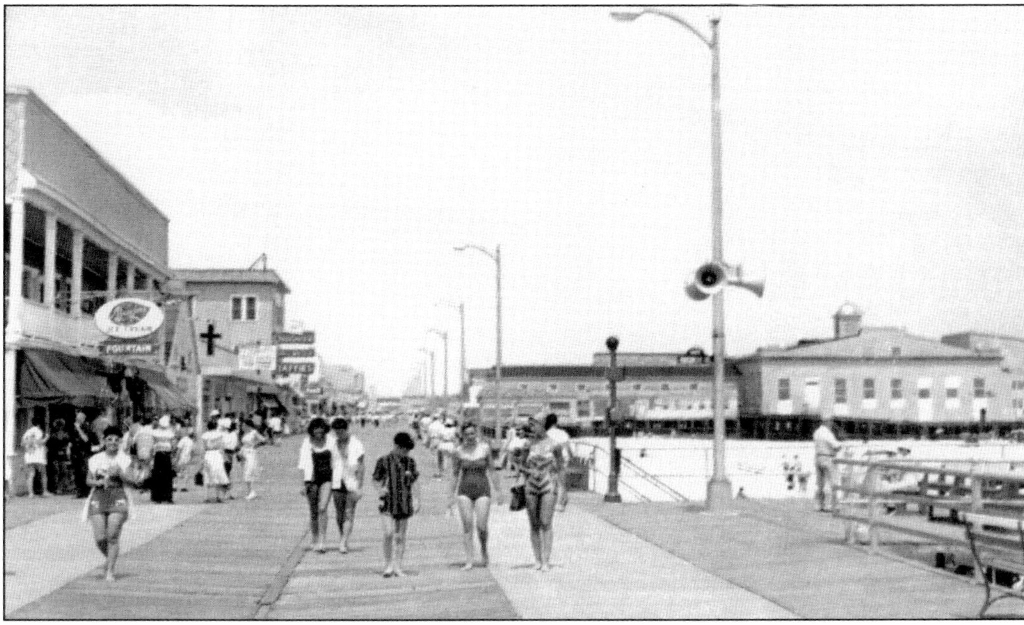

This view from the 1950s shows the boardwalk at Montgomery Avenue. The large structure in the distance and to the right is the former convention hall. In the immediate foreground, an old sign advertising Breyer's Ice Cream can be seen. Just beyond the sign is a cross hanging over the boardwalk, indicating this spot as the home of the Boardwalk Chapel. Although these stores have changed over the years and convention hall is no more, the Boardwalk Chapel is still in existence.

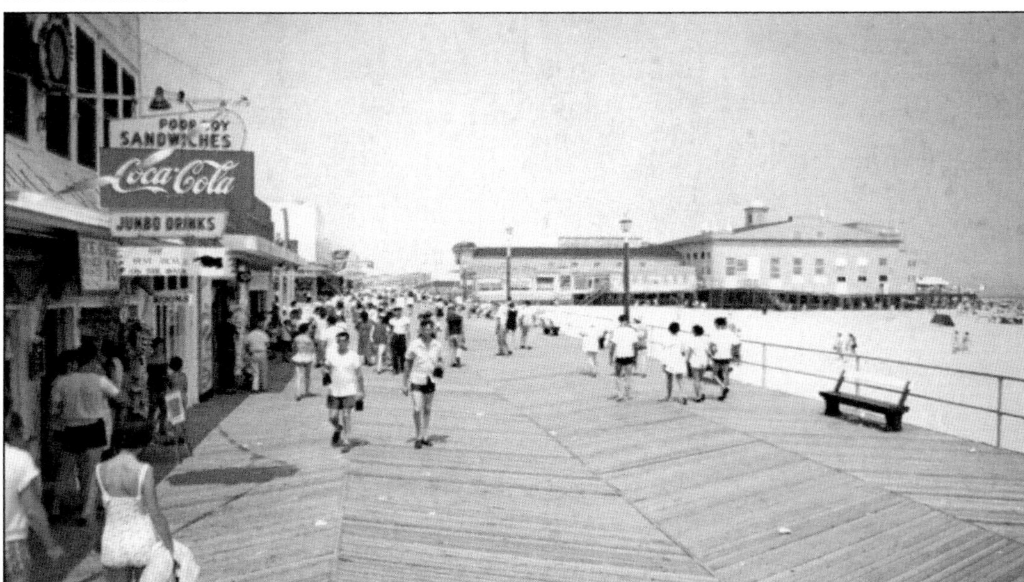

This postcard from the 1950s shows the boardwalk looking north from Montgomery Avenue. The Coca-Cola sign at the left advertises jumbo drinks in addition to "poor boy" sandwiches. Although these sandwiches are less familiar to residents of the northeastern United States, the poor boy sandwich is a favorite among people from Louisiana. With more than 50 years having gone by, this scene along the boardwalk looks quite different today.

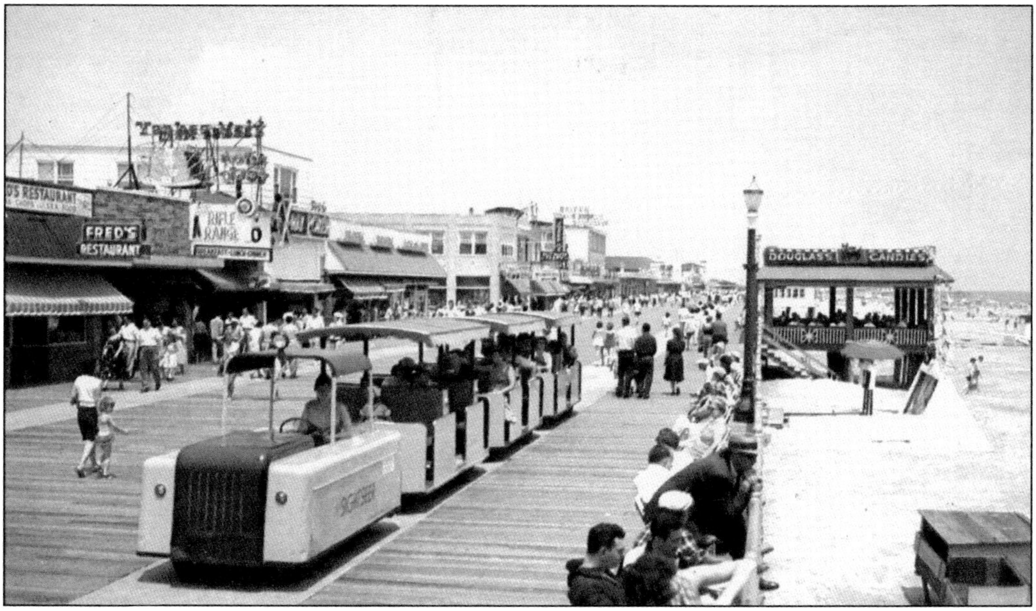

This postcard from the 1950s shows a view of the boardwalk looking north from Oak Avenue. Some of the businesses visible include Fred's Restaurant, the Rifle Range, as well as Douglass Candies. Across the boardwalk is a seating area sponsored by Douglass Candies, and the familiar tramcar travels south in the foreground. With the exception of Douglass Candies, none of these other businesses are still in existence today.

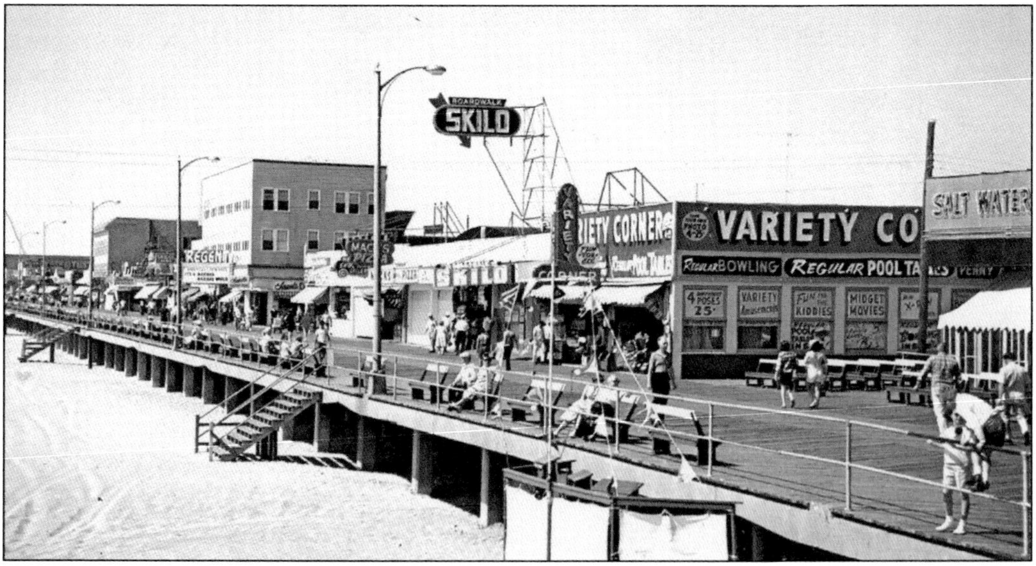

This postcard from 1963 shows the boardwalk looking toward Garfield Avenue. In this view, one can see the popular Variety Corner, which featured bowling, pool tables, and photographs. Moving along further, the Skilo game, Mack's Pizza, and the Regent Theater can all be seen. Today the theater has been converted to the Boardwalk Mall. Virtually all of the stores in this picture are a thing of the past today.

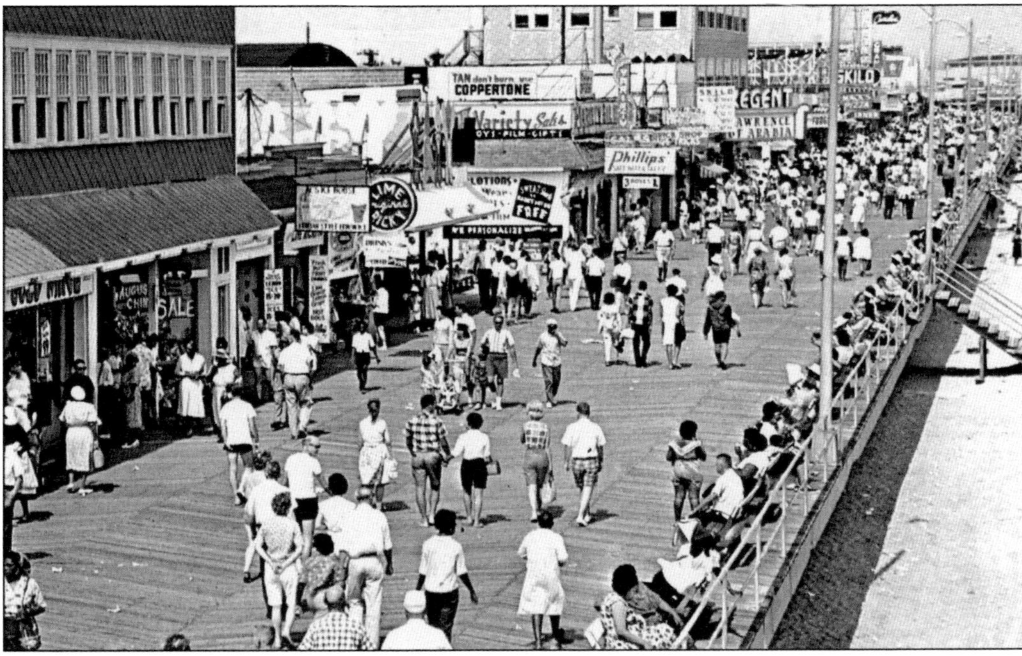

In this view of the boardwalk at Spicer Avenue, it is evident that *Lawrence of Arabia* was playing at the Regent Theater in 1962. Some of the other signs visible in this view tout an "Original Lime Ricky," Star Variety, Phillips' Salt Water Taffy, Mack's Pizza, and Sagel's Candies. More than four decades later, most of these businesses have become just a memory.

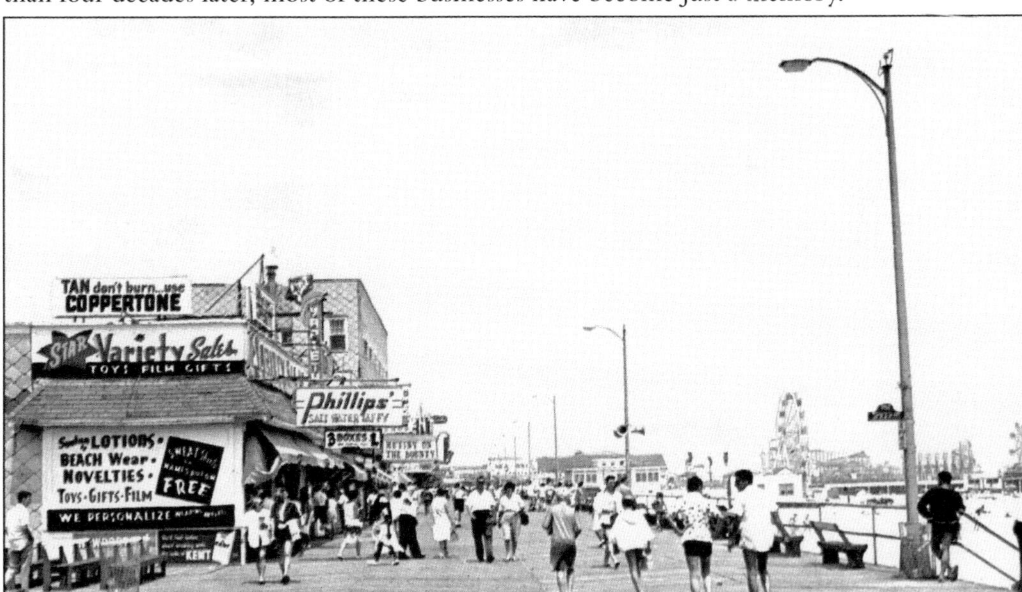

In yet another view of the boardwalk at Spicer Avenue, one can see that the Regent Theater's marquee now advertises *Mutiny on the Bounty*, another film released in 1962. In this view, the Coppertone advertisement crowning the variety store is clearly visible, in addition to an amusement pier off in the distance. Although visitors still stroll the boards at Spicer Avenue, this area looks quite different today.

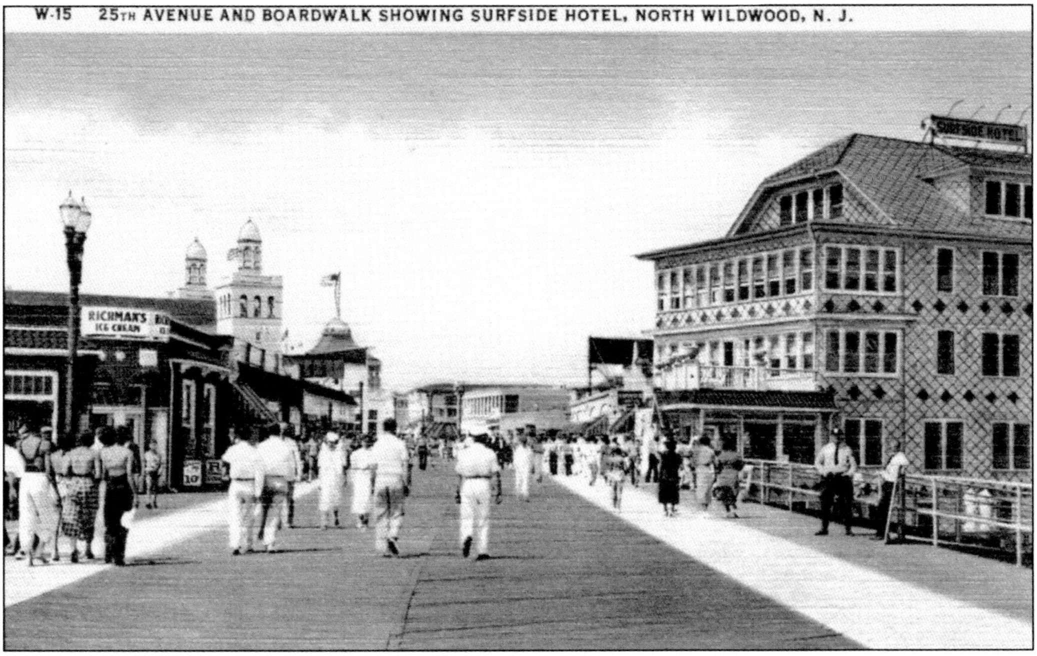

This view from the 1940s shows the boardwalk scene at Twenty-fifth Avenue in North Wildwood. The store at left advertises Richman's Ice Cream, while the Surfside Hotel is visible along the right of the boardwalk. The Surfside Hotel was one of the few hotels actually situated directly on the boardwalk. Virtually all of the buildings seen in this picture are but a memory of the past.

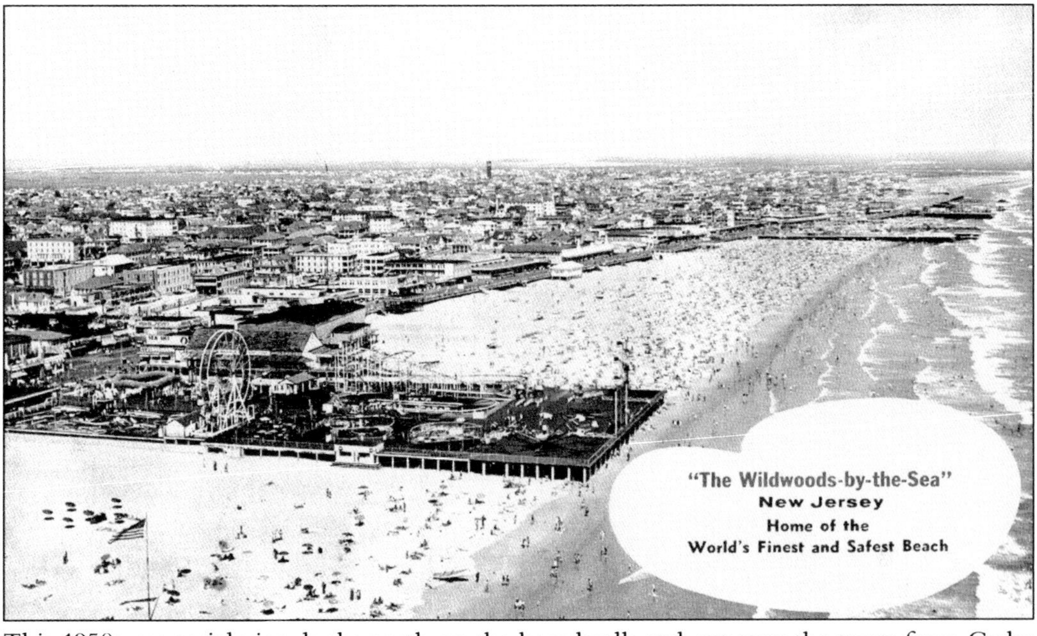

This 1950s-era aerial view looks north on the boardwalk and out over the town from Cedar Avenue toward the left of the image. Beyond the beach in the foreground, one can see the Playland Amusement Pier. Today a significant number of the Wildwoods' older buildings that were visible in this picture have been lost to time and progress.

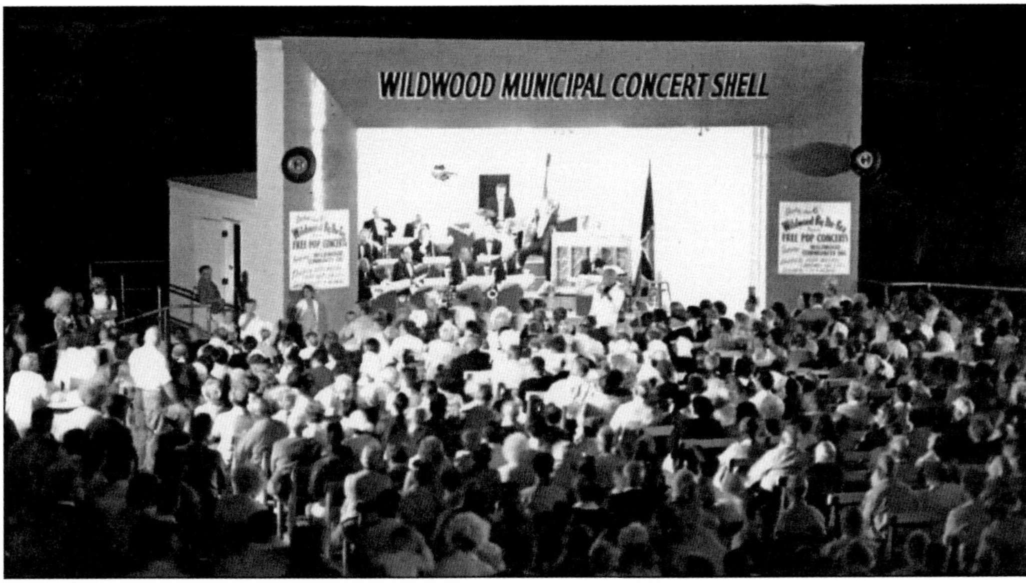

This postcard from 1964 shows the Wildwood Municipal Concert Shell located on the boardwalk at Montgomery Avenue. The signs adorning either side of the concert shell exclaim "Free Pop Concerts" in "Wildwood by the Sea." Today someone standing on the boardwalk at Montgomery Avenue can only imagine the presence of the former concert shell.

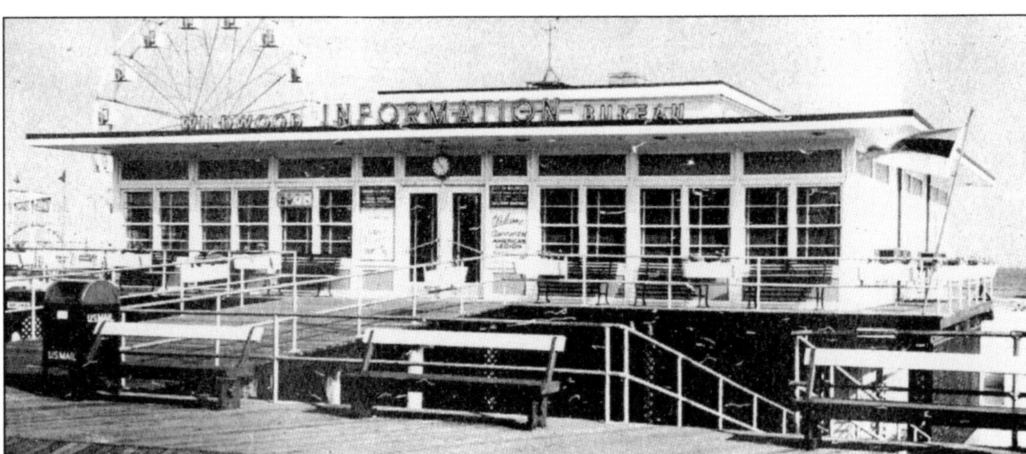

This view from the 1950s shows the Wildwood Information Bureau located on the boardwalk at Schellenger Avenue. Although this building would be updated over the next few decades, the visitor center is still located in this spot along the boardwalk. The Playland Ferris wheel is visible in the background of this image as well.

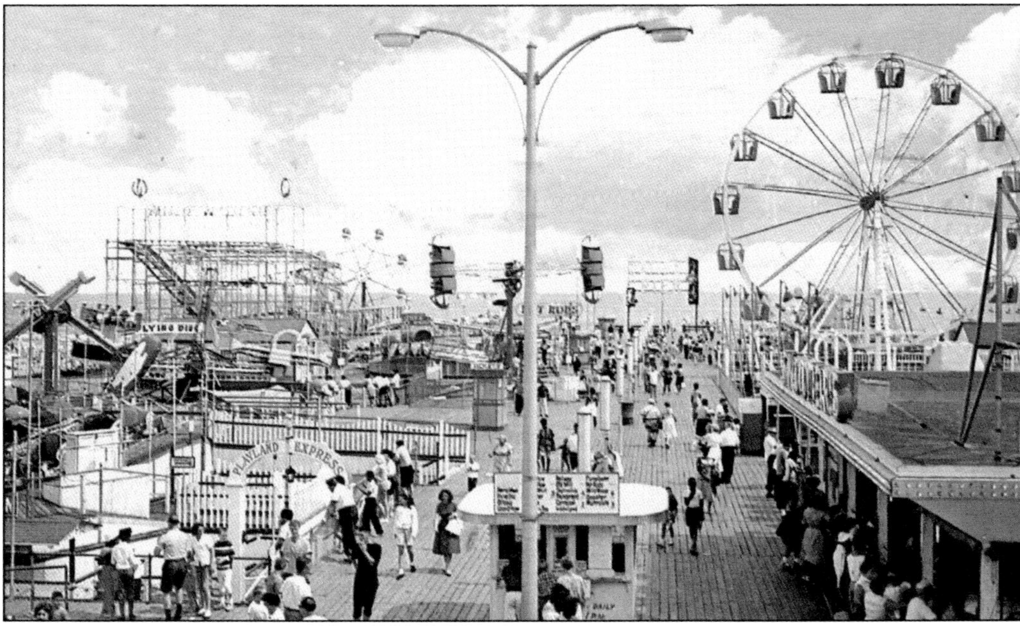

Formerly known as Playland Amusement Pier, this 1960s postcard shows Marine Pier West, located on the boardwalk at Cedar Avenue. There is still an amusement pier located in this place today, although the rides and amusements have been updated and changed many times over the years.

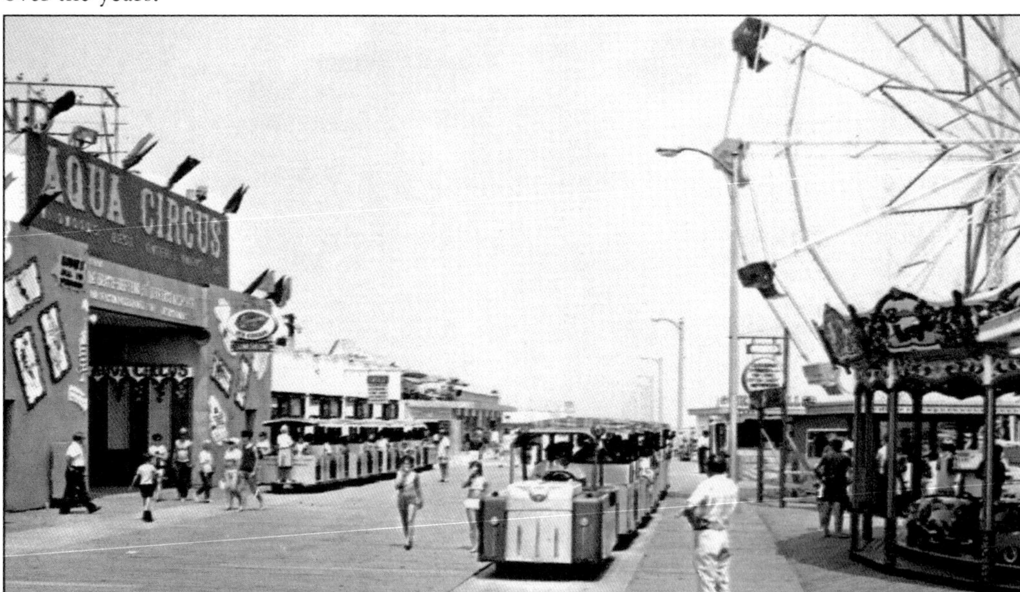

This postcard from the 1960s shows the boardwalk at Twenty-third Avenue in North Wildwood. The most prominent feature in this image is the Aqua Circus attraction, billed as "Wildwood's Best Entertainment." A Breyer's Ice Cream sign hanging from the front of the Aqua Circus can also be seen, just across from Sportland Pier, which featured a Ferris wheel and merry-go-round. Today the Aqua Circus is just a memory, and this area of the boardwalk looks quite different than it did 40 years ago.

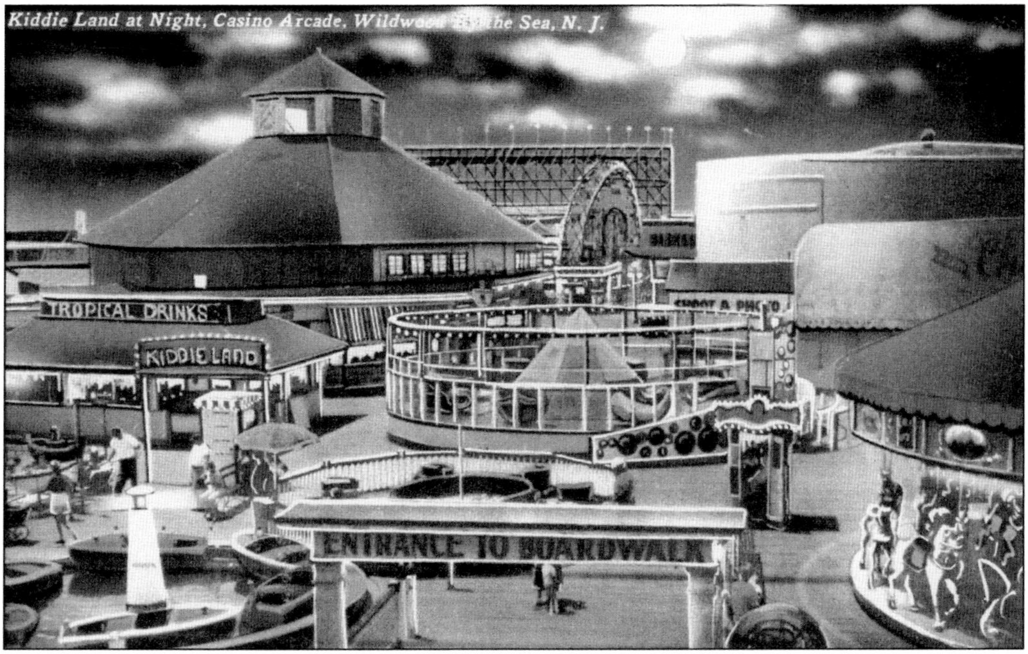

A postcard from the 1940s shows Kiddie Land as it appeared at nightfall. A variety of rides targeted for younger children can be seen in this view, in addition to a concession stand offering tropical drinks. Today Kiddie Land has been given a new name, and the rides seen in this view have long since been removed.

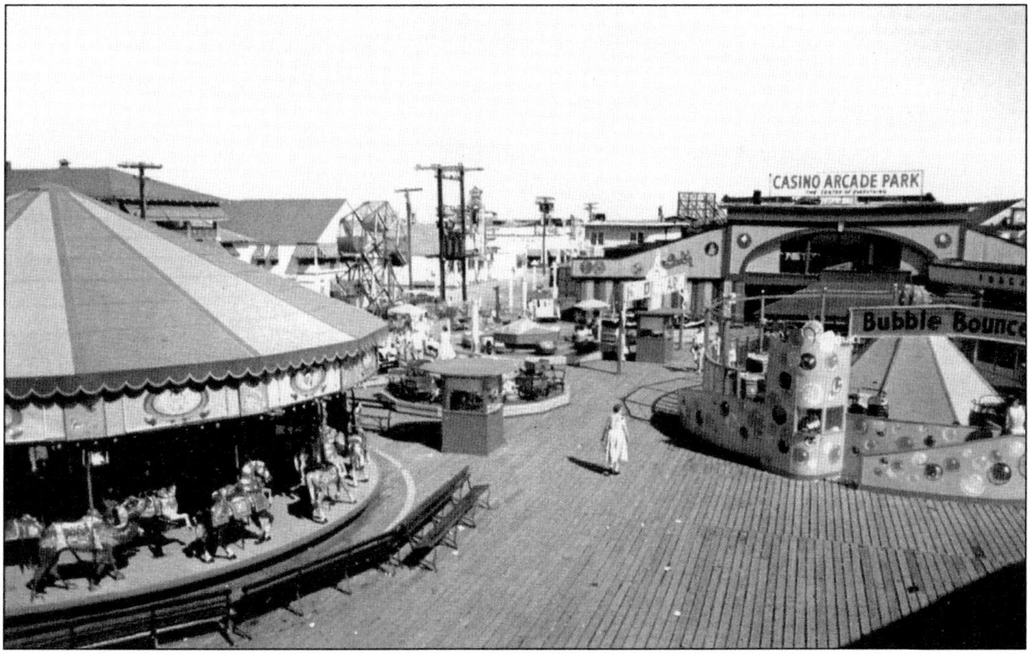

This postcard from the 1960s shows Casino Arcade Park, which featured the Bubble Bounce ride, in addition to a merry-go-round and other rides. The Casino Arcade was located adjacent to the boardwalk at Atlantic and Oak Avenues. Today the Casino Arcade Park is but another attraction relegated to Wildwood's past.

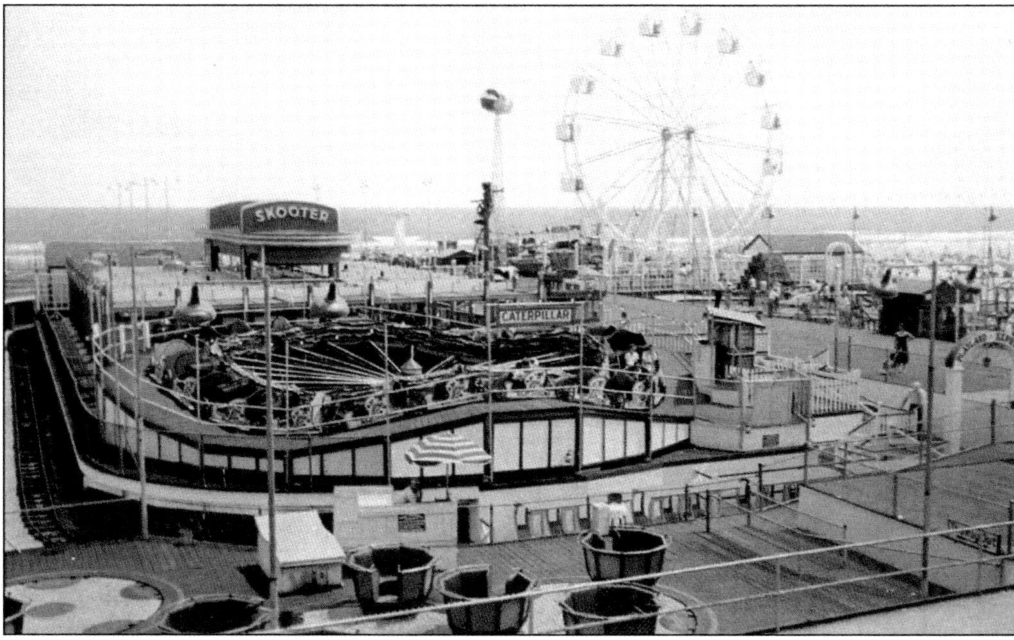

Playland Amusement Pier is seen in this postcard from the early 1960s. In this view, one can see the Playland Express, Ferris wheel, Caterpillar, and Skooter. The very popular Tea Cups ride is seen in the foreground at the bottom of the image. Today the area that was Playland Amusement Pier has been completely reinvented.

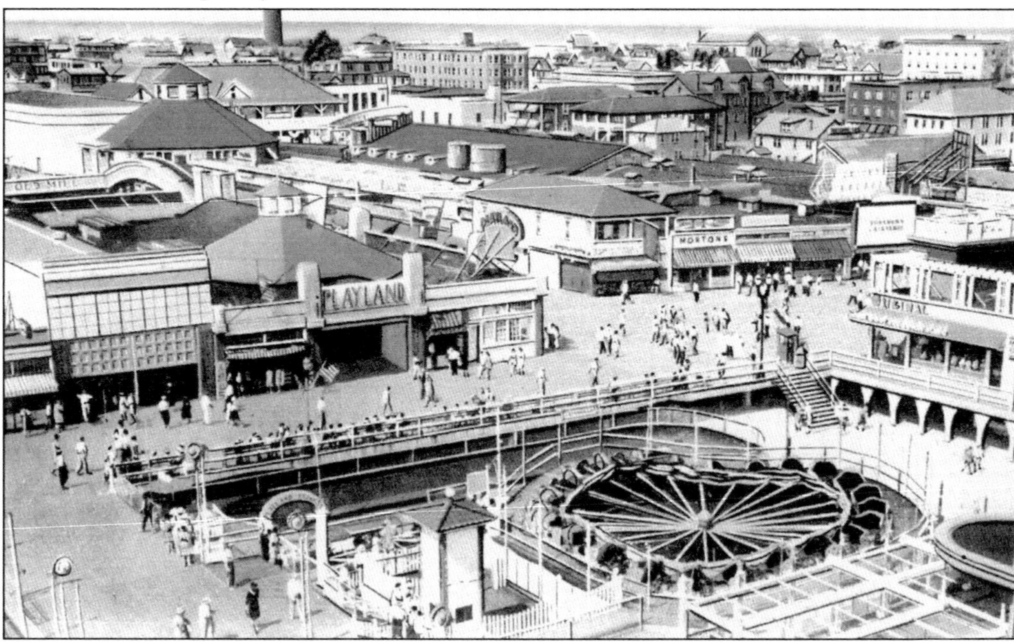

This view of the boardwalk and beyond was taken from the Playland Ferris wheel during the 1940s. The merry-go-round can be seen in this view, in addition to a variety of rides, amusements, and food stands located on the boardwalk at Cedar Avenue. A picture taken from this same vantage point today would be quite a contrast to the scene visible below, taken more than six decades ago.

Six

The Beach

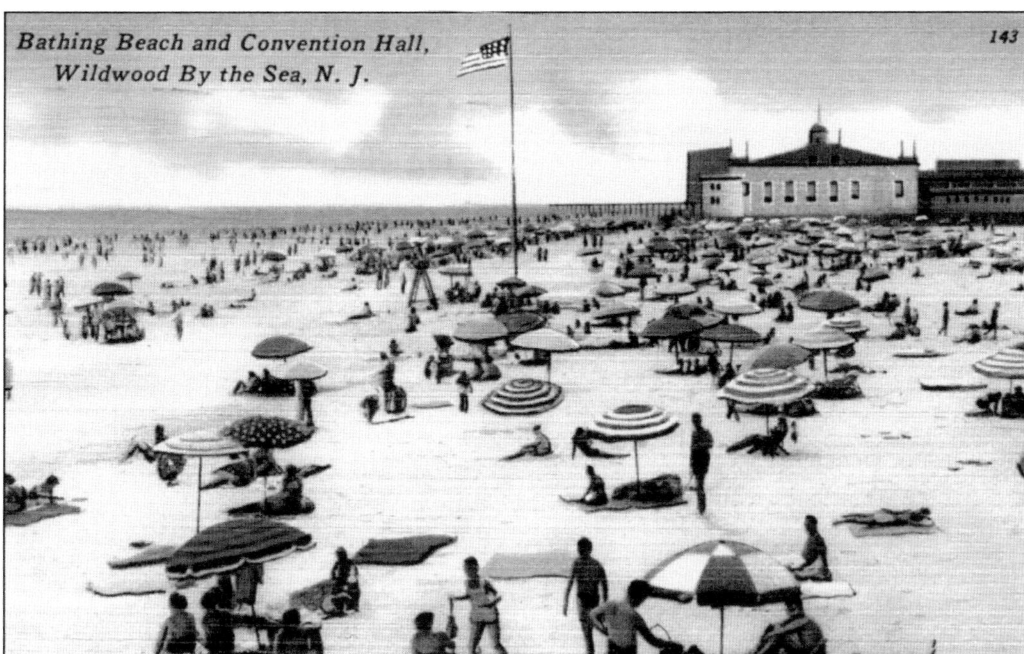

This postcard from the 1940s looks south on the beach, toward the original convention hall located at Youngs Avenue. The large building was built as convention hall in the 1920s and would later be converted to Fun Pier by the late 1950s. Ultimately a devastating fire would destroy what remained of Fun Pier in the 1980s.

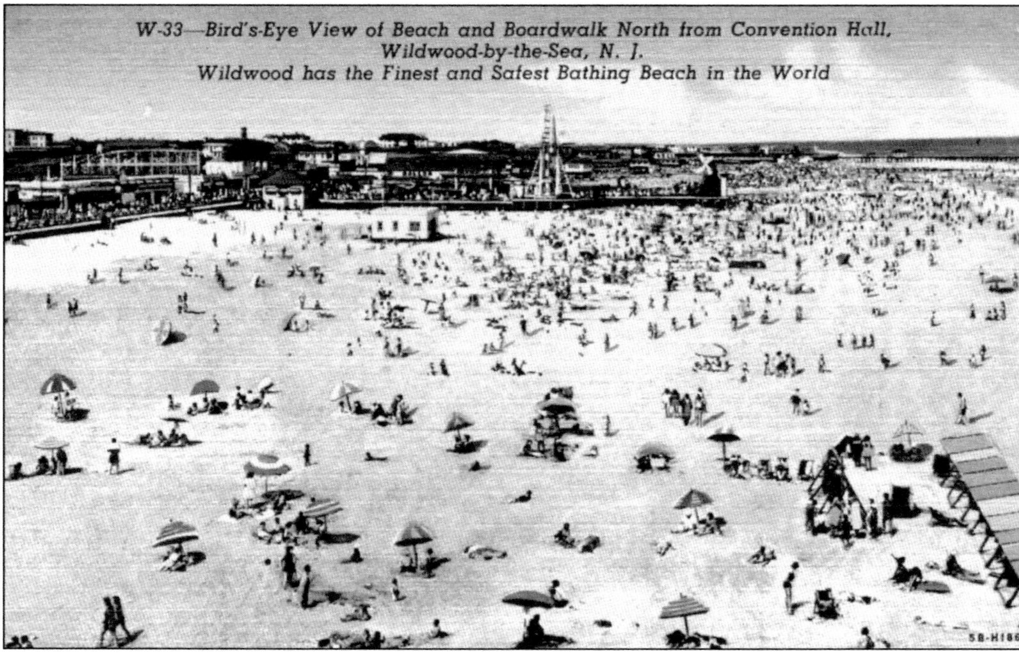

This postcard from the 1940s shows the expansive Wildwood beach in a view that looks north from convention hall in the area of Youngs Avenue. In the distance, one can see the Playland Amusement Pier, along with a variety of boardwalk shops. Hundreds of beachgoers have turned out on this summer day to enjoy Wildwood's beautiful beach.

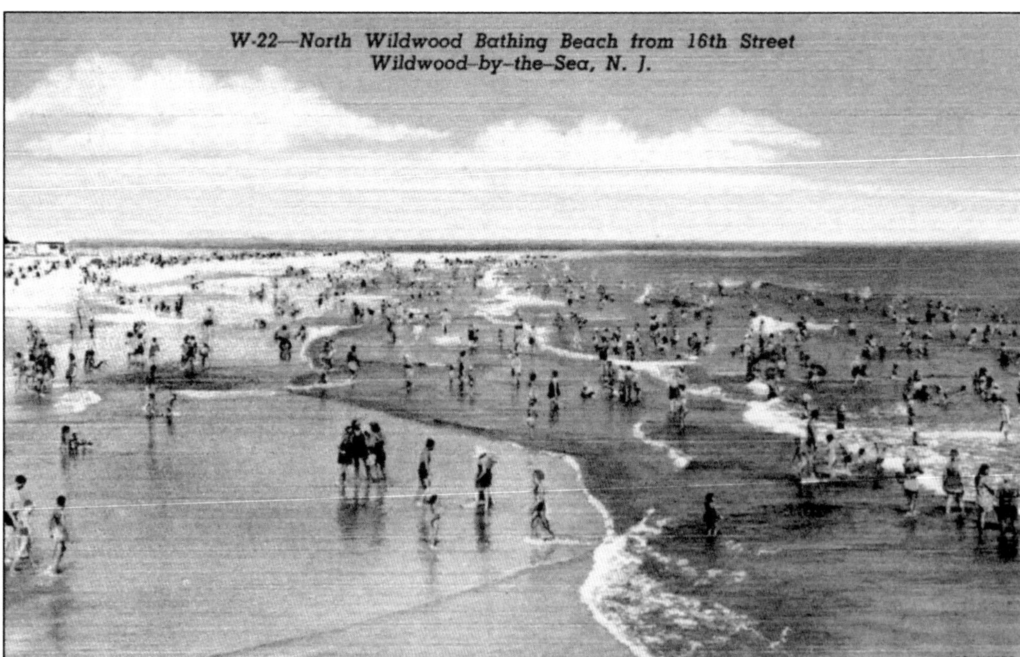

A portion of North Wildwood's beach is seen in this postcard from the 1940s. In this view, the beach as it appeared from Sixteenth Avenue is seen, erroneously identified as Sixteenth Street on this postcard.

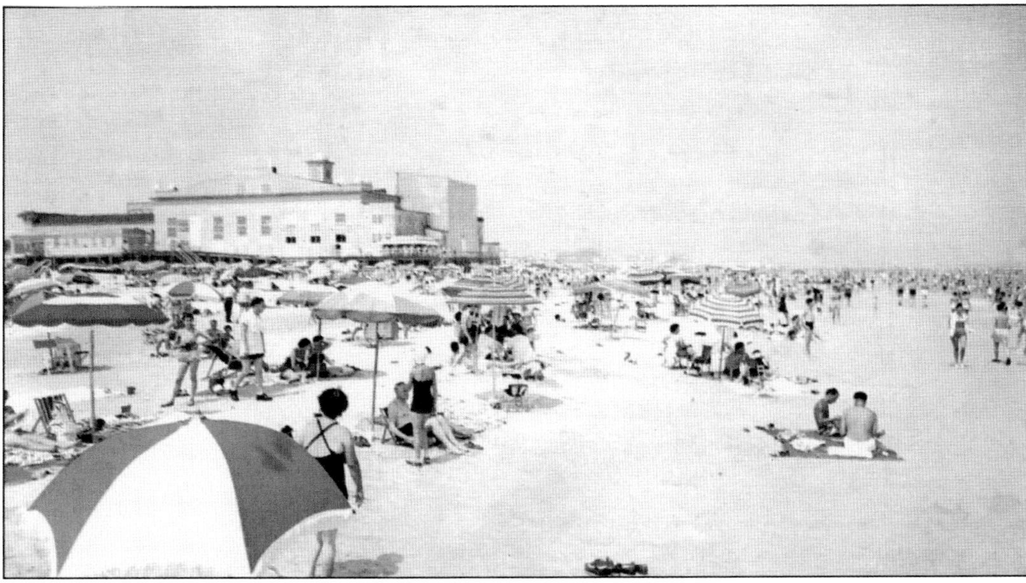

This postcard from the 1950s shows a very crowded beach in Wildwood. Hundreds of people were soaking up the sun and surf in an area just south of Youngs Avenue. The beautiful sand beaches of Wildwood continue to attract tens of thousands of people on any given summer day.

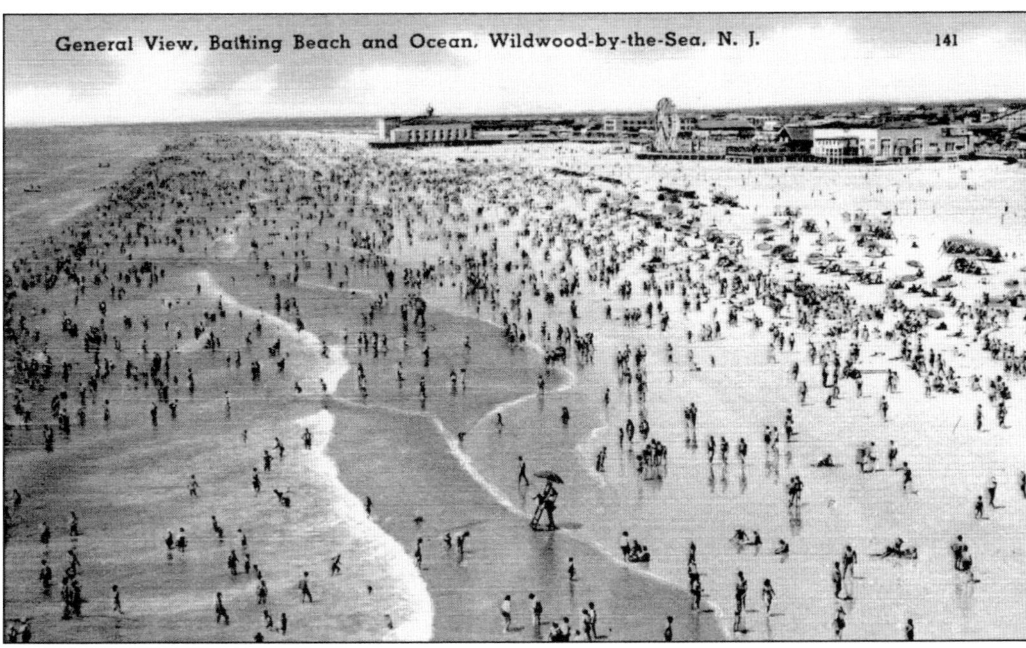

This aerial-view postcard from the 1940s shows a crowded beach in Wildwood. This shot looks south toward the convention hall, located at Youngs Avenue. Also visible in this view is Playland, identifiable through the well-known Ferris wheel on its amusement pier at Cedar Avenue.

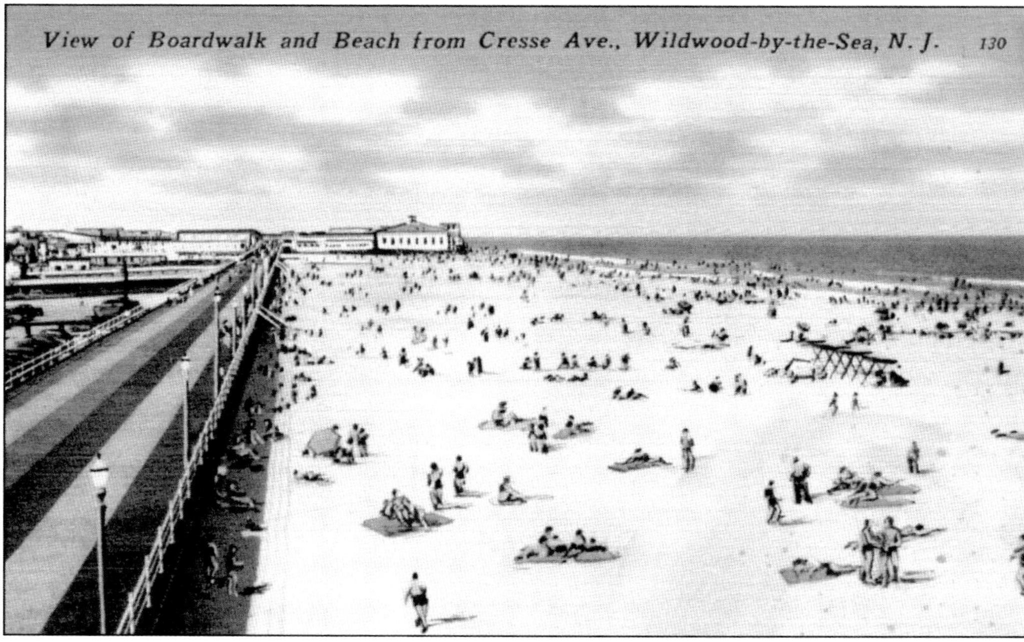

This postcard shows a view of the beach and boardwalk, looking north from Cresse Avenue in the 1940s. In the distance, one can see the convention hall located on the boardwalk at Youngs Avenue. Cresse Avenue is typically referred to as the dividing line between Wildwood Crest and Wildwood.

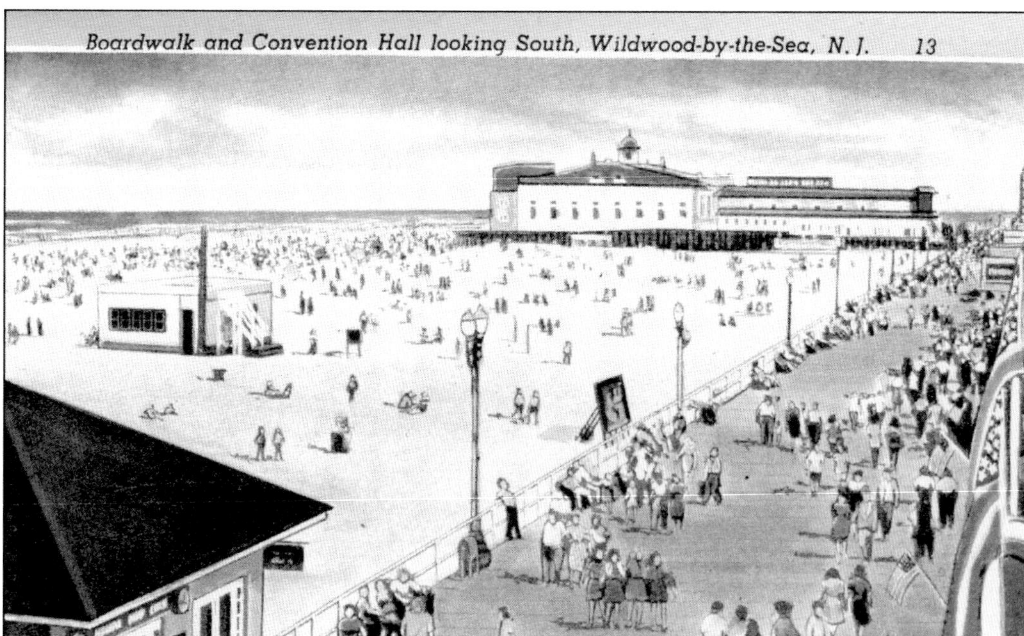

This postcard from the 1940s shows a view looking out over the boardwalk and beach, toward convention hall. Just barely in view at the lower left portion of the image is a first aid station located on the boardwalk at that time.

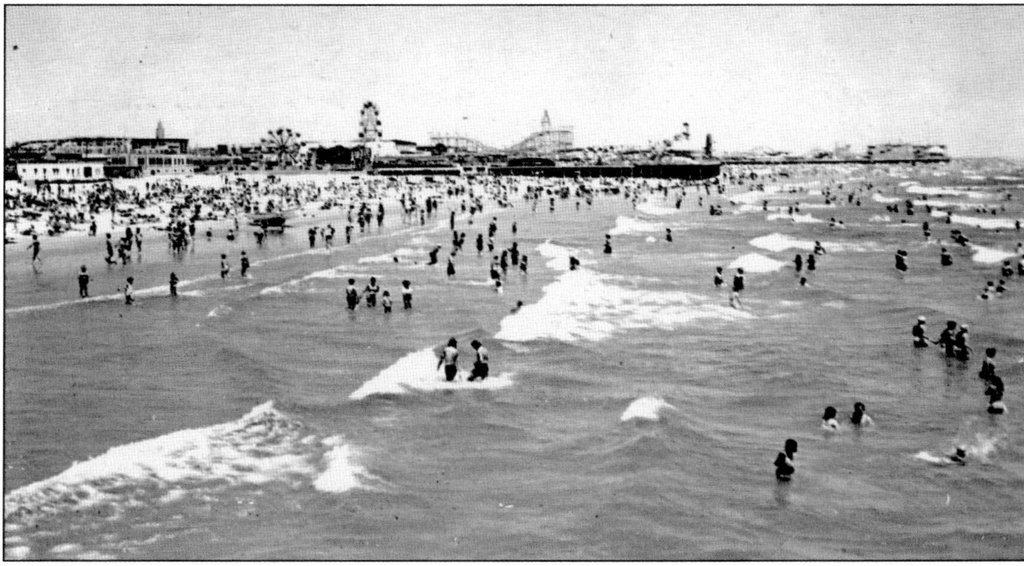

This postcard from the 1950s shows hundreds of people enjoying the beach and ocean surf on a warm summer day in Wildwood. There is no doubt that the children seen in this view must have been looking forward to an evening of riding the amusements on the boardwalk, seen in the background of this image.

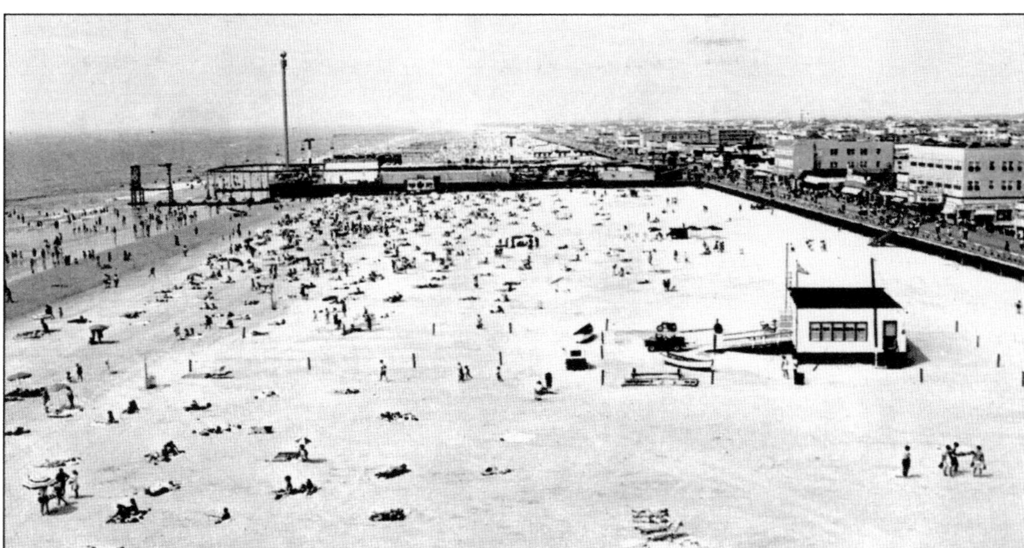

This postcard from the 1960s shows a view of the beach looking south from the Ferris wheel at Marine Pier West. The large amusement pier off in the distance was known as Fun Pier. The small structure located on the beach in the right side of the image was a lifeguard station.

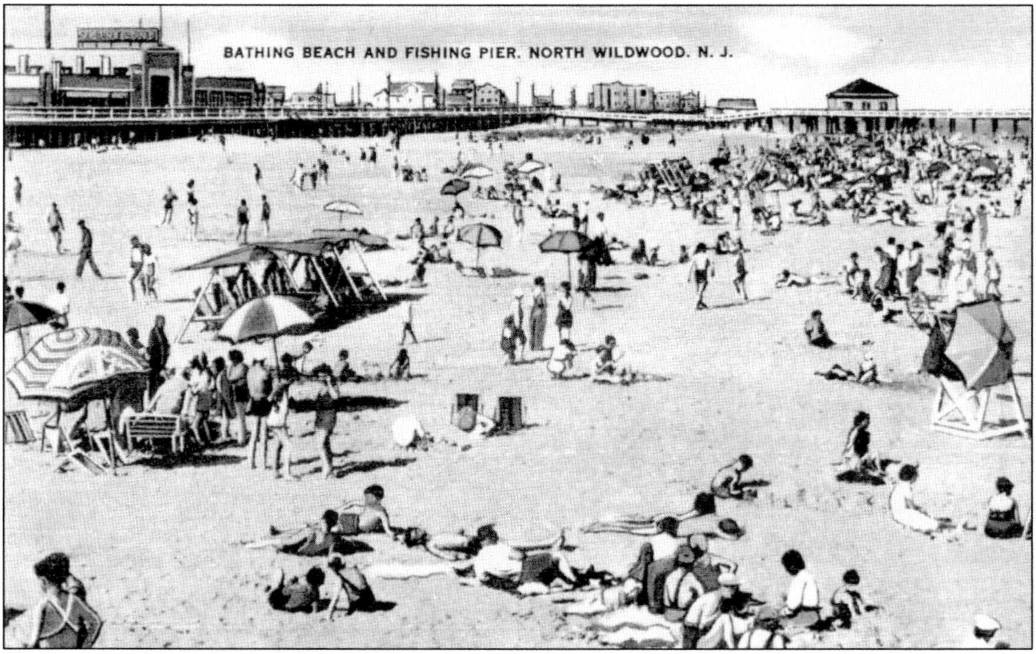

A postcard from the 1940s shows a view of the beach and fishing pier in North Wildwood. In the background on the boardwalk one is able to see the sign for Sportland Pier. Although hundreds of people still flock to this section of beach on any given day, the view of the boardwalk and pier has changed quite significantly since this time.

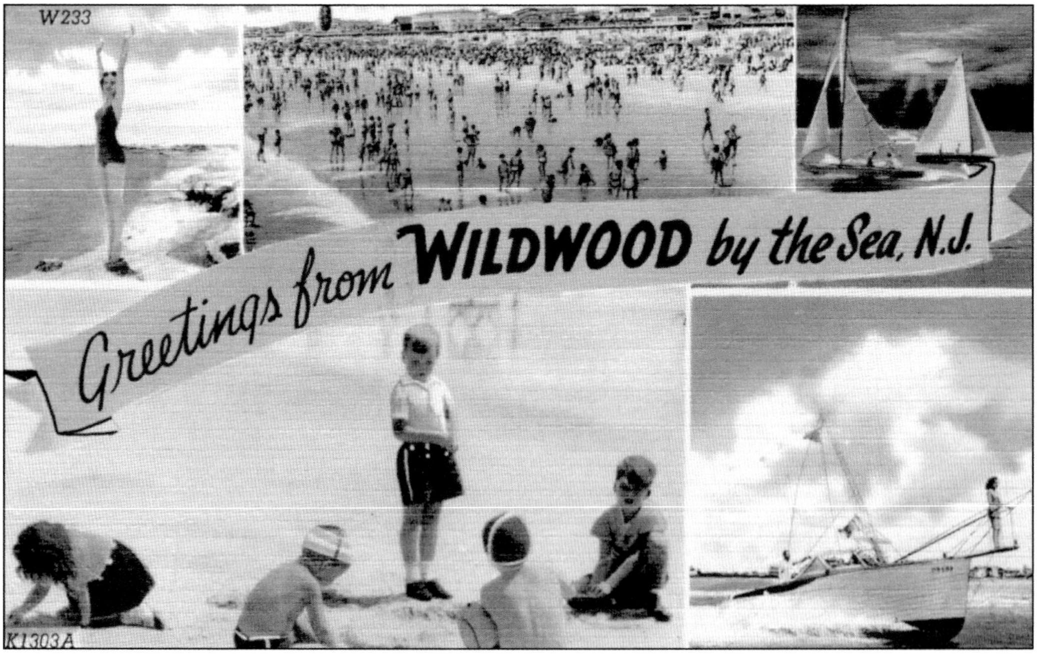

This multi-view postcard from the 1940s shows various scenes from the beach and surf. In one shot, some children with bathing caps can be seen playing in the sand. In another portion of this postcard, a crowded beach view can be seen, where hundreds of families are enjoying themselves on a hot summer day.

Seven

COMMUNITY

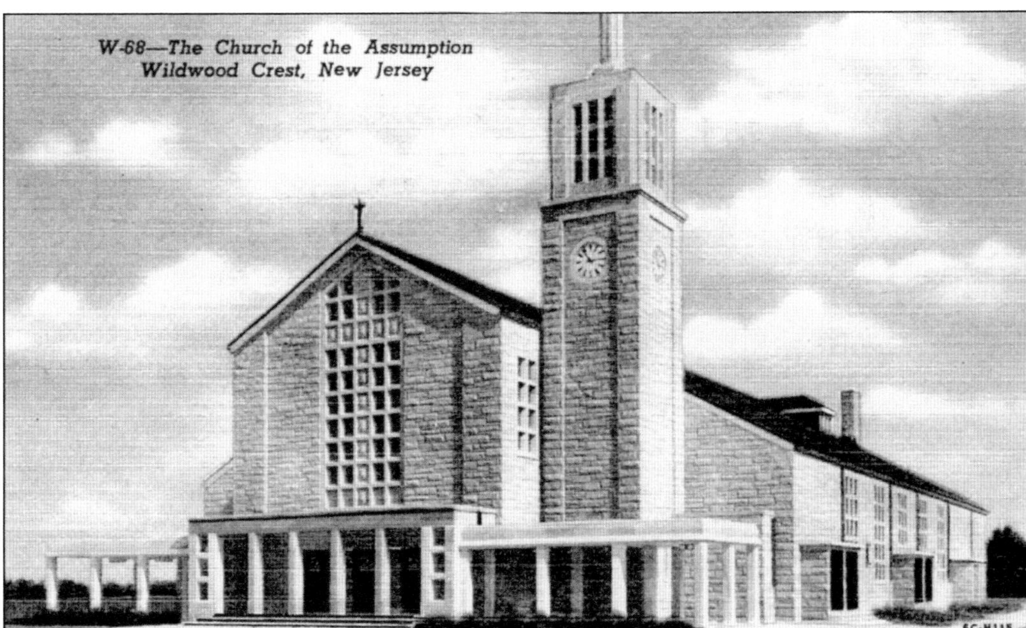

The Church of the Assumption is seen in this postcard from the early 1950s. This Catholic church is located at 7110 Seaview Avenue in Wildwood Crest. The church maintains a steady year-round congregation, although masses held in the summer also accommodate many vacationers to the area. The structure still looks quite similar today as it did when this postcard was produced more than 50 years ago.

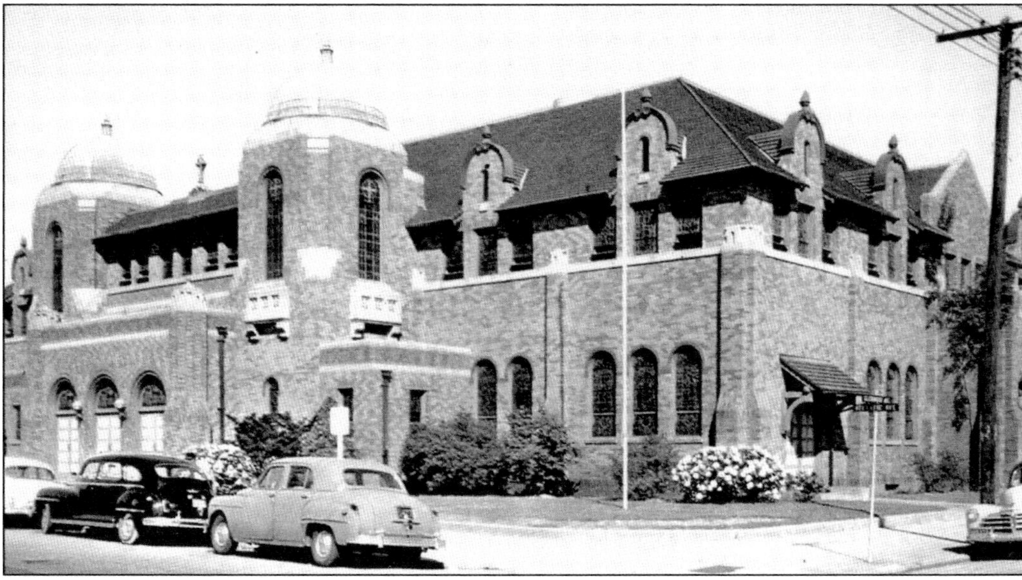

This postcard from the early 1950s shows St. Ann's Catholic Church located in Wildwood, along Atlantic Avenue between Glenwood and Magnolia Avenues. This large church welcomes residents and visitors alike, although the summer months most assuredly mark greater levels of attendance. The church looks quite similar today to what is seen in this postcard view.

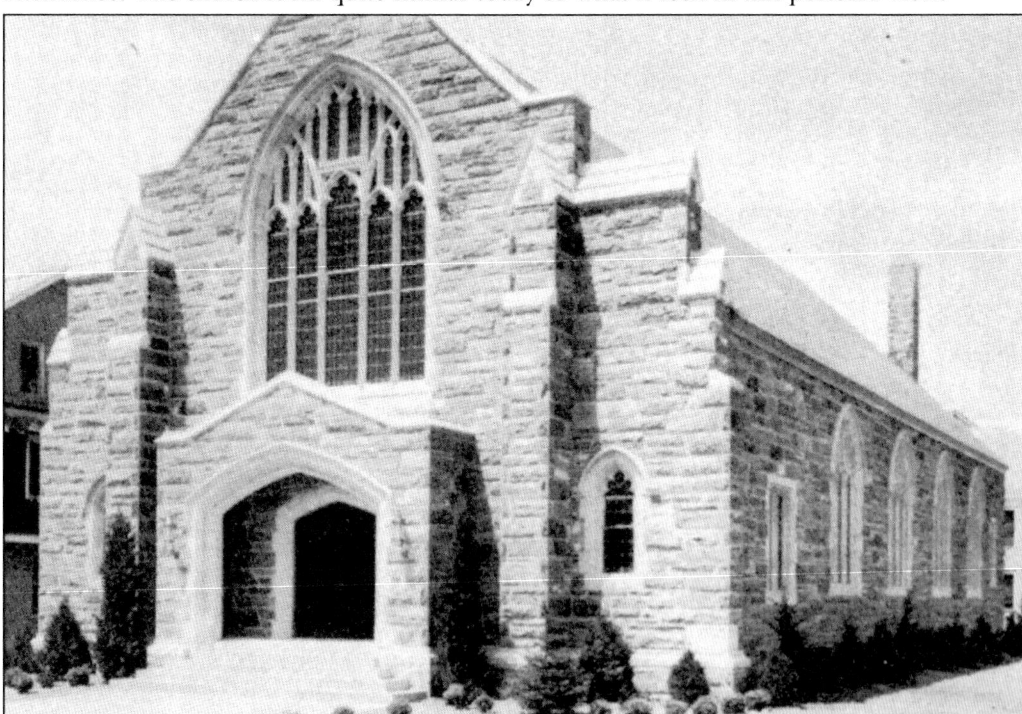

The Lutheran church is seen in this view from the 1940s in its location along Atlantic Avenue at Poplar Avenue. This is just one of many houses of worship located in Wildwood that serve a diverse population of residents and visitors. The church is still there today and looks very similar to the way it did more than six decades ago.

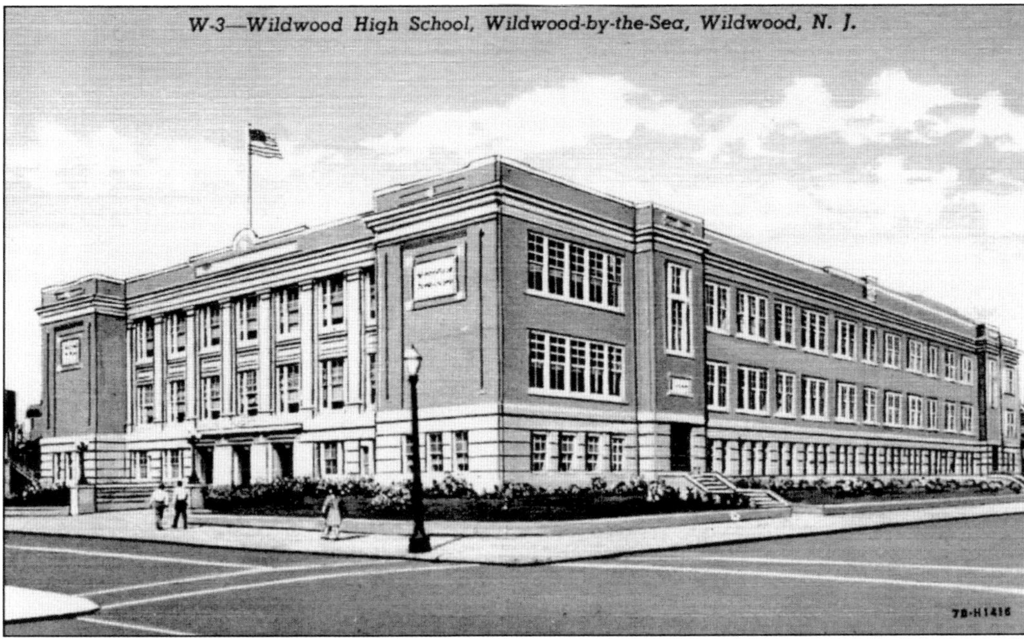

This postcard from the early 1950s shows the Wildwood High School located in downtown Wildwood along Pacific Avenue at Montgomery Avenue. This school has educated generations of Wildwood's youth. Today the building looks strikingly similar to how it did when this postcard was produced more than 50 years ago.

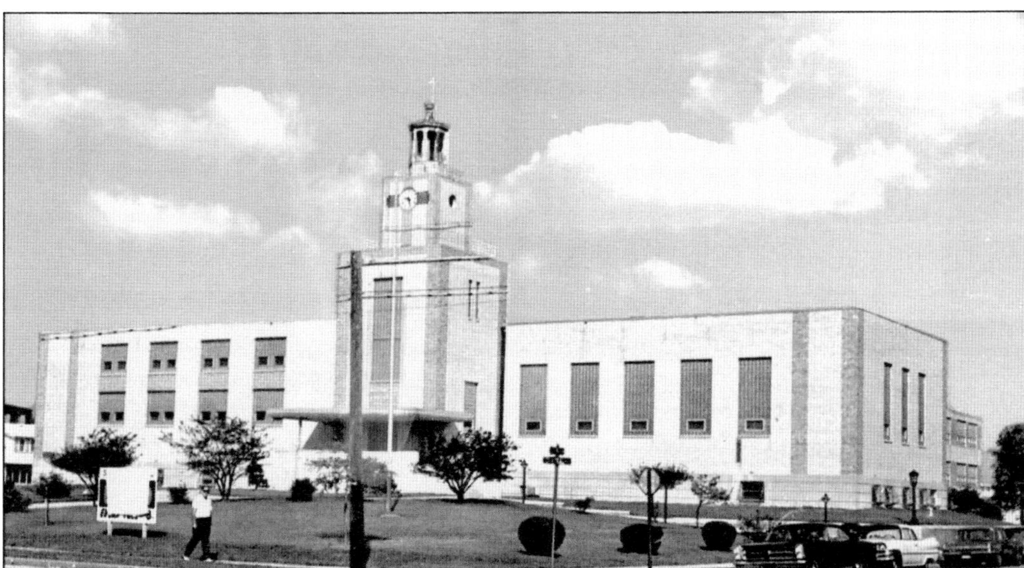

Wildwood Catholic High School is seen in this postcard from the early 1960s in its location at 1500 Central Avenue in North Wildwood. Although the cars that might be parked outside the school today would look a lot different, the school's exterior has seen only minor modifications over the last few decades.

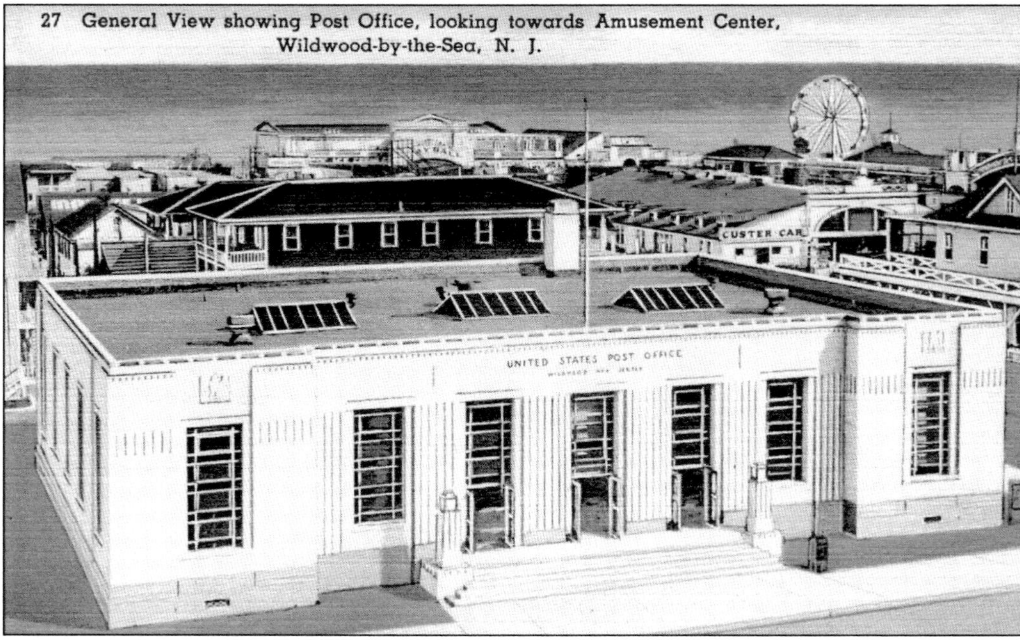

The United States post office is seen in this postcard from the early 1950s. This building is located at 3311 Atlantic Avenue in Wildwood and has served residents and visitors for more than five decades. Although most of the amusements and buildings seen in the background of this view no longer exist, the Wildwood Post Office looks quite similar today.

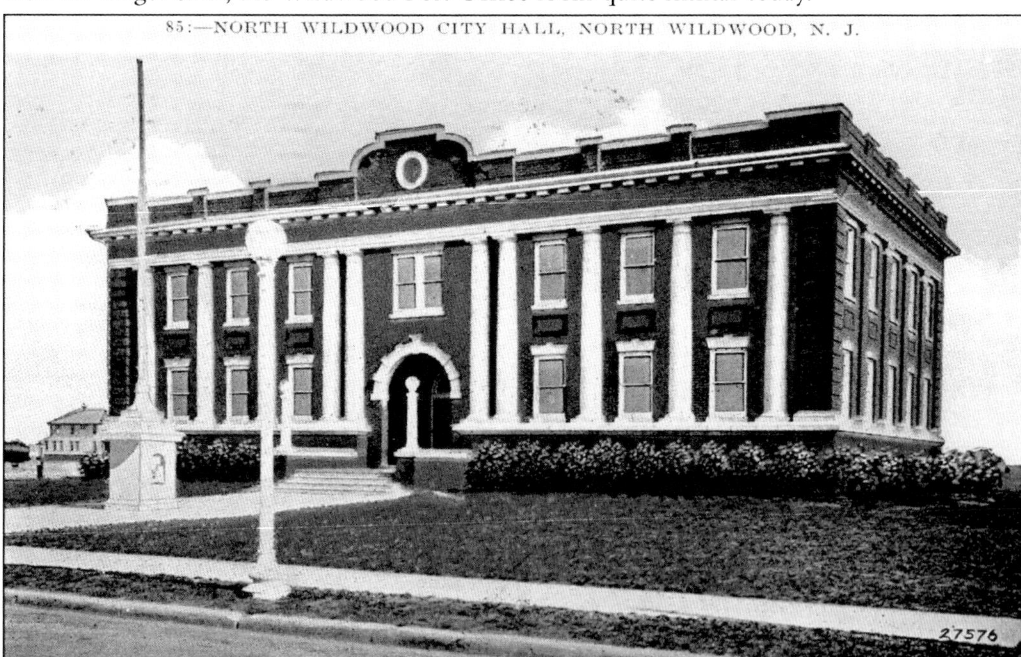

This postcard from the 1940s shows city hall in North Wildwood. This building is located at 901 Atlantic Avenue and continues to serve the community in this location several decades after having been constructed. Remarkably time and progress have not been able to erode the appearance of city hall. The building's exterior looks almost the same today as it did then.

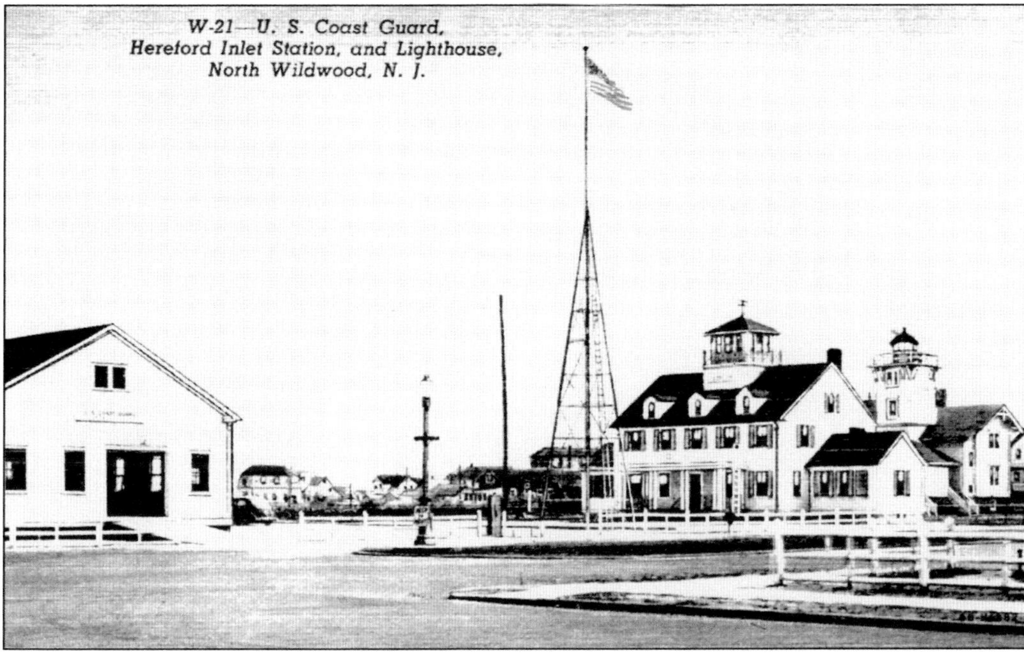

A postcard from the late 1940s shows a view of the United States Coast Guard station at Hereford Inlet. Additionally one can also see the lighthouse in the background and to the right. Located near First and Central Avenues in North Wildwood, the lighthouse continues to attract tourists who wish to visit this 19th-century beacon of safety.

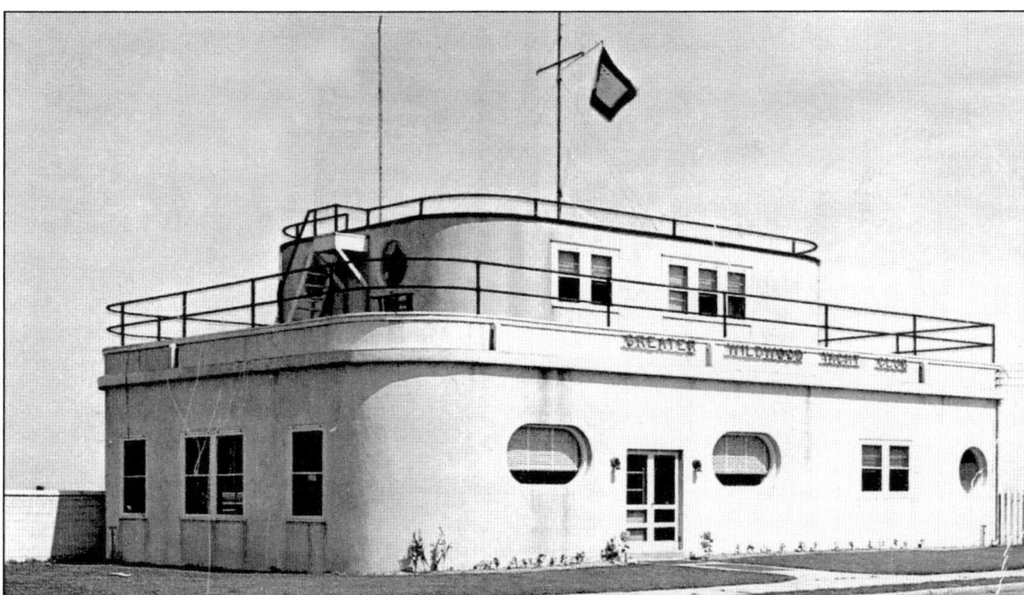

This postcard from the early 1950s shows the Greater Wildwood Yacht Club. This building is located at 6510 Park Boulevard in Wildwood Crest and overlooks beautiful Sunset Lake. Although a full second story has been added to the structure, the unique shape of the first floor windows reveals the identity of the building. More than 50 years later, this structure is still used in its original intended capacity.

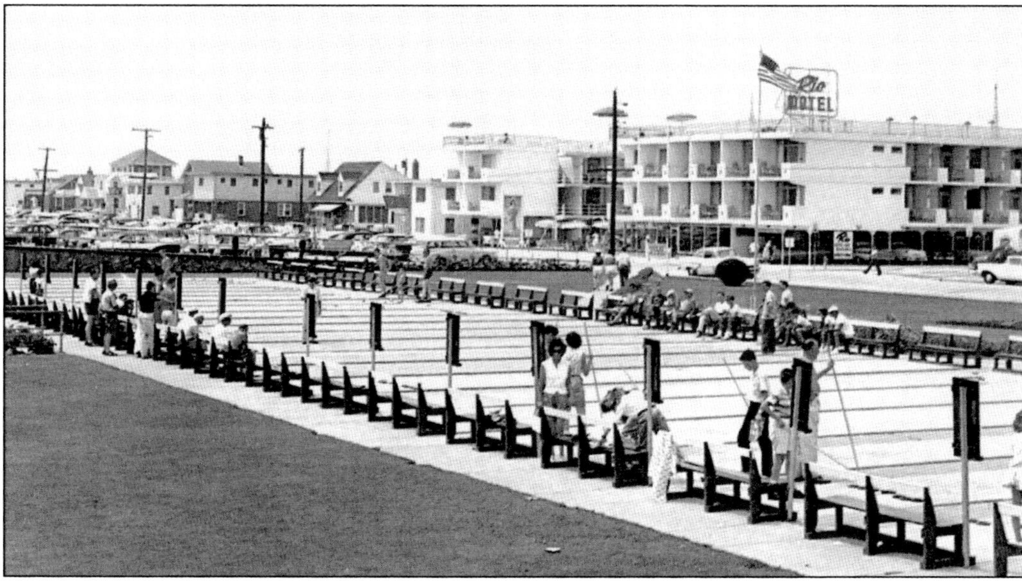

A postcard from the 1950s shows a view of the shuffleboard courts located along Ocean Avenue in Wildwood. The Rio Motel can be seen in the background of this image in its former location at Ocean and Rio Grande Avenues. Today the Rio Motel is gone, and the shuffleboard courts have been paved over to provide parking for Wildwood's new convention center. As the popularity of shuffleboard has waned over the years, this piece of oceanfront property was just too valuable to be allowed to sit idle.

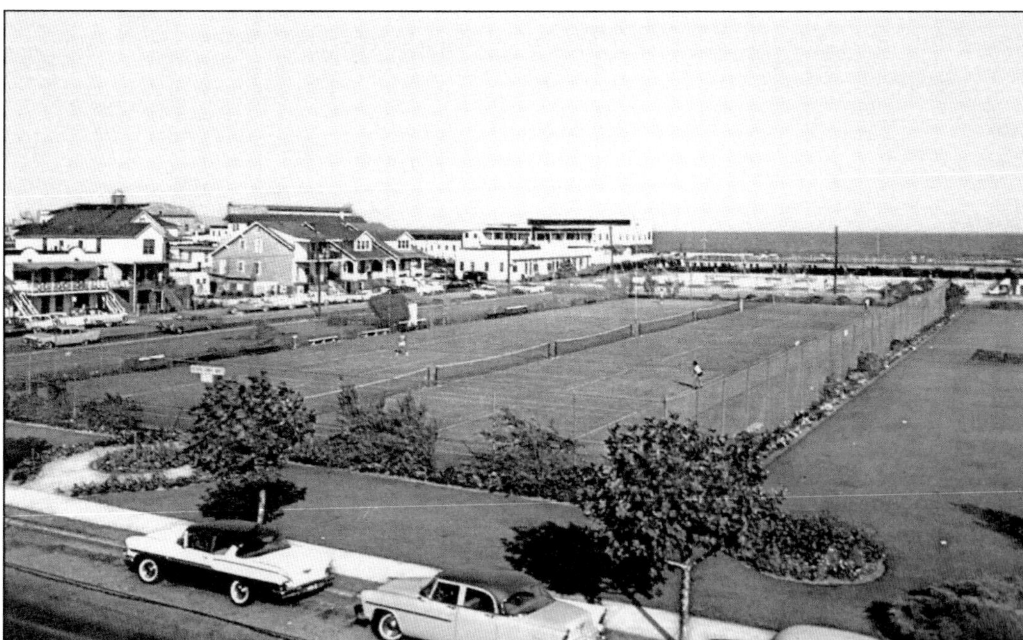

This postcard from the 1950s shows the tennis courts at Fox Park. The entrance to the park is located along Atlantic Avenue at Davis Avenue in Wildwood. Although the neighborhood and cars around the perimeter of the park would look quite different today, the facilities of Fox Park are still in constant use by residents and visitors, as they were then.

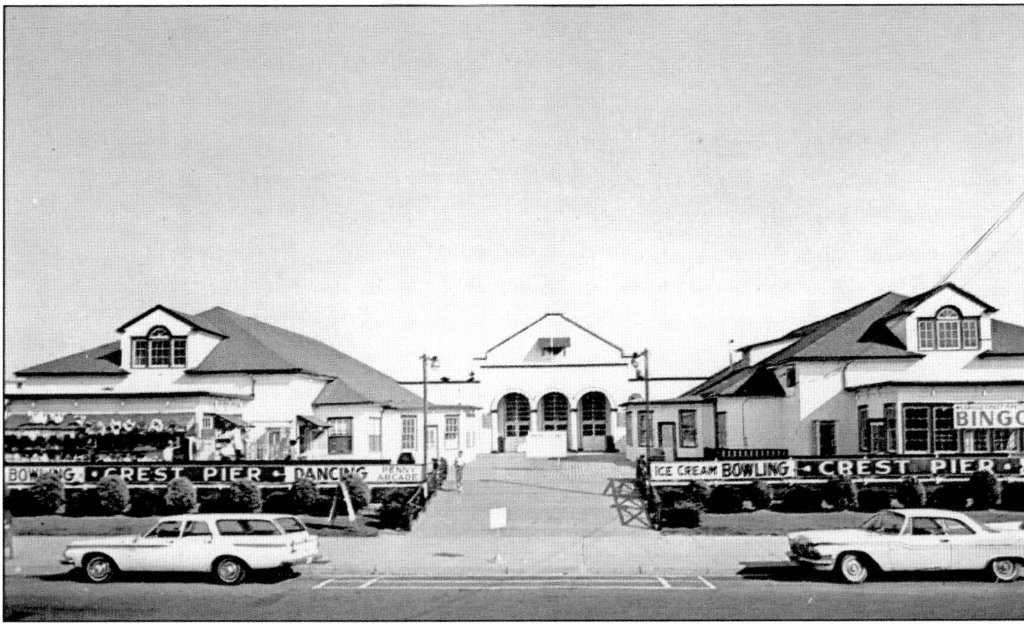

Crest Pier is seen in this postcard from the early 1960s. This structure was located between Atlantic and Ocean Avenues at Heather Road. Some of the signs visible in this postcard advertise bowling, dancing, a penny arcade, ice cream, and bingo. This structure was demolished in the 1980s and replaced with the current building that serves as Crest Pier.

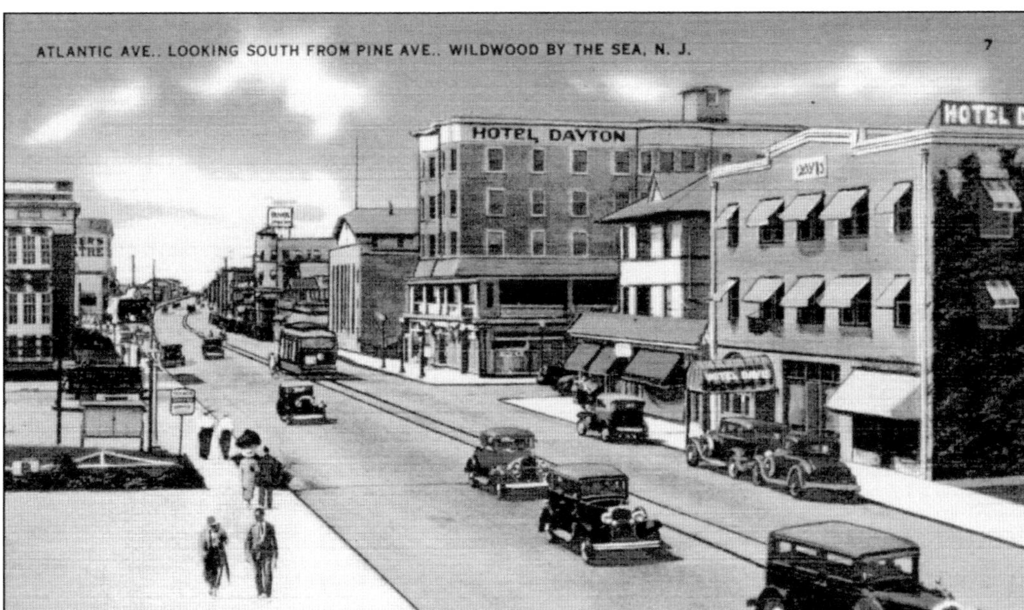

This postcard dates from the 1930s and shows a view of Atlantic Avenue in Wildwood, looking south from Pine Avenue. Among the structures seen in this view are the Hotel Dayton, Hotel Davis, as well as a portion of the Wildwood Title and Trust Company, seen at the left side of the image. The aforementioned businesses are all gone today, their buildings being just a memory. Today a variety of newer motels and businesses occupy this strip of Atlantic Avenue.

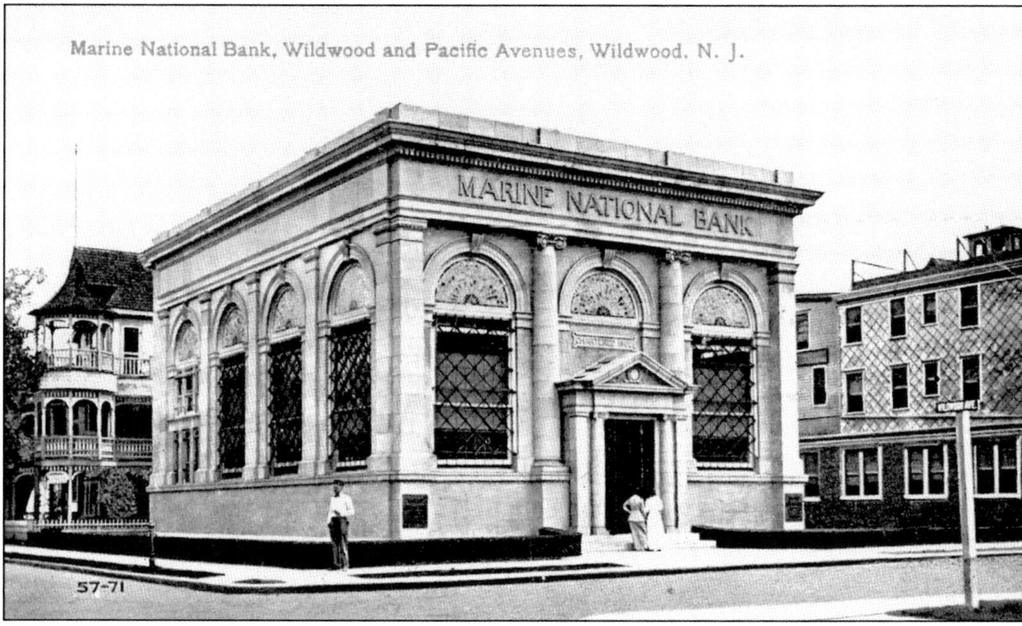

The Marine National Bank is seen in this postcard from the 1920s. This structure is located along Pacific Avenue at Wildwood Avenue in downtown Wildwood. Although the bank has received a couple expansions over the years, elements of the original structure are still visible today. As of 2007, the bank is still in operation as Crest Savings Bank.

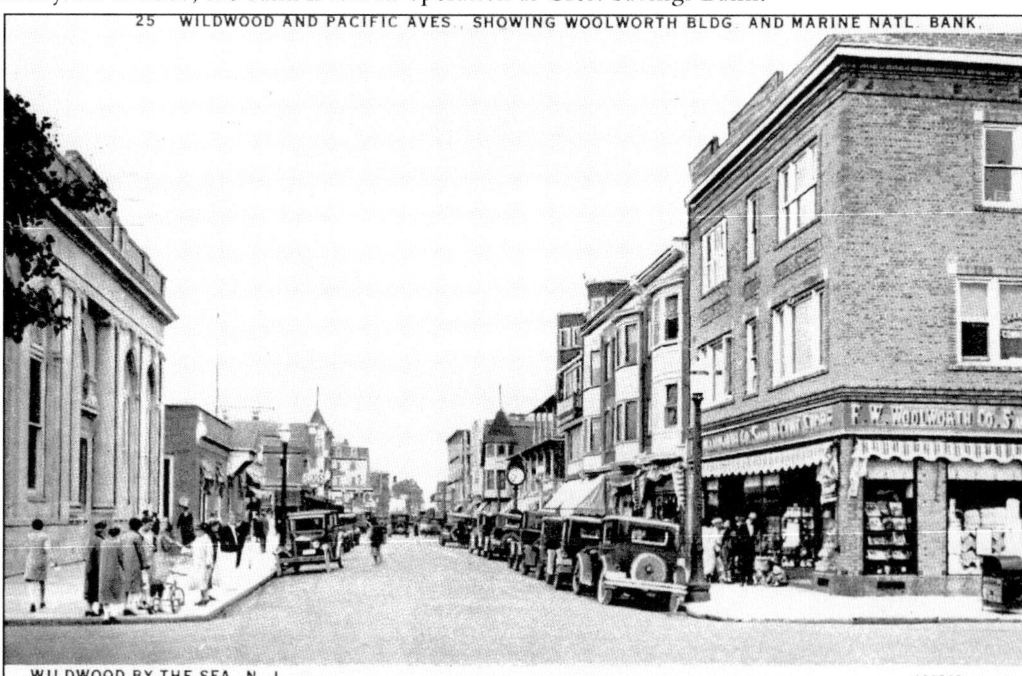

This postcard from the late 1920s shows a view of Wildwood and Pacific Avenues. At left is the Marine National Bank and at right is the F. W. Woolworth's five-and-dime store. Although F. W. Woolworth's is a thing of the past, many of the buildings pictured here have survived well into the 21st century, albeit with a multitude of exterior modifications.

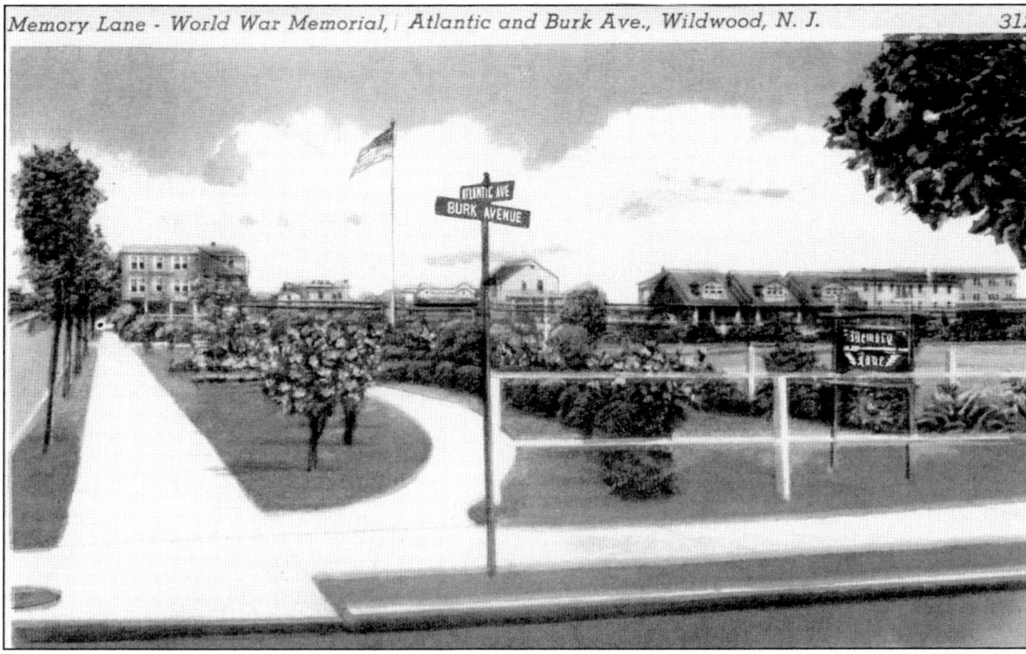

The Memory Lane War Memorial is seen in this postcard from the early 1950s. The memorial is still located within the boundaries of Fox Park at Atlantic and Burk Avenues in Wildwood. A commemorative sign marks the location of Memory Lane and bears an inscription which reads, "In memory of those who gave their lives in service of our country."

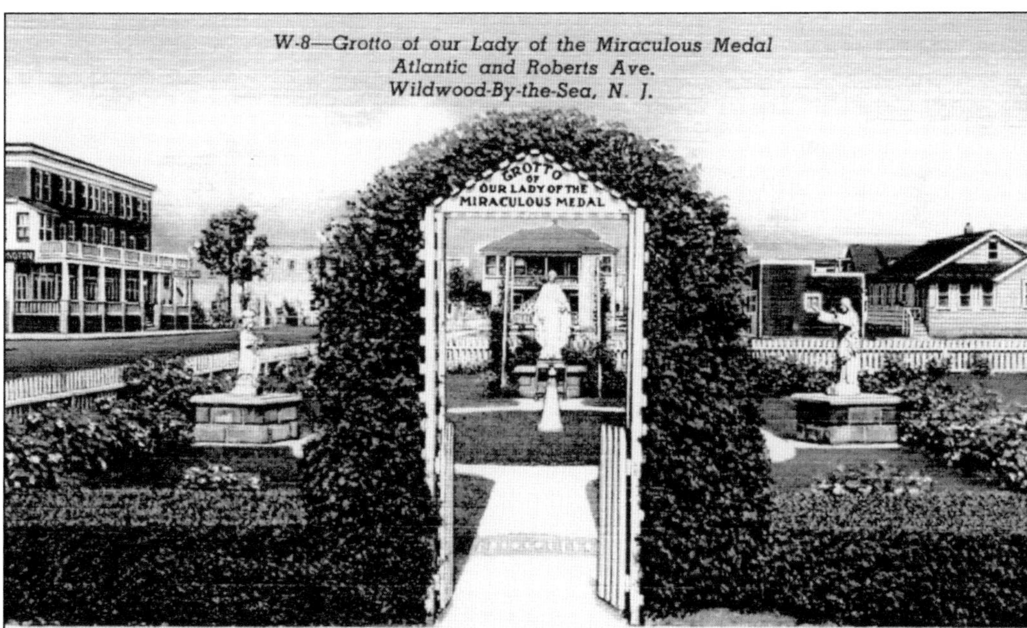

This postcard from the early 1950s shows the Grotto of Our Lady of the Miraculous Medal located at the corner of Atlantic and Roberts Avenues. The Catholic statuary seen in this image no longer exists at this place today. Additionally the area around Atlantic and Roberts Avenues has changed quite significantly over the last five decades.

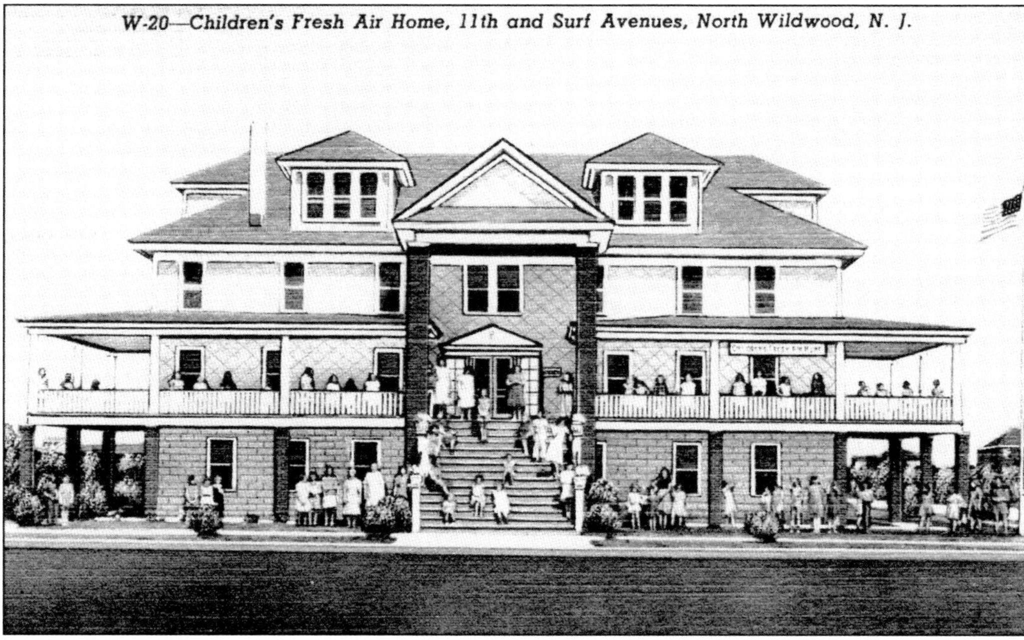

The Children's Fresh Air Home is seen in this postcard from the 1940s. This building is located at Eleventh and Surf Avenues in North Wildwood. The structure dates to the 1920s, but the mission of the Children's Fresh Air Home was wrought in the late 19th century. The Fresh Air Home continues to operate in the same capacity as it has for decades and the building looks very similar in 2007.

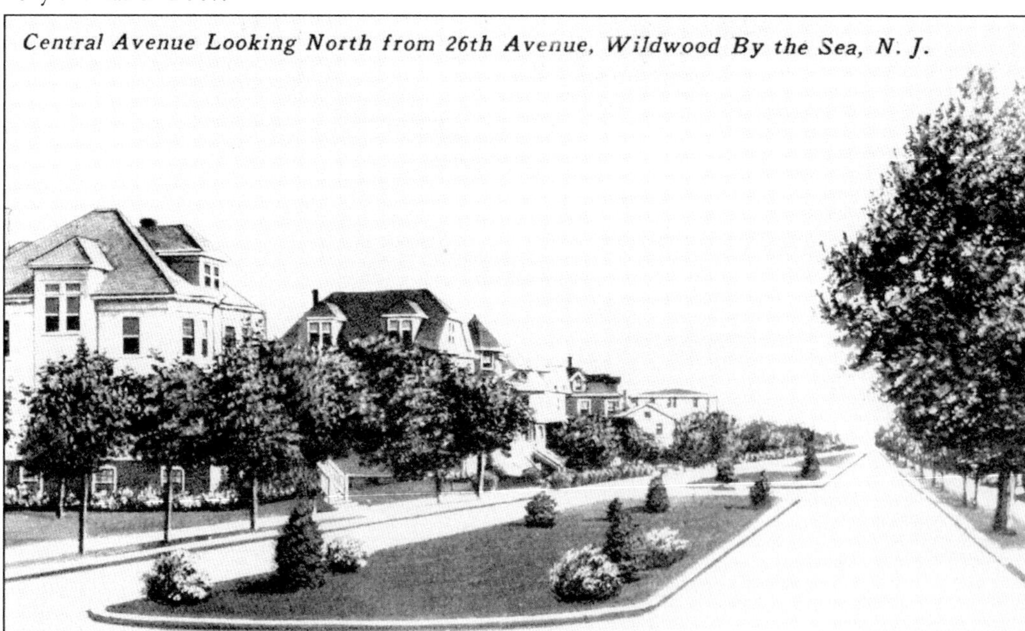

This postcard from the late 1940s shows Central Avenue looking north from Twenty-sixth Avenue in North Wildwood. Central Avenue is easily recognizable because of the grass islands that run through its center. Although more than 60 years have elapsed since this postcard was produced, many of these houses remain in place in 2007.

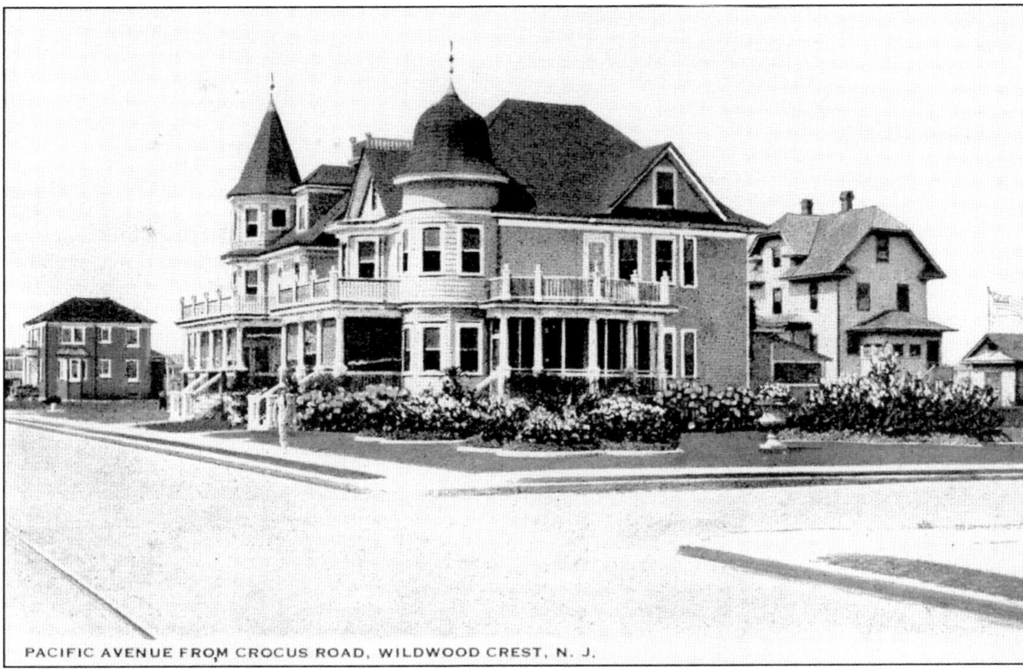

A postcard from the late 1920s shows a view of Pacific Avenue from Crocus Road in Wildwood Crest. These large, ornate homes still exist as of 2007, although another home has been built on the lot where gardens are visible in the foreground of this postcard image. These homes are located in the approximate area across the street from the Crest Community Church.

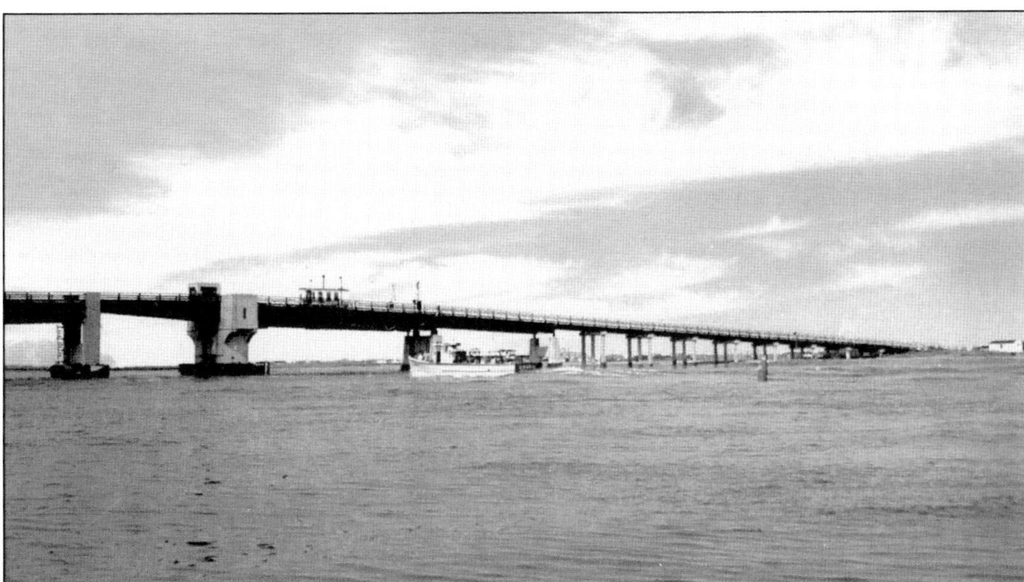

This postcard from 1960 shows the Ocean Drive Bridge that spans the water between the Wildwoods and Cape May. Although more than four decades have gone by since this postcard was produced, the bridge looks remarkably similar today. The open space in the background at the bridge's terminus, however, has seen moderate development over the years.